Memoirs of

Waldo Frank

Edited by Alan Trachtenberg

Introduction by Lewis Mumford

The University of Massachusetts Press 1973

Library of Congress Catalogue Card
Number: 73–123541
Manufactured in the United States of America

Grateful acknowledgment for permission
to reproduce photographs is extended
to Mrs. Jean Frank, Walker Evans,
Lewis Mumford, Paul Strand, and the
University of Pennsylvania Library.

Contents

Photographs follow page 120

Editor's Preface

At his death in 1967 Waldo Frank left a large body of unpublished work, including two novels and the present autobiographical work. He had begun writing his autobiography in 1962, and as late as a year before his death, during a period of rapid physical decline, he was at work on the concluding section (Part III), which remains incomplete and unrevised. Frank had conceived of the project late in 1958. "I have decided," he entered in his notebook in December of that year, "to note in this book thoughts on my life, which might serve as material in a *Memoir*." For the next several days he called up memories from his boyhood, sketching out in effect the opening chapter of the present volume. However, other projects drew his attention. And it was more than a year later that he recorded words of encouragement from Lewis Mumford to "write my memoirs, principally of the 1920s." A clearer conception of such a book began to emerge. He set down a tentative title, "The Boy Outside," explaining to himself: "I've always felt myself as an *outsider*—yearning, struggling to *get in. Into* my own home, *into* N.Y. of the people, *into* France (later Spain), *into* literary America (7 *Arts, Our America* & the 1920s), *into* the Revolution (the People). I've never succeeded—whence the growing stress and importance of "*into* the Cosmos." The theme of failure, of being always and everywhere the "outsider," would provide a focus, much as Henry Adams' sense of estrangement provides theme and focus for his *Education*. Shortly before undertaking serious work on the manuscript he wrote:

> To go into, Last Words. To solve for myself the problem of whether my life (work) has really been a failure. What were my motives? What organic relations between each book, each professional act, and myself—my integration of self into its times and its essence. I see: not a linear narrative but a series of progressing scenes.

Like Adams Frank would view his life as a "problem," and would search for a solution within the process of self-interrogation.

The book is, then, less an autobiography than a deliberate reflection upon a life. How well Frank realized his desire for a "solution" to his life is, of course, beyond our knowing; the book must be considered as unfinished at his death. Yet in essentials of style and point of view the book is a complete act, certainly complete enough for us to evaluate in light of Frank's intentions. In regard to subject matter, for example, the book contains less overt discussion of "failure" than we are led to expect, less even of the private man, the inner life, than promised by the notebook entries. We find only sparse discussion of his books, a quite scrupulous avoidance of details of private family affairs, and given the occasion, surprisingly little introspection. Instead the book is in large part a chronicle of the public career of Waldo Frank, an inventory and stocktaking of an American writer whose activities intersected virtually all the significant artistic, intellectual, and political movements of the period from 1910 to 1950.

To read the *Memoirs* exclusively as a chronicle does not, as shortly becomes apparent, do justice to its fullness. But on this level alone the book is a welcome new source of material for the cultural historian. In spite of his abiding sense of failure and of being "outside" the main currents of his times—a feeling abetted in the last two decades of his life by the outrageous neglect he suffered, in no small portion for political reasons, such as his association with the Communist Party in the 1930s and his support of Cuba in the 1960s—Frank enjoyed a remarkable career. When he died in 1967 hardly any of his published works were in print (none of his books has yet been reissued in a paperback edition); yet at one time his name stood for the radical cultural and aesthetic aspirations of a whole generation of writers, including such figures as Sherwood Anderson, Hart Crane, Alfred Stieglitz, Van Wyck Brooks, Randolph Bourne, Jean Toomer, Paul Rosenfeld, and Lewis Mumford. No other of this group equalled his range of association and friendship, extending to the intellectual capitals of America, England, France, Spain, and America Hispana. By virtue of his mobility, his ease with several cultural traditions, and his access to a remarkable variety of experience, Frank's perspective upon his times was unique. But in an important sense his career was also typical. His life embodies several common predicaments of an American intellectual whose childhood and youth witnessed the breakup of a cultural order. The opening chapters of the *Memoirs* are especially interesting for the light they shed on the formative years of twentieth century intellectual life in America. Frank composed this work with a keen sense of the historical moment—indeed, with the cultural historian's eye for the revealing detail, the typical episode.

As a historical document Waldo Frank's *Memoirs* adds considerably to our picture of the immediate past—not only its personalities and events but its characteristic dilemmas, as manifest, for example, in the chapters on the *Seven Arts* and on the 1930s. But the book's value does not end here; it is not simply a recollection but a literary act artfully conceived. The book is, after all, the concluding expression of a writer who considered himself "first (and last) an artist: a story-teller." Composed with a deliberate concern for structure—"not a linear narrative but a series of progressing scenes"—the book can be taken as the final of Frank's many formal experiments in narrative. Although much of Frank's fiction is autobiographical in the general sense of drawing upon scenes and persons and issues from his actual life, none of his full-scale works is openly autobiographical. That is, in none is the literary problem defined as how to present the materials of his own "real" life in such a way that the process of recovering memory and the process of interpreting (or *solving*) the remembered life appear as a single act. Frank makes it clear that his purpose in this book is to find grounds for accepting his life as necessary and self-sufficient, all evidence of "failure" to the contrary. The formal equivalent to this purpose is the problem of point of view, the choice of perspective from which the "I" of the narrative recovers and witnesses the experiences of his earlier self. Point of view is, of course, the function of the on-going voice or self of the narrative, and it was precisely in portraying this voice and its relation to the past that Frank encountered his chief compositional challenge. The most overt expression of the difficulty is the shift—one might say equivocation—between first and third person prominent in early drafts of the manuscript and still apparent in the present version. Frank's reasons for presenting himself in the third person are undoubtedly complex: in his journals characteristically he refers to himself as "he." Whatever the psychological factors in this habit, in the *Memoirs* the uncertainty of point of view is a symptom of the large problem which the book itself undertakes to confront: the problem of his identity. One senses as a steady single-keyed note reverberating through the text the question: who is the author of this work? Who is the subject of this book? Does he stand in the eyes of others as he wishes to stand in his own eyes? Are the same terms of self-justification available to others for a public justification of this life, now doubled as a life lived and a life recollected? Who will want to hear of this life— the life, Frank recognizes in his journals, of "an author of un- findable books"?

Frank's problems in creating this book typify the main problem of his entire career: the relations to an audience, of an author committed to attempted reconciliations of a felt absolute world with the phenomenal world, of God with history. In earlier works Frank presented himself as a seeker of new forms of resolution, of "true Words by which man, living in phenomenal times, knows and experiences absolute Values" (Journal IX). Described in the *Memoirs* as a virtual covenant to provide in word and deed "proofs of God," this intention led Frank into difficult literary paths; he seems to have constrained his talent to follow experimental directions at the expense of furthering and deepening his best achievements. Frank himself took measure of this expense in a remarkable journal entry at the end of 1928, titled "The Public Position of Waldo Frank in 1928 (notes for a future historian)"— the following section is titled "The Inner State of Waldo Frank at the Close of 1928 (notes for himself)." He speaks of having "no definite audience" and accounts for the "nebula" of his reputation in the following words: "Each portion of his work, superficially separate from other portions, had won a certain audience for him —in fact, no part of it had failed of some interesting response. But the publics so won were separate: . . . [no] appreciable group of readers had organized his image and influence into a whole." A potential audience was, he felt, "drawn away by more accessible novelists—such as Dos Passos, Hemingway, Virginia Woolf, Joyce.

> The reason was, that on the whole there had been no deep understanding of his novels which had hence been vaguely grouped with these other works. . . . His work puzzled, irritated, stimulated—it seldom enthused. Its basis of a mystic vision and of a philosophy and fundamental logic, held off readers who, on the whole were used to more immediate sensory approaches. . . . No body of readers had been fastened to him, yet so much interest had at some time been generated by his various books, that, if all these groups were to be organized together, he (who had no real audience) might have the most real audience of any contemporary writer.

This, as he saw it in 1928, was his "anomalous" public position.

The accuracy of Frank's appraisal is less important than the light it sheds on basic needs for "deep understanding," for acceptance entirely in terms set by himself, and for a conviction of the potential if not actual significance of his experimental course. The *Memoirs* reveal that Frank had not given up any of these demands upon himself and his readers. But now he was able to reflect upon them, to see them operating in memories charged with heightened meaning, in the patterns which linked his life to history. The *Memoirs* are not a plea for acceptance so much as a revelation of how deeply that need emerged from Frank's nature. Driven by his own inner logic alternately to the center and to the periphery of his times, Frank here confronts the accomplished facts and wishes to provide for them an adequate literary form.

As Frank made clear in his notes and in the opening paragraphs of Part III, he did not count on chronology alone to provide that form. His preference for a "series of progressing scenes" rather than "linear narrative" suggests a novelistic approach, and indeed parts of the book resemble fiction in their use of description, dialogue, and scene. The organization into three books each with seven chapters suggests too an intended symmetry of form, perhaps meant to produce a counterpart rhythm with the progressing movement of the narrative. But more important than these devices is a less conspicuous formal element, a prevailing idea which guides the construction of the book. By this I refer to Frank's idea of "the person." This idea lies at the base of his thinking, perhaps his most cherished construct, and one that links him directly with Emerson. Frank's "person" is his most vital measure of culture and of individual life. It is a measure implicit in his point of view toward his own career, so finely woven into his language that he does not feel it necessary to make its assumptions explicit.

The idea of "the person" rests upon the notion that the "self" ("that which is feeling, acting, thinking") consists of three parts, a "trinity of dimensions." One is a "group" or social dimension, another is an "ego-somatic" or individual-body dimension, and the third "vector" is the "cosmic." The "cosmic" is not to be confused with an abstract "spirit"; rather, it is found within the self's other two dimensions, its group and ego relations. In *Rediscovery of Man* Frank writes:

> It is a harmony of man's empirical relations. His work, his love,
> his needs and aspirations, all individually within the group
> and ego dimensions, create an overtone which transcends them.
> This is the "spiritual," and it is universally human.

The "cosmic" appears, or is revealed, as an "overtone" in common life. The mystical element in Frank's writings needs to be understood in light of this stress upon the "empirical" dimensions of human life, precisely the dimensions which provide the stuff of the *Memoirs*. Frank's concern is with the conditions necessary for intactness of experience and the fulfillment of character in history and social relations: thus the great emphasis in his life on action. It is telling that his best books, the ones most likely to win readers in the future, are not his fictions but his cultural studies such as *Our America* and *Virgin Spain*, those works rooted unequivocally in historical fact and firsthand observation. Frank's mysticism was neither ascetic nor self-denying; it was a cultivated sensitivity to those moments of felt integration when the "whole" seems revealed in the particular styles and actions of peoples.

The *Memoirs* are not an argument on behalf of integration, but the terms of Frank's theory cling to the bones of the text. What we have in the narrative are the interacting relations of the separate vectors of his own "self" (a self, as I have indicated, he tended to objectify in third person constructions). More room is allowed the group dimension, the social aspect of his life, but the ego-somatic and cosmic dimensions are present in episodes recounting sexual and autistic experiences. But informing the narrative, somewhat like the theory of "force" in Henry Adams' *Education*, is the implicit measure of the integrated "person" as the elusive culmination of experience. The ideal is expressed in the following passage from *Rediscovery of Man:*

> The person is the individual whose functions, included in the
> broad realms of the group and ego dimensions, are not
> suppressed, not distorted, and not dominant; but are constantly,
> inwardly, informed by his sense of the whole self in which
> the cosmic is an active vector. This person will eat, play, love,
> follow a trade, have friends and enemies, predilections and
> aversions; suffer joy and pain, defeats and victories, fight for
> causes or against them—all within the pattern of his culture
> and within groups of similarly centered persons. But each of his
> acts, expressing a function of relation with his somatic ego
> and his group, will be suffused and transfigured by his
> experience of the whole, not as exterior cosmos but as cosmic
> quality within him; tincturing his empiric emotion and
> thought, yet beyond them; formed as spacetime, yet beyond it.
> *The person is the individual made real.*

The arch burden of Frank's entire writings is a painstaking account, frequently in strained and difficult language, of conditions which block personhood. Overriding all other interests was his concern with the deprivations of American culture, the barriers thrown up by Puritanism, by mean-spirited reflexes of the pioneer experience, by technological willfulness, to the achievement of personal integration. A remarkable trait of the *Memoirs* is the relative absence of such generalized cultural criticism, replaced by an unsparing light cast upon his own responsibility for failure and loss, and upon the handicap he inflicted on himself by pledging to remain an "outsider" rather than compromise his own visionary view of himself. What matters for the reader of the *Memoirs* is not simply the wealth of detail of a life lived, after all, richly, but the quality and form of self-awareness. The book witnesses a life devoted to a rigorous, probably an impossible ideal of selfhood. Such a life is always vulnerable to attack. But Frank avoids the more blatantly sentimental or recriminatory methods of self-defense. The book is a disciplined vision of a complex American life, and deserves to be read in that light. Certainly as an act of humility on the part of a proud man toward the inexorableness of the past it is a remarkable document.

NOTE ON THE TEXT

Parts I and II exist in final draft in typescript; Part III exists in typescript marked "unrevised and unfinished," although it includes numerous corrections made in pencil by Waldo Frank. Editing consisted only in eliminating minor errors, such as repetitions, and some very light changes of person in order to bring the text into conformity with Frank's intention to regularize his use of the first person. The notes are supplied chiefly for bibliographic purposes, in order to suggest further readings which bear on Waldo Frank's career and its place within the cultural history of the twentieth century.

ACKNOWLEDGEMENTS

Mrs. Jean Frank offered indispensable and thoroughly understanding aid in the editing of this book, and I would like to express my appreciation for her hospitality and sympathy, as well as for her willingness in undertaking to solve several specific difficulties. Without her special insight and her industry a number of matters would have remained obscure. Lewis Mumford provided encouragement along with his invaluable advice, and I would like to thank him for many kindnesses, especially for indulging my frequent digressions into matters beyond the immediate details of this text, though relevant to its ambiance. I received excellent help from Neda M. Westlake and the staff of the Rare Book Room, University of Pennsylvania Library. Donald Gallup of the Beinecke Library, Yale University, also provided important help. I thank, too, for their assistance at various stages of preparation of the text, Victor Spector, Jan Costello, and Glenn Reiter.

ALAN TRACHTENBERG

Introduction

Today the name of Waldo Frank is almost unknown in his own country. But half a century ago Frank seemed to many of his contemporaries one of the most vital literary figures of his generation, then rivalled only by Van Wyck Brooks. His was a robust spirit, in tune with his age, eagerly exploring new paths in the novel, the drama, and in criticism, testifying by his presence to that general upsurge of creativity which brought back to the twenties the self-confidence that Emerson and his contemporaries had expressed almost a century earlier.

Before Frank was thirty he had come to the fore as an editor of the *Seven Arts*, interpreting the spiritual ferment that was working no longer in Europe alone but in *Our America*. In confirmation of his American fame Frank was welcomed as a colleague and a potential equal by the leading writers of Europe, from James Joyce to Romain Rolland and Jules Romains, the Romains whose "unanimism" permeated Frank's *City Block*. As early as 1926 his *Virgin Spain* was widely accepted as a classic interpretation of Spanish culture by the Spanish-speaking world, beginning with the Rector of the University of Salamanca, Miguel de Unamuno. Though Frank's own countrymen have undervalued this work, the intelligentsia of Latin America have continued to admire it.

Who could have guessed, after such a swiftly mounting career, that this rocketlike reputation at the height of its trajectory would lose its momentum and plummet erratically to earth long before its energies were used up. But so it happened. During the last quarter century of his life Waldo Frank felt himself disdained and ignored by his countrymen, and during the final years no publisher would even consider his fiction for publication. When he died on the ninth of January, 1967, he left behind the manuscripts of two novels, the voluminous diaries he had kept all his life, and this still not quite completed autobiography. Though the present memoir presents one of the most illuminating pictures of the period that I know, and has even greater value as a personal confession, this manuscript went begging, even when offered to publishers who had brought out Frank's earlier work.

For most of Frank's contemporaries after 1950 he was no longer a star but a dead planet, almost invisible even by the reflected light of other stars. Critics who had either ignored or disparaged Frank's current work did not hesitate to dismiss him as "unreadable." Whether he is in fact unreadable the reader of this memoir will find out for himself: but certainly he, who had prided himself on being one of the avant-garde, was no longer fashionable. This anticlimax was not the temporary fading out of a reputation that so often follows a writer's death. Established writers, even great ones like Goethe or Hugo, or popular ones like H. G. Wells and Arnold Bennett, often become "unreadable" or rather invisible in their old age, like pictures that have hung too long on the same wall. But Frank met a worse fate, for while still alive, still productive, he vanished from the scene. Without dying he ceased to exist as a literary presence in his own country, though he still kept his Latin American readers. He had become too obscure even to be attacked.

This would have been a harsh outcome for an author whose writings were less significant than Waldo Frank's. But no matter by what standards one may rate Frank's work, such total indifference was not only unkind, it was unjust. If any proof were needed to show that Waldo Frank was still indeed a writer to be reckoned with, this autobiography should suffice. Though it is not an exhaustive work, and though it hardly does justice to his genuine achievements, the fact that Frank exposes and assesses his own errors and weaknesses, sometimes with scarifying objectivity, gives the true measure of the man. This memoir, backed by the testimony of his major books, should re-establish him as one of the important writers of his generation. This is the generation that includes J. E. Spingarn, Van Wyck Brooks, Paul Rosenfeld, Sherwood Anderson, and Frank himself at one end, and Ernest Hemingway, Scott Fitzgerald, William Faulkner, and Edmund Wilson at the other.

My task here, as I conceive it, is not to make a fresh evaluation of Frank's literary achievements, but to throw a light on them with the aid of his own belated discoveries about himself. This is a genuine problem, and it admits of no facile answer. How is it, I have often asked myself, that such an abundantly endowed personality, such a well-seasoned mind, at home in the literatures and religions of the world, such an active participant in the intellectual and political turmoil of our times, should have left on his own generation such a faint and often distorted impression of his genuine talents? If my claims for his work as a whole are not just the indulgent inflations of a friend, how is it then that they must be made at all? Though Frank and I had known each other for almost forty years, I lacked the inner clue to his fate until I read this memoir. Until then I was almost tempted to say of Frank, as he did of Simón Bolívar: "The more I delved into the man the less sense I had of understanding him." Fortunately Frank himself has provided in this memoir, with unsparing honesty, all that anyone needs for understanding. What remains baffling is that he himself seems to have been unable to use this self-knowledge in guiding his own development.

The only satisfactory answer for me takes the form of a paradox. Perhaps Waldo Frank's greatest handicap was that he started in life with so few handicaps, or to speak more accurately, with such a surfeit of advantages. At birth some wicked fairy played the sinister joke of giving him a magnificent largesse of natural abilities, supplemented by all the cultural furniture that an upper middle-class household, well-stocked with books and music scores, free from importunate financial pressures or obsessions, accustomed to European travel, could afford. Everything that a youth of the highest potentials needed for his education and maturation was at hand for the asking—everything, that is, except hardship, deprivation, resistance, natural difficulty. Frank himself, even as a youth, seems to have been uneasy over this economic favoritism; and in fantasy, he took the side of the deprived and the subordinate—as in the incident of the carpenter who was kept waiting in the kitchen while the family finished its leisurely dinner. Though spurred by his democratic convictions he later made many separate gestures of sharing the lot of the underdog, he never in fact flew far from this well lined bourgeois nest.

Our generation is only beginning to realize fully the perils of the Affluent Society, now that great masses of the population have a share in mass-produced abundance. But this is a peril that ancient aristocracies have often confronted, and what is worse, succumbed to. Many of Frank's convictions and much of his conduct could not be interpreted fully until the same traits—the same inordinate expectancies, the same demand for instant compliance —were magnified in the imperious conduct of the younger generation today. In following Frank's account of his childhood and adolescence, I find myself concluding that the surfeit of gifts and opportunities he enjoyed from the beginning coddled his exorbitant ego and kept him from making the best use of his many native capacities. At sixteen an immature novel of his was even accepted for commercial publication; only the prompt intervention of his family prevented that embarrassing "success." More such restraints and rebuffs might have seasoned his talents.

Part of Waldo Frank's affluence was organic and innate, the expression of a sturdy body and an active, highly sensitized brain; so even as a child his cultural precocity matched his material advantages. As a boy of ten or twelve he had passed beyond Dickens and was already reading Tolstoi and Balzac, and as a senior in high school he refused to attend the required course on Shakespeare because he felt he knew Shakespeare better than his teacher. (When he was older, I might add wryly, he transferred his sense of superiority from his despised teacher to Shakespeare himself.) That characteristic act of juvenile insolence deprived him of his high school diploma, but did not prevent him from entering Yale. There he had a brilliant scholastic career, being graduated with an M.A. as well as a B.A., with an Honorary Fellowship to boot. Who could doubt that his was a mind of the highest calibre: self-propelling, audacious, original?

Somewhat small in stature, though compact, as a youth Frank counterbalanced both his size and a kind of feminine sensitiveness with a show of defiant energy; and to the end of his life he was protected by an almost incredible naiveté from understanding the impression he made on others by his innocent assumption of superiority. To put it bluntly, on the evidence he himself offers, in early adolescence Frank was dominated by a mythical sense of his bodily self, or rather of his penis, contemplated in erection while floating in his bath, as the very center of his personal universe—a universe he actually named "Waldea." In all our intercourse he never mentioned this central motif to me, any more than Jung related to anyone his own comparable phallic dream. But the fact that Frank returns to this image at the end of his memoir offers a central clue to his personality, and above all, to his repeated failures to take into account and come to terms with the experiences of other men. If the cosmos was already within Frank, as he deeply believed, what else did he need?—except the willingness of his countrymen to acknowledge this myth and do homage to the ruler of "Waldea." Once Frank's authority was accepted, once this revelation stirred the masses, then what Frank conceived as the "deep revolution" would take place.

Here again Frank's most serious defect sprang from his remarkable gifts: not alone his early intellectual maturity and his over-abundant talents, but his unabated, seemingly uninhibited, sexual energy. Unfortunately his sense that he possessed magical powers which might transform the world, a sense he shared with a long succession of religious prophets, major and minor, undermined his ability to work with others or command their unreserved loyalty. "Waldea" cut him off from reality. In a sense Frank secretly anticipated the rebellious London University student, by scrawling on his private wall: "I want the world and I want it now." As a result, Frank did not even get that part of the world to which his actual achievements entitled him.

Many exceptional minds achieve their growth in a spiritual cocoon, unconscious of their special gifts until ready to break forth. That is their good luck, the luck that both Whitman and Melville enjoyed. But young Waldo could not help being aware of his many genuine talents and gifts. As if to confirm this sense of himself, he came under the spell, he tells us, of Max Stirner's once famous book, *The Ego and His Own*, which was translated into English at a critical point in Frank's adolescence: 1908. Though he mentions this book, Frank unfortunately does not appraise its influence upon him, perhaps because it only confirmed and reinforced an ego that was already tumescently visible. Yet even his friends would admit—and who sooner?—that the most trying aspects of his personality could be summarized in that title, *The Ego and His Own*. Just because Frank's original endowments were so large, the demands of his ego became correspondingly inordinate, and the more his ego was slighted or denied, the more visible homage it demanded.

On this matter, Paul Rosenfeld's criticism,* timely though emotionally somewhat ambivalent, might have helped release Frank's creative potential if Frank had not armored himself against criticism by seeing in Rosenfeld's analysis only hostility and envy. With full foreknowledge of how he was endangering their friendship and with many misgivings which he confided to Sherwood Anderson, Rosenfeld seized the publication of *The Dark Mother* to analyze Frank's central weakness. "Don't think for a moment," he wrote Anderson, "that I wrote this merely because of the failure of the D.M. If I thought the failure of the D.M. merely a fluke, an ill chance, I would let the book pass unnoticed. But I perceive something at the base of the faulty esthetic of the work that is the very devil in Waldo, in me, in everyone. I hope to hit it wherever I catch

*"The Novels of Waldo Frank," *Dial* (January 1921).

sight of it. I hate it in myself, and give everyone the right to point to it whenever they spy it. . . . I have got to break that false circle which Waldo has drawn about himself . . . the circle that forbids anyone to be frank with him about his work, and that threatens everyone who dissents with excommunication."

Unfortunately Frank's early successes stood in the way of his reducing the ego's demands to more reasonable proportions. He found himself at the top of the mountain without having been toughened in a slower, harder ascent by scrapes, falls, freezing winds. Success came to him too quickly and effortlessly, in every possible form: money, adulation, countless erotic adventures, flattering publicity. And much as he might despise popular journals with large circulations, it was there that, right into the thirties, he found receptive editors and a mixed audience that was no less responsive than those who attended his lectures. Such early acclaim may handicap a young writer far worse than twenty years' indifference; for thereafter any failure to gain the same measure of approval becomes a major misfortune: a sign, as Frank felt after the publication of his uneven collection of essays, *Salvos*, of public neglect and alienation.

But even more than popular acclaim, Frank needed the recognition of his peers, and his patent efforts to achieve this too often evoked skepticism, if not suspicion. Regrettably the premature appraisal of his writing by Gorham Munson, in a book published in 1925, when but a single major work of Frank's—*City Block*—had appeared, had an effect like the exposure of an embryo to X-rays: it helped to bring on the leukemia that eventually vitiated his literary reputation. Frank did nothing to block this exposure; indeed, in his desire for early acknowledgement as one of the great writers of his generation—which he potentially was— he helped to nourish doubts about his genuine achievements and even perhaps to foster an unfair revulsion against his whole work.

Though at the outset I promised myself to write about Frank's life without discussing his literary work, I shall not be able to carry out this intention; for where else does one come closer to the essential being of a writer than in his mode of expression? Frank's early choice of words and metaphors provoked unfavorable criticism and eventually evoked the pat response I have noted, that he was "unreadable." How far was this reaction justified? Frank shared with many writers of his generation, long before unintelligibility became the badge of avant-gardism, the effort to freshen language by dissociating words from their traditional context and creating meanings through shattered metaphors: witness James

Joyce and Boris Pasternak. In his early novels he sometimes strained too hard to embellish commonplace events with a bizarre prose. This, as Chekhov kindly tried to show young Gorki, was not originality but fake poetry.

As a boy, Frank had fallen in love with Edgar Allan Poe and admired the least admirable part of Poe, his pretentious use of esoteric words. Frank tells us that he then would observe at the dinner table that he was two "lustrums" old, or that his hair was too "planturous" to be combed. In time he came to write in his best moments a strong, supple prose; but he never entirely mastered the childish temptation to trot out an unusual word. Bittner points out that he ruined a whole passage in *The Invaders* by needlessly inserting the strange word "inspissate." But in his best work after the twenties, this trick does not often intrude. He shook off these Poesque gewgaws; so it was his ideas, not his words, that the more hostile critics found hard to swallow. But since only those who were capable of thinking on the same plane as Frank were equipped to criticize effectively his vision of life and the program of action that he sought to derive from it, it was easier to dispose of his ideas by pointing to occasional verbal idiosyncrasies.

Obviously, most of the traits that I have noted are common in some degree in all artists and writers. Though Robert Frost's efforts to establish himself as the poet of his generation were more private, they have the same unpleasant characteristics; for it is only a rare Shakespeare or a Bach who dares to stand aloof and let his work speak for itself. But in Frank the claims of his ego had a retarding effect on the efflorescence of his extraordinary talents. As to his original gifts, all his friends—Adolph Oko, Roderick Seidenberg, Alfonso Reyes, Reinhold Niebuhr—could warmly bear testimony. Certainly he was one of the educated men of his generation: no other contemporary I know of had read more widely, had reflected more deeply, had ranged so far in travel both at home and abroad, had encountered such a wide variety of people, both distinguished and humble, or had lived with so many different types, often on intimate terms—on a Wyoming ranch, among the populist farmers of Kansas, among French intellectuals on the Left Bank of the Seine, or even, once, in a prison cell with a low-grade Communist politician.

Not only was Frank an eager explorer of cities, landscapes, and cultures, but he had disciplined himself to record his day's experiences every night in his diary, and his outward explorations mingled there with inner probings of his personal life. What perfect training for a novelist! one instinctively exclaims. But here again Frank's life presents contradictions. For his finest qualities as a writer came forth, not in his novels, but in his perceptive interpretations of other cultures and ways of life: not merely Spain and Latin America, but Russia, Israel, and Cuba. Even in old age he was eager to explore China when invited to speak there at the Walt Whitman celebration.

In this brief sketch I cannot attempt to separate the tangled skeins of Waldo Frank's life. At best I can only point to the problems that a new generation of critics, beginning with Professor William Bittner, has now begun to explore. Central to any appraisal is the philosophy that consciously underpinned—and alas partly undermined—his entire work. Two large themes, with religious foundations and political consequences, dominated Frank's whole career. One was his personal mission, addressed to restoring the individual's sense of cosmic unity and personal commitment: a unity that, on his historic analysis, had been lost with the breakup of the "medieval synthesis" in Western Europe. This belief in his special mission was secretly attached to his juvenile Waldean myth; for though he ostensibly sought love and personal union he also carried with him a Stirnerian demand to satisfy the ego on his own terms, without concern for the interests or feelings of other people.

Frank's innate sense of being one of the elect was flatly opposed to his conscious democratic sympathies; but unfortunately it went far deeper and led him, as he himself ruefully recognized at the end of his life, to nourish fantasies as private and as high-flown as Don Quixote's. Who but Frank could for a moment have supposed that by aligning himself with the party Communists in the thirties he could convert them, overnight, from orthodox Marxist Stalinism to the more religious "Waldean" concept of the "deep revolution" founded on the expression of the whole personality? This quixotism marred both his personal relations and his social hopes, and in the end, without a Sancho Panza to bring him down to earth, it left him lonely and abandoned without even the solace of his utopian dreams.

The other dominant theme, present from Frank's youth too, was his desire for union with God. To feel that God or the cosmos was within one and to surrender utterly to it was, on Frank's readings, the key to human salvation. This openness to transcendent realities that cannot be put into words or rationally explicated gave Frank a vivid understanding of the historic function of religion. That mystic sense was so lacking in his generation that many who still considered themselves religious and regularly attended church or synagogue utterly lacked it. In believing that the mystery of life was an essential aspect of its meaning Waldo Frank was on firmer ground than most of his own intellectual generation. This partly accounts for their total rejection of him. To the popular pragmatists and rationalists, the very word mystic was anathema: they held that the ultimate mysteries would either be explained—that is, devaluated—by science or erased by the advances of technology. Thus Frank was separated from his contemporaries by one of his positive virtues: his concern for meanings and values above and beyond those which the here-and-now world admits. As a result of this breach, his religious conceptions never received the rigorous criticism they deserved. For had Frank's contributions here been taken seriously, he might have become conscious of the fatal isolationist streak in his interpretation of the "Great Tradition."

In his boyhood Frank had identified himself with a cat he encountered, as part of the same cosmic whole: a profoundly Hindu conception of cosmic unity, which Emerson had put to perfection in his poem, "Brahma." But for a man who had such an intuition of unity, Frank's philosophy was a singularly Western one: what he called the Great Tradition was essentially the Western tradition, or at least that part of the Western tradition which had taken form about the Mediterranean, mainly in Palestine, in Egypt, Greece, and Rome. Frank's fixation on that Great Tradition was, to say the least, one-sided, since upon a mere count of heads it excluded about half the human race. Strangely Frank seemed untroubled by the fact that this was far from being a universal solution, even if by some miracle the "deep revolution" he sought could be brought about. This was a flaw that ran through all Frank's thinking.

But the errors of an original mind are often more fruitful than the truths of a more limited one; and by understanding the background of Frank's thought and seeing into what he sought to do, one has a more comprehensive insight into vital problems affecting the whole future of mankind, not merely the intermingling of the races but the marriage of cultures and the efflorescence of personalities than one would otherwise have. Let me here confess my own debt to Frank's earnest concern with the most central area of life, that of religion. It was partly by wrestling with Frank's passionate metaphysical convictions, which I could never make my own, that I opened the way to an answer more satisfactory to me—one that, as Emerson had put it, includes the skepticisms as well as the faiths of mankind.

The issues that Frank raised in book after book are the essential issues of human life: they deal with its meaning and value and question all those institutional routines and ideological fixations which limit man's consciousness and his potentialities for further growth. That Frank wrestled with these problems at a moment in Western history when even the Churches, in the main, had lost sight of them or had lost faith in the standard solutions is more significant than the fact that Frank's own answer was inadequate.

The contrast between Frank's ego-dominated energies and his vision of social justice and personal love brought exacerbating inner conflicts, and those conflicts were never to be resolved, even in the period of self-criticism and personal humility that marked the last decade of his life. To judge by his quotations from his own diaries, he was engaged in endless moralistic battles with himself, nagged by a persistent sense of guilt. This self-examination started early, for when his own conduct brought his first marriage with Margaret Naumburg to an end just at the moment when, with the birth of their first child, he confessed to himself his readiness to accept the joys and obligations of fatherhood, he realized that he had not only failed in marriage but cheated himself. But even this realization did not cause him to alter his course: "The supreme sin," he told himself, "is not to be able to forgive yourself."

That self-absolution was naive. With Frank's deep understanding of Christianity, with his admiration for Thomas Aquinas, he surely should have remembered that the only way to earn forgiveness is to repent and change one's ways. Like the defiant high school boy who forfeited his diploma rather than apologize for or alter his conduct, Frank chose to feel guilty and not to repent. So too, though in time he regretted his unkind portrait in the *New Yorker* of his English professor, William Lyon Phelps, who had greatly stimulated and nourished him, he reprinted it later in a book. Even worse, he held up to scorn in *Salvos* a popular poet who, on Frank's own interpretation, was not worth his attention. Though he felt rejected by his countrymen, it was only belatedly that he realized, in his description of his relations with the Washington Square Players, how ready he had always been to scorn their values and reject their advances. Frank needed comrades and colleagues of equal gifts to give body to his own vision, but what he actually sought was disciples who would accept his "total commitment to either revolution or revelation." On those terms he was forced to disparage even his best friends because they did not share his peculiar commitment, though by excluding the rest of the world he crippled and ultimately excluded himself.

Little though Frank's contemporaries appreciated his true worth, they were nevertheless justified in their sense that there was a discrepancy between his professions and his actions. Toward the end of his life he became bitterly aware of this disparity, one long ago acknowledged in the famous words of St. Paul. But despite Frank's critique of empirical rationalism, he pinned too much of his hopes for personal improvement on new techniques for achieving "wholeness," especially that based more or less on the therapeutic exercises of Matthias Alexander which had attracted John Dewey. Though the book in which he elaborates this prescription, *The Rediscovery of Man,* has like the earlier *Rediscovery of America* many pregnant passages in it, this mode of "salvation by posture" proved on his own pathetic confession an imposture, for it had not operated successfully in his own life. In asking for a quick personal remedy Frank was, in opposition to his own valid insights, denying both the complexities and the depths of anything worthy to be called a good life, for such a profound transformation demands a lifetime of effort, without any promise, apart from moments of grace, of some final consummation. Alexander's sword could not sever *that* Gordian knot. Only in "Waldea" could the collective transformation Frank passionately sought be achieved.

So once more we come back to the struggle between Waldo Frank's expansive genius and his insistent, self-defeating ego. In his youth, Frank explains in this memoir, he had made a covenant with God to give up "the expected rewards of an author, money (Kipling), disciples (Tolstoi), World Fame (Hardy, Meredith, Shaw) in order to search for Truth." But this was a brazen self-deception: in his heart he had given up none of these rewards. To judge by his actions, Frank valued money, disciples, and fame almost as much as Ernest Hemingway did, though less blatantly. Yet the means that he took to achieve these ends only put them further away, so that he became toward the end of his life what he had called the hero of his first book: The Unwelcome Man.

The allusion I have just made to Hemingway would have shocked Frank, but it is more than a haphazard reference. Looking at Stieglitz's portrait of young Waldo Frank in the frontispiece of Gorham Munson's study, the intense innocent face, the intent eyes, the fierce black hair, the bravado moustache, one realizes that he was physically a smaller counterpart of the younger Hemingway I met once at one of Rosenfeld's soirées. From a literary standpoint, the two were of course diametric opposites: Hemingway's marvellous ear for the spoken word, his studious underemphasis, his affectation of a limited vocabulary in which "good" served as a stand-in for all other adjectives and adverbs—this was the opposite of Frank's strained, overflorid early prose, in which buildings or furniture often showed more life than the human characters.

In actual life, however, there were many points of resemblance between Frank and Hemingway. Both were wilful men, both were restless for physical adventure, both failed in their early marriages, and above all, both were licensed egoists in the old-fashioned nineteenth-century style. Not least, their early triumphs kept each —though in different ways—from fulfilling his potentialities; so at the end each was sunk in black despair. But the fact that Waldo Frank could nevertheless face his life and expose his weaknesses with the candor he shows in this memoir, gives him a large margin of superiority over Hemingway in moral courage.

As for physical courage, Frank had that too, in more than usual measure: he was equal to facing the blows of the posse that ran him and his fellow-investigators of a coal strike out of Harlan County, Kentucky, back in the thirties: he was equal, too, to flying over the Andes in an early single-motored plane, to standing up to the Fascist thugs who laid him low with a blow on the head in his apartment at Buenos Aires, and, not least, early in the twenties to exploring the South, with Jean Toomer, disguised as a fellow-colored man and accepting the indignities that the Negro endured. This courage wore perhaps the armor of innocence; he did not believe evil could befall him. Yet after one has reckoned with Waldo Frank's egotism, one must remember this heroic side of him which nobly offsets it. Whatever his need for public appreciation, he never boasted of these heroic encounters, still less attempted to capitalize on them. And in this respect, too, he stands as a man in happy contrast to Hemingway.

If I have been as unreserved as Frank himself is in appraising his life, it is because, after due allowance has been made for all the idiosyncrasies and faults that alienated so many of his contemporaries, much of Frank's work actually remains admirable: full of luminous perceptions, challenging interpretations, vibrant calls to further thought and action. If Frank felt himself in his own words a Jew without Judaism and an American without America, it was partly because he had by his own efforts transcended these limitations and become a true man of the world. Not alone was he at home in all the new movements in the arts, realizing that the modern world had disclosed social and esthetic values no earlier culture had been aware of. To counterbalance this he had a special sense of older treasures that the modern world was, to its own loss, ignoring or brutally destroying. These values he found through repeated intercourse with the fundamentally primitive peasant cultures of Latin America, with their vivid emotional responses and erotic expressions. And it was here, I suggest, that Waldo Frank made his unique contribution. On this matter the verdict of his ranking Hispanic contemporaries deserves to be taken seriously; and if Frank had at an earlier point fully understood his own gifts, it is in this realm, I believe, that he would have concentrated a major part of his energies.

In making this judgment I am in effect depreciating Frank's novels; and that would have grieved him; for he regarded his imaginative fiction as his central life work. Let him then speak for himself. "I was not a politician, not an economist or a preacher; I was a poet. My method was simply to tell stories that revealed—within the heartbreak, within the dark and terrible mystery of being born and of living—that joy which is the presence of God made known beyond knowledge."

Yes, that was his conscious intention. And if he had indeed achieved it in his fiction, he would now rank with Gogol, Dostoevski, and Tolstoi. But as earnestly and sympathetically as one may read Frank's novels, this joy is just the redemptive quality one fails to find in them. That note one finds in Tolstoi's description of the mowers in *Anna Karenina*, and one finds it again in Father Zossima's deathbed injunctions in *The Brothers Karamazov:* some of it pervades all their works. But despite Frank's effort to impart this divine joy through his fiction, the place where it naturally arises, organically and magnificently, is in his imaginative representation of other cultures: pre-eminently in *Virgin Spain*, in *South American Journey*, and in his biography of Bolívar.

Now it is in Frank's major works, where he himself is least visible, least seeking to manipulate events and experiences in order to reveal his ultimate philosophy and plan of redemption, that the poet comes out and his true virtues as an imaginative writer, as a kind of lyrical anthropologist and historian, rise to the surface. In this realm Frank has few American rivals, and for any comparable gift one must go back to writers like de Tocqueville and Taine. In these books Frank actually comes close to what he dearly wished to achieve in both his life and his novels: the surrender of himself to a movement of life that transcends his personal limitations. What Frank saw, felt, grasped, understood of the elemental Hispanic world completely absorbed him; and he surrendered himself to it like an imaginative lover who, by his very self-effacement, gives more of himself to the object of his love.

Though I regard Frank's interpretation of nations and cultures as offering the best evidence of his special gifts, there are other works that have stimulated and challenged me, and may still do so to later readers if only as mementoes of past historic occasions and now buried hopes. These begin with *The Rediscovery of America* and come to a climax, as a further summation of his conscious philosophy, in *The Rediscovery of Man*. In between lies his timely and often cogent *Chart for Rough Water*. If Frank's autobiography sends the reader back to these books, he will not, I promise, come away empty.

But enough! Far more important than anything I have been able to say in this Introduction, by way of either appreciation or negation, are Frank's own reflections on the whole course of his life: for this memoir, written in the loneliness of old age, while inwardly battered to the point of almost suicidal despair, exhibits such an access of self-knowledge, such desperate candor about his human misjudgements, his political naivetés, his Quixotic fantasies, as few men dare to display even at the height of their powers. In his latter years Frank had in fact achieved a humility and an honesty that should disarm all petty personal hostility. Here, as repeatedly in his latest letters to me, his grief over the cold indifference of his contemporaries mingles with a remorseful wonder over whether the fault may not in fact have been his own.

Looking into his own heart, Frank plainly did not find "the whole and integral man" who was to "create the fertile revolution." Both had turned out to be mythical projections, disappearing below the waves with the sinking continent of "Waldea." For consolation he turned to the image of Don Quixote, whose heroic illusions would still be needed to quicken the ass's pace of the multitude of sober, down-to-earth Sancho Panzas.

Too late Frank had acquired the self-knowledge that might have altered his whole career and earned for him in his own generation the place that his redoubtable talents originally promised him. It had taken a lifetime of experience for him to understand that though he might have "the egoism of the martyr" he had utterly lacked "the shrewdness of the saint." He realized in these final hours that his bravest ambitions had been thwarted, his most generous social hopes had been betrayed, his prophetic announcements had remained unheeded: in short, his cosmos had fallen apart and his God had deserted him. Yet out of that funeral pyre of Waldo Frank's ego, a living writer arose: the brave man who in his last days wrote this memoir of his life.

LEWIS MUMFORD

Chronology

1889	Born 25 August at Long Branch, New Jersey.
1902–1906	Attended DeWitt Clinton High School, New York.
1906–1907	Attended a private preparatory school in Lausanne, Switzerland.
1907	Entered Yale University.
1911	Graduated from Yale University. Received bachelor of arts and master's degrees concurrently: Phi Beta Kappa. Summer: worked as rancher, Wyoming and Montana.
1911–1913	Reporter for *New York Evening Post* and *New York Times*.
1913	February–September: lived in Paris.
1914–1916	Lived in New York, Greenwich Village. First fiction published in *Smart Set*.
1916–1917	November 1916–October 1917: associate editor and regular contributor, *Seven Arts* magazine. 20 December: Married Margaret Naumburg.
1917	January: first fiction, *The Unwelcome Man,* published (composed 1914–1915). *Seven Arts* suspends publication. June: registered for the draft in World War I as a pacifist.
1918	Traveled through midwestern and western states. *The Art of the Vieux Colombier* published.
1919	November: *Our America* published (composed 1918–1919).

	November–December: served for four weeks as organizer for Non-Partisan League in Kansas.
1920	Traveled through the South with Jean Toomer. *The Dark Mother* published (composed 1917–1920).
1921	Trip to Spain and France.
1922	May: son Thomas born. *City Block* published (composed 1920–1922); also *Rahab* (composed 1920–1921).
1923–1924	Visited Algeria and Spain; met Alfonso Reyes and other writers in Madrid. *Holiday* published (composed 1922); also *Chalk Face* (composed 1923–1924); and *Salvos*, collected essays, 1916–1924.
1925	April: began series of "profiles" for the *New Yorker*. November: named contributing editor to *New Republic*.
1926	Divorced from Margaret Naumburg. March: *Virgin Spain* published (composed 1921–1925). May: named contributing editor to *New Masses*. Trip to Cuba and Isle of Pines with Hart Crane. *Time Exposures, by Search-Light* published anonymously. Visited eastern Europe and Palestine; traveled with Adolph Oko.
1927	March: Married Alma Magoon. Lectured at New School for Social Research, New York, on modern art. "Rediscovery of America" appeared in serial form in the *New Republic*.
1928	Visited Charlie Chaplin in Hollywood.
1929	March: *Rediscovery of America* published; also *New Year's Eve: A Play*. July–December: lecture tour of Latin American countries: Mexico, Argentina, Bolivia, Peru, Cuba; also Chile, Colombia, Brazil, and Uruguay.

1930	*Primer mensaje a la America Hispana* (the Latin American lectures) published in Madrid. Daughter Michal born.
1931	May: father died. July: daughter Deborah born. September: *America Hispana* published (composed 1930–1931). August–November: tour of USSR.
1932	February: heads committee of writers, aiding striking miners in Tennessee and Kentucky. 10 February: assaulted by vigilantes and expelled from Harlan County, Kentucky, when on expedition taking supplies to strikers. Headed writers' delegation to protest treatment of Bonus Marchers in Washington.
1934–1935	*The Death and Birth of David Markand* published (composed September 1932–July 1933). Visited Argentina and Chile. Addressed the American Writers' Congress; elected chairman of League of American Writers. Delegate to International Congress for the Defense of Culture, Paris.
1936	Resigned as chairman of League of American Writers. Joined committee of writers to support Communist Party candidates Earl Browder and Robert Ford. 30 September: arrested with Browder at Terre Haute, Indiana.
1937–1938	Delegate and speaker, Congress of Revolutionary Writers and Artists of Mexico, Mexico City; visited Trotsky in Mexico. Traveled in Europe, including France and Republican Spain. Lived in London, friendship with Sir Richard Rees. *In the American Jungle (1925–1936)*, collected essays, published; also *The Bridegroom Cometh*, published in London (composed 1935–1938).
1939	Toured southern Mexico with President Cárdenas.

1940	With Lewis Mumford, resigned from *New Republic*. *Chart for Rough Water* published (composed 1935–1938).
1941	*Summer Never Ends* published.
1942	April: revised edition of *Virgin Spain* published. April–September: second Latin American lecture tour. 1 August: declared *persona non grata* by Argentine government. 2 August: assaulted by fascists in Buenos Aires; hospitalized.
1943	May: *South American Journey* published (written April 1942–January 1943). August: divorced Alma Magoon in Reno. Married Jean Klempner.
1944	August: *The Jew in Our Day* published (collected essays written for periodicals 1926–1944).
1946	*Island in the Atlantic* published (composed 1940–1946).
1947	Son Jonathan born.
1948	May: *The Invaders* published (composed February–August 1947). Early 1948–early 1949: trip to Venezuela, Colombia, Ecuador, Bolivia, Peru. Research on Bolívar for biography commissioned in 1948 by Venezuelan government (overthrown before work completed).
1951	September: *Birth of a World: Bolívar in Terms of his Peoples* published (written 1948–1951).
1952	February: elected to membership in National Institute of Arts and Letters.
1953	May: *Not Heaven* published (composed 1948–1952). May: son Timothy born.
1954	April: began a monthly, syndicated series of critical essays for Latin American periodicals.
1957	June: *Bridgehead: The Drama of Israel* published.

1958	*Rediscovery of Man* published.
1960	Visited Cuba and Fidel Castro.
1961	*The Prophetic Island: A Portrait of Cuba* published.
1962–1967	At work on autobiography and other writings, including two unpublished novels.
1967	Died 9 January in White Plains, New York.

I

Winter Looks at Spring

1

The World of West 78th Street

The house on West 78th Street was one of the solid rows of three-and four-story dwellings that made a phalanx between the Hudson River and Central Park.[1] Through the phalanx, darkening Columbus Avenue, ran the "El" whose puffy little engines, until the line was electrified, belched their hot cinders into parlor windows. These flats were dingy before they had a chance to age. Despite the crowding, neighbors did not know each other. Next door to our house in the middle of the block lived a Cuban family named Marino. Not one of them was ever inside the Frank house and none of the Franks ever visited the Marinos. Yet, altogether, the inhabitants of the blocks of private dwellings felt themselves distinct from the dwellers in the flats of Amsterdam and Columbus Avenues. I recall a little episode of no importance which tells much. My father had ordered a carpenter on Amsterdam Avenue to come and give him an estimate for shelves in the basement to house the overflow of law books for which there was no room in his downtown office. The man came just as the family was sitting down to dinner. Father gave orders for him to wait in the kitchen and proceeded calmly and slowly to enjoy his dinner. The workman's long wait made the boy nervous: not the father, nor probably the carpenter. The boy felt guilt, although he did not even try to guess whether the guilt came from the indifference of the parent to the comfort and time of the workman or from his—the boy's—failure to take his superiority for granted, which would have made the discourtesy to the carpenter a small matter.

What can take shape here is not a picture of a spring so much as a picture of a winter looking at a spring. For the man and woman who in the early eighties bought the house on West 78th Street and through the fullest years of their marriage lived in it with their four growing children, the world was at spring. But the recollector of this spring is a man past seventy, older than his parents were when they moved out of the old house; and all I can set down now and here must be the revealment of my ageing self reflecting upon that now lost green world. It was green, but it was also brown. It was full of a sap of love, a flowing and a flowering, but hard as the tough oak. God was acknowledged in it, a fatherly and orderly God who listened to the prayers of little boys and girls if they were good, promising them prosperity when they grew up, if always they were good: a God of justice and also, in contrast, a God of nature—of Darwin's nature: the survival of the fittest. For the life of the house (and of similar houses of relatives and friends and fellow-citizens throughout the land) was carried on within the rules of a fierce competition, within the laws of a jungle defending the rightful booty of the strong against the disorderly weak.

None of this was conscious in me, of course, the youngest of the four children. But it was implicit, I now see, in my earliest attitudes. The house was a warm fortress, with coal in the cellar to keep it warm through coldest nights. The laws of property were the fortress ramparts, taken for granted as a child always takes his environment for granted. The substantial, comfortable furniture including the Steinway grand piano was simply *there*, unarguable as the clothes covering each body. The good food, deliciously prepared, stated the master's right to the best of the earth. And the house domestics and the tradesmen who served the family were examples of the human race decent and permissible so long as they remained in their places. These places were of permanent subordination. No one doubted the lowliness of labor, least of all the servants, foundations of the house and of its security within. But the cook or maid who lost her place and carried no "reference" from her last mistress to her next was a lost life.

The Freudians surely would find much to make of the fact that my sustained and substantial memory hardly begins before my seventh year. (I was born August 25, 1889, in Long Branch, New Jersey, in a white frame house with a porch around it, a block above the sea, where the family was spending the summer.) Of my fifth summer, two episodes stand out. The old wood hotel in Forest Park had a tower rising above the long second story. There was a violent thunder-storm, and the lightning seemed to strike the flimsy building. Little Waldo saw a ball of electric fire, bigger than his head, roar down the tower stair and vanish. The tower was not struck, there was no fire, but my memory remains firm and invincible against the evidence. This was the first occasion when my exact recollection runs counter to what must have been the precise fact. That same summer I found on the hotel grounds, under a window of an annex, a nest of wasps or hornets; and began pelting it with stones. The angry insects came out and swarmed around my head. My mother, or my governess, found me in a ferocious cloud of swarming, yellow beasts which with cries of terror the two women tried to beat away from my eyes. I was not stung. It was a cold day, and my father ascribed my escape to the hornets' sluggish condition in the unseasonable weather.

Two events: both violent, one largely distorted, one unreal. The last decade of her life, my grandmother, the mother of my mother, who lived with us, was blind. I see her in her widow's black which she wore in perpetual mourning for her husband, who died just before my birth. (She used to say her husband's soul had entered the body of her grandson.) In this memorial event, she is not blind, and therefore it can be reckoned I was five or less. She and Frieda, one of the servants, are seated sewing together, a pile of clean but unironed wash before them, and little Waldo is with them. Suddenly I ask: "Is there a difference between the bodies of men and women?" Without hesitation, a bit sternly, grandmother says, "No: there is no difference." Frieda, large-bosomed German peasant with black hair and a splotched complexion, gives a little whinny of amusement. Soon grandmother sets her sewing aside and leaves the room. I repeat the question. Frieda giggles, I jump up and with both hands lays hold of her mighty bosom, lifting a huge breast free of the loose brown cotton blouse. Frieda feigns anger and thrusts back her treasure whose sight has overwhelmed me half with ecstasy, half with disgust. In all the other earliest memories of the gentle little grandmother with a black lace cap on her grey hair, she is blind. And as far back as I can remember, in my nightly prayer (after the perfunctory one I must repeat with my mother) I beg of God: "Save me from blindness."

The common denominator of these remembered moments is aggression or the fear of it, my own or nature's. I adored my grandmother who saw in me consciously the prolation of her husband. Her blind face was the mask of peace. Her voice was never raised. And in the Japanese cabinet across from her bed she kept treasures, of some of which I was invited to partake: a candy, a candied fruit, or piece of ginger. Was I afraid of blindness because the blind face of my grandmother was sweet? Perhaps it is natural that violence of some sort should first jog a child's memory into order.

There is a photograph of me standing on a chair, which doubtless dates with these earliest memories. The black-haired, doughty little fellow looks sullen, near bursting into tears of anger, and one guesses that the hand on the carved mahogany chair arm might easily become a fist. The joined black eyebrows over the nose make a perpetual scowl of temper. I was all of seven, it seems, before any peaceful remembered rapture displaced aggression.

I fell in love with my first grade teacher at Horace Mann School. The print that stands now in my conscious mind is of a woman, ageless, in pale blue, colored and textured, I now see, like a figure of Puvis de Chavannes with soft luminous hair and the countenance of an angel. One day, when class was dismissed, I was told to wait (doubtless some problem had arisen of transport home, two miles away). But I thought I was being "kept in," for some untold fault. I howled inconsolably, and Miss Schuster, not understanding, tried to comfort me. The touch of her hand brought heaven into my hell. Here too is violence: what could be more aggressive than chastisement for an unjust accusation, more pervading than a guilt without cause? The little fellow I was seemed to like to have pretexts for joy in pain. What was punishment if the executioner was lovely?

There seems, then, to be factual evidence that around the age of *seven* my organic memory begins: the house of 78th Street as a whole, the family as a whole, begins . . . and the world outside becomes a whole of negation of the far greater world "within."

A little after seven, I became the high priest—and the body—of a religion: a new one or at least my own. Friday is bath night for me. I luxuriate in the hot soapy water. I lie stretched out in it, on my back (the tub longer than my stripling length), all immersed except my penis. It stands up, erect, the island apex of a continent which a pressure of hand and foot on the bottom of the tub reveals above the water. This is the Waldean continent,[2] with the male organ as its center. . . . So far as I can recall, that is all there was to it: no dogma to this religion, no ritual: solely the fact of the continent of my body to be contemplated and that has my name, Waldea, and is centered at my member. But the grandiloquence of this childish game translates, we shall see, into childish deed . . . ambition.

I am the youngest. I adore and also envy and hate my big brother who is the oldest, almost seven years my senior. My sisters I envy and resent for they look up to their brother and look down on me, the baby of the family. My love for Joseph is a hot glow. I melt in it and it threatens to destroy me. This is a permanent attitude in the group which threatens war, and war is never far away. I raid my sisters' dolls and break them. When they play house with sheets for walls and ceiling, I tear the sheets down. I let fly a hairbrush at my brother, which crashes on his cheek. I hurl an iron fireman at sister Enid which barely misses her eye and leaves a scar forever.

Of course, love is in this spiced brew—and desire. On one recalled occasion, my elder sister, Edna, dries me with a rough crash towel after my bath and the touch of her hand on me is a delight I can control (lest it bring shame) only by clowning. She too is kindled and the war between us is forgotten.

Mother creates the home anew, each day. The house lives and works, nurturing and guarding, because of mother. It is lovely to look at, full of music, because of mother. Yet the house does not bound mother. She transcends it, as a sun transcends its planets. She is immensely occupied running the house, holding the servants up to her standard which allows no speck of rust on the library mantel, marketing and shopping; when there are guests to dinner superintending the high culinary arts in the kitchen before they arrive; practicing her music daily (she was a radiant soprano and before her marriage Leopold Damrosch, her teacher, father of the less gifted Walter and Frank Damrosch, wished to train her for the opera—to the horror of her conventional parents). When she sang for the company after dinner I, long since sent to bed, sat on the stair outside my fourth-story room, shared with my brother, and drank in the fire and honey of her voice in the romantic songs she loved best: Schubert, Schumann, Brahms, Hugo Wolf, Richard Strauss, and Franz.

That walk to bed through the dark house was a constant bad dream I had to master before the good dream of the music could save me. So I learned the partnership of pain and joy. I recall my dread at table as I waited the word I knew was coming: "Waldo, bedtime." Slow as I dared, but at once, I go from face to face, saying good night, and at last leaving the light. It is a generous house, but electricity and gas are saved in the now empty upper stories where I must venture alone, being the youngest and the first to bed. Demons of fear inhabit this dark; and terrifying questions: What would I do if I met a burglar—or a murderer!—or a face so horrible that it made me mad?

Wherever she was, my mother . . . efficient lady . . . was a presence. Yet I did not see her objectively; some force within her was always interposing. She was an artist, and a disappointed one. Her little private audience or charity bazaar recitals were no surrogate for the wide applause she craved. Her children felt a lack in her, and suffered. As a parent, their father was more whole. He was away, of course, all day practicing law. But when he was there, he was complete. In mother there was always a subtle discord between what she gave her children and what they wanted. When I was ill, father's step was the most soothing. He accepted the sickness, which in some recondite way mother *protested* as if the child's illness was a burden on her.

I am quite sure now that I was a pretty bad boy because the badness brought my mother closer, warmed her into a more malleable being. Mother would run desperate hands through her hair; she would sob: "Aren't you *ashamed?*" and this brought her perversely near to me. What did the naughty boy do? I stole raisins and cooking chocolate tablets from the kitchen closet, sneaking down the circular stair from the butler's pantry so still that cook and laundress at the kitchen table before a cup of coffee never heard me. I smuggled bananas into my bureau drawer upstairs and when mother confronted me days later with the rotted fruit staining my underwear I brazened it out, denying my guilt. I dirtied my pants, almost daily. And when I was scolded or prayed over, my nose twisted like a rabbit's. . . . Until one day, in desperation, my mother took me to a famous doctor.

I recall his name: the celebrated Dr. Janeway: and his brown beard and his eyes quietly observing—as they dwelt within him. He took me alone into his study: everything brown and heavy, and asked me to sit down, and smiled, and when a few questions had been answered leaned smiling toward me and said in a voice that was half whisper—and that filled the world: "You know, Waldo, this weakness of your bowels is not your fault. Not in the least your fault. If you had a weak leg, so that sometimes it failed to support you, would you blame—blame anyone? Simply, you'd get that leg fixed. *And we're going to fix it.*"

I felt *good;* never had I felt so *good.* I did not need to go back to Dr. Janeway. The dirty pants—barring a few accidents—were past. I had other problems, almost as serious. When I fought or romped with the boys, after school, I cried! I wasn't hurt; I might even be winning the fight. But in the struggle, I cried; I needed to cry and so the boys called me cry-baby. I was perhaps a coward, or needed to be a coward. My mother must see me cry as I fought with the boys on the block. I could be tough—but she must see me.

On the adjacent 77th Street, off Broadway, there were two fire-stations, an engine and a hook-and-ladder. It was a joy when my brother took me there. The alarm rang, the horses rushed forward from their stalls and stood under the suspended harness which needed only to be buckled into place. Meanwhile, the men hurtled down the poles from the floor above, finishing their dressing as they came.

Soon, seemingly without trace, as I grew enough to go about alone, the Waldean continent vanished. I now knew my destiny! I would be a fireman. For several years I was the intrepid hero leaping and living among flames, succoring children and women: I had by now a room to myself on the fourth floor. It became the cabinet room where the president admonished his secretaries. It became the army tent from which I conducted victorious campaigns against the rebels. On the same top floor slept two of the maids. I was delivering a long speech to the people, standing before the mirror. President, commander in chief, great and humble democrat, the common ground of all my roles was my long suffering before all the others. It wasn't fun, it was a burden like Lincoln's. I would hear footsteps on the stairs. Annie was coming up to bed. Swiftly I stripped myself stark naked and opened the door a little. Annie had mahogany colored hair and blue Irish eyes and a sunken chest which hinted at malnutrition in some Irish hamlet. The door was ajar. Annie said: "Good night, Mr. Waldo," and went on to her room.

Like everyone, I accepted the status of the servants; but my rebelliousness making me a naughty boy soon gave me a sense of them that was subversive. My mother patronized them, and was a severe mistress, and they loved her. How comparatively successful she was came out when the other ladies on her Wednesdays at home told their latest servant troubles. I did not like my mother's popularity with her slaves. The status became ritual on Christmas Eve when gifts were dispensed. The servants came in, one by one, and received fruits, raisins, packages of candy, and a few articles of personal wear, a scarf, lace handkerchiefs, embroidered bedroom slippers. They came forward, received their gifts and retired. I never liked it.

From about seven to twelve, my development was explosive rather than linear. I read a number of the novels of Scott, of Dickens, and of Thackeray, in that order. I did not like them. I trudged sturdily through one or two George Eliot, and was bored. The house was pro-Thackeray; the girls loved *The Mill on the Floss;* father rather shamefacedly favored Dickens, as a man might secretly enjoy cigars. (He did not smoke.) I began to frequent the public library on Amsterdam Avenue and 82nd Street. Here, for the first time, I read the exotic names: Balzac, Tolstoi and Flaubert. I knew at once these writers were for me. A whole winter and spring, the bananas and chocolate in my bureau drawers were replaced by forbidden volumes. Then I encountered *Hedda Gabler*. My mother, baffled, watched me roam the house in a spell that both exiled and freed me from my ordinary life. I did not know what the play meant—but did Hedda know? Somehow, Ibsen came closer, cuttingly closer, than the exalted words of Shakespeare, the Old Testament, and Tennyson, which my father read aloud to the children after dinner.

Already I had discovered Poe. In a small notebook I put down every word Poe used which I did not understand; I looked it up, and at the next meal practiced the use of it—often to the family's hilarious laughter. I would say, "I am two lustrums old," or "My hair is too planturous for a comb." I decided to read the entire *Comédie Humaine* (in translation). I earned my first dollars copying names and addresses from the school files for a mail order house and with them bought a complete Balzac. I would never forget the sensuous joy of those volumes standing in columns before me. There was a cosmos in them, palpable in each story. This of course is the triumph of Balzac: in the self of any of his greater tales the spirit of the universe is revealed: not in a character or group of characters but in the whole of a town, a business, an intrigue. No other novelist approaches this, except perhaps Tolstoi in *War and Peace;* I was right. But my reading soon branched out. The enjoyer of Balzac's self (as I would say today) with its cosmic and social dimensions cultivated also the anarchist Max Stirner, in whom the ego overwhelms the social and the cosmic.

I had an older cousin, Eddie Fried, who at the time introduced me to *Leaves of Grass.* I suspect that Eddie loved Whitman chiefly for *Calamus*, Whitman's love of "robust comrades." But the encounter was a thrill I never lost. Whitman found multitudes within his self, within all selves. That was the first part of the miracle. The rest was that he designated America as the home of this mystic revelation; and sang his discovery in rhythms broad as the continent. I still have the green-bound copy of *Leaves of Grass* given me by my father (who, I believe, found Whitman unreadable) and rededicated by him to the fifteen-year-old boy. The worn book is filled with pencilled notes, most of them quite childish, and defensive as if I needed to protect my preference by odious comparisons . . . with Longfellow and Whittier.

There was an annual oration contest at DeWitt Clinton. The high school had not yet moved to its new building on West 59th

Street, and the tourney was held in a long, narrow, uncomfortable hall. In one of the last rows of seats I saw my parents. They should not have come! For a few moments I lost control of my fears. My classmate, Vincent Gilroy, finished his address on "The Spirit of 1776." Then I faced my first public. Most of the audience, including the teachers, had never read a line of Whitman. Somehow, I succeeded in making them ashamed of their "neglect." My method was simple: I read a few lines of the poet, and dared the listeners to deny that this was poetry. What moved me to this passionate partisanship? Whitman shared with other mystic poets his sense of the Whole and of participation in the Whole. The unique in Whitman, and the irresistible appeal for me, was that he *naturalized* his sense of the cosmic Whole into the body and shape of America. They gave me the gold medal. I did not know that in other Americas and in other tongues, poets and mystic warriors were making the same heroic revelations.

I was already keeping notebooks, filling them with exalted resolutions—even with titles of books I would never write. (I recall two: *The Will without a Way* and *The Way without the Will.*) I put down about this time: "All the books that I shall write shall be proofs of God." This, of course, was pure Walt Whitman.

But do not imagine that I spent most of my hours in intellectual pursuits and speculations. The house and home of which I was a member was a dynamic unit and above all it kept going. Moreover, it kept going from certain premises not too complex and never challenged. Thus, there was sharp antagonism between me and my father, but the father's right to govern in accord with certain values was not questioned. There were tensions; not war, nor war's dissolutions. The home housed three nations: the servants, the elders, and the children. The servants lived in their top-floor bedrooms and in the kitchen and laundry. Mother alone could rightfully invade them. I never saw my father in the kitchen, and went there myself only for snacks and raids. The elders (mother, father, grandmother) lived on the second floor, but the first floor library and parlor with its piano and organ (played by father) was also their terrain. Yet access to it was free, even compulsory when Edna practiced piano, Enid the violin, and I the cello. The basement (for breakfast and lunch) and the dining room (exclusively for dinner) were of course barred to the domestics except in so far as they served the masters. Despite the large library, dark with its one window (soon shaded by a single ailantus tree), its dark bookshelves, its colorless pictures; the home expressed itself more through music (which mother stood for) than through books. Mother sang daily.

Her eldest brother, Herman, lived in a like house on the same block. He was a rich business man, and he played the fiddle badly; but he got up in time every morning except Sunday to practice a half hour before breakfast. Every Wednesday or Thursday night (I forget which) he had a quartet in his home. He played the second violin; a cousin, Alexander Bloch, played the viola. The first violin was the professional, Mr. Edouard Hermann, who taught my sister, Enid; and the cellist was Emile Schenck, my teacher—a poor cellist who scratched when he played fast, but a sweet, large, gentle and indolent man for whom music was simply language, not requiring instruction to those *native* to it, beyond grammar. (He wanted to make a cellist of me, who did not see myself practicing twelve hours in succession.) Alex Bloch suddenly gave up a lucrative business job, went to Europe to study with Leopold Auer, became a professional musician, and finally a famous teacher. For this he was universally condemned; in particular by the ladies who on the musical nights sat in the room beyond the music room and gossiped.

Mother had six brothers (one of whom died early), all in the family business of making varnish. Since they had all come from the South, their childhood home, after the War between the States they settled where business dictated. Business was life; therefore it is not surprising that they all seemed to fit where they lived. Herman, the amateur violinist, whose son, Arthur, was my dearest friend, whose daughter Helen was a ravishing beauty, and whose home was down the block from ours, was a quiet, simple man, the opposite of brilliant, but intelligent and firm. He was the president of this family concern which at its height was the largest of its kind in the world with factories widespread from Chicago and Toronto to New York and London. After Herman came Theodore, a resident of London. I was supposed to resemble him, which may somewhat explain why we so warmly liked each other. He came to New York frequently, and often invited me to an English breakfast in his hotel room which smelled of heavy leather luggage and the best tobacco. In accord with British form, he always "tipped" me—a five dollar bill or a gold sovereign. Uncle Theodore was a sober, dependable man, in sharp contrast to Oscar, who headed the Chicago branch, a somewhat raucous little sport, bubbling with vitality and quips, the archetypal salesman whose jokes with ladies present were never too risqué and whose taste for his sister's succulent dishes—whenever he came to town—

inspired his lyric praise. Willie, whose son, Bill, I loved in a friend-ship which our differences often strained but never broke, lived ten blocks farther uptown in an elegant house near Central Park West and the Park, with an "American basement" in lieu of the old-fashioned stoop. He too was the perfect salesman, but he was also a gourmet (he would have said *Feinschmecker*). I can still see him, savoring the smoke of a choice *Habana* as if it had been a fine cognac. He was a little man (the brothers were all short) who compensated by the largeness of his spending. He was the first of the family to own a car (a Panhard-Lévasseur), and al-though he made good money he was often broke. The youngest, younger than their sister, and tallest, was Edward, who also lived in London. Edward was more entrepreneur than standard busi-nessman. He drew his excess profits out of varnish and at an early date invested—among the first—in plastics. He lived in a mansion, enclosed in its own park with a high iron grille around it, near Regents Park with over a dozen servants, gardeners, and chauffeurs to run his establishment. Indeed he was one of the privileged commoners with whom Albert Edward, Prince of Wales, liked to play cards, doubtless savoring their raciness and push.

Uncle Edward was something of a practical joker. On one oc-casion, when my mother was in England with her children, he took us for a day's outing. We stopped at an inn for lunch, and mother, who could not tolerate even a glass of wine, was served from a tall decanter of fruit juices, masking champagne. The in-nocent lady became suddenly quite gay—and giddy. Uncle Ed-ward thought the gaiety was worth the price of a bit of sickness.

Friday nights, at home, became a source of my education, at least equal to music and books, school, and the boys on the block. Father's two celibate brothers, Alfred and Jerome, and their spin-ster sister, Celia, came to dinner at least twice a month, except in summer. There were stormy arguments about politics here and abroad. After dinner Leo, the other brother, might come and usually one or two of mother's brothers. With the best trained mind in the family to back up his priority, father would override the weak logic of the others who usually opposed his liberalism. Gentle Jerome was for peace at any price; gruff Alfred was peppery and loved a fight with his elder brother. Jerome was the chemist in the varnish business; Alfred was a manufacturer and importer of papers; lived frugally, died rich. Both adored their elder brother who, on their father's death, had helped support the family by teaching at "Workingmen's Night School" while he was studying law at Columbia Law School. I soon noted that no one ever changed his judgment, despite whatever devastating proofs against it. Aunt Celia was a forerunner of the modern woman. She belonged to a Portia Club and she too adored her brother, which perhaps explains why she never married. There was a wildness in her, manifest in bursts of temper. And she made it plain, even to the children, that in her judgment their father had married "beneath him"—which would have been the case whomsoever he had married.

When the after dinner folks arrived, the men sat around the table, while the wives retired to library or parlor. And this was Aunt Celia's tragedy; she would have preferred to discuss politics or books with the men, rather than servants and the latest sale at Altman's with the women. In truth, the explosive little lady had a quite untrained mind and was run entirely by her emotions, which despite the Portia Club remained feminine. The children all loved her. When we were ill, Aunt Celia helped to nurse us; and we knew that her touch, under her brusqueness, was as sensitive as father's.

Non-relatives were not invited to the Friday night dinners, which were strictly family . . . with exceptions. One was Julius Fehr, a Catholic Rhineland German, equally at ease in German, French, or English which he spoke with rhythms that now remind me of W. C. Fields. Family friend and family wine merchant, he came on business every year from Europe, and while he was in town he attended our Friday nights, loving mother's sweet-sour fish, planked steak, mushrooms *sous cloche,* and potato *puffer* as much as anyone. He came, always, with personal gifts for each child: superb chocolate cigars for the boys, dolls and pretty handkerchiefs for the girls, puzzles and German picture books for everyone. He was a tall, lean man, slow moving as if his joints needed some of the oil he lavished in his conversation. He would sit at table at father's left hand, and father would ask: "Well, Mr. Fehr, what have you done today?" Whereupon Herr Fehr would give a detailed account of his day, hour by hour, minute after minute, place by place, bar by bar—recording everyone he had met, everyone he had missed, everything he had said, with a meticulous completeness that would be the envy (since humor was in it) of the "new realists" now writing novels in Paris. He was never boring; he was always delightful because he was always, himself, *delighted.* The people he saw were mostly his customers. And he would sail back to Europe with exact instructions of each patron's orders in Bordeaux, Rhine wines, Tokays, and sherries. I loved Herr Fehr—and envied him, for he was always having a good time—I, a bad time; always loving, whereas I always seemed to myself to be "griping." Herr Fehr kept on coming until 1914 . . . until the genial, relaxed little world he represented vanished.

Of course, those Friday nights were the remnant of the Jewish Sabbath dinner; and the family's religious status is well revealed in the surprising fact that—until I grew up—I never knew this. "Friday night" was to me simply a family gathering, held at my father's house since he was the head of the family; and the dinner was a feast representing my mother's culinary genius. She trained her cooks. Her repertory was famous unto the most remote family frontiers. None of the ladies questioned this superiority, as none questioned her singing art, which was usually sampled around ten o'clock when the arguments of the men and the confidences of the women about "servants—troubles or treasures"—flagged. Not a word, not a ritual act, ever reminded anyone that this was the Sabbath meal, the weekly Sabbath hour after the days of grinding battle for survival, when every Jew must rejoice in sumptuous food and wine, *as if* the Lord Jehovah were indeed caring for his people.

If talk at these reunions had been recorded, no direct clue that these men and women were Jews would have emerged. Yet they all knew they were Jews, would have been shamed even implicitly or indirectly to deny or hide that they were Jews, and were proud of their Jewish values. None belonged to a synagogue or temple. They were more cosmopolitan than the average gentile business family, and they were also more cosmopolitan than the run of Jews pouring into New York from eastern Europe. In Alabama, the parents of my mother had disapproved of slavery and for servants hired the slaves of others. But this was not uniquely Jewish. In the 1850s, my mother's father invested in New York real estate and a Pennsylvania coal mine. When war came, he sold out and exchanged his good northern securities for Confederate paper—of course, losing every cent. Was this Jewish? My father was a trustee of the Society for Ethical Culture (horrendous name!). Its founder, Felix Adler, a watery neo-Kantian but a great preacher, *lectured* on Sunday morning. The society had a Sunday school, to which I went once. I refused to go again, and father did not insist. Years later, in *Our America,* I attacked the basic premises of this pseudo-church. My father said nothing. The society attacked me, still my father was silent.

I came to know the workers' houses: the long, dark, musty halls, the bedrooms giving on airless and lightless inner courts, the front parlors with a cheap chromo calendar on the walls and tinsel bric-à-brac, above all the pervading smells of boiled cabbage and pork chops. Class distinctions, I found, suffused into the family. There was a cousin, whose business had failed and who was now a mere employee, living in a cheap little frame house near Broadway ("the Boulevard") and 149th Street. He, his wife, and the children were of course welcome at family gatherings, although they seldom came, and nothing was ever said to embarrass them. But the stigma of un-success was implicit on them all, despite the fact, as I soon discovered, that the children of Cousin Pinky were the brightest and the best musicians of the entire lot. There was also Uncle Leo, my father's brother, a rustic and sweet man who never read a book. I suspect that today his I.Q. might be found to be quite low and he might never get to college. He didn't try. He was a businessman, and a good one, with the wits to marry a woman whose brothers were getting rich with stores all over town. He was warm, crude, a little deaf, and loud-voiced. He, too, and his whole family were in the thin outer circle of acceptance.

I began to wander away from our block in ever wider circles; the poor, the "failures," I found everywhere. Was I moved in my discoveries by a principle of "social justice"? I doubt it. I was first of all "against" my father, whose democracy was Jeffersonian. And Jefferson had tolerated slaves. My father, too, as a practicing lawyer, accepted the foundations of society as I found them. But Jefferson had believed in "revolution, every thirty years." I rode the contradictions.

Was it in the third, fourth or fifth grade that I was expelled from Horace Mann School? The teacher, Miss P——, looked like a cat, a scrawny cat with a small head, and without beauty. In the class was a bully, a big fellow and the teacher's pet. He persecuted the appreciably smaller Waldo who got no protection from the partial teacher. Thus, resentment was built up in the small boy, especially against the teacher. One day, when the bully tormented me, I lost my temper. I lunged, we grappled and spun round the room, pounding each other while the rest scampered for safety. On teacher's desk, on a platform raised a half foot from the floor, Miss P—— had a cheap plaster statue of the head of Jupiter. The boys' writhing bodies struck it and it fell, smashing to smithereens. That stopped the battle. But Miss P—— made an issue of it before she would sign a peace. The boys must tell her that they were sorry for what they had done. The bully complied; I refused. I was *not* sorry. Miss P——— and her Jove "had it coming to them." Miss P——— kept on insisting: I must be sorry, and say so. My father was called in and could not make me in my new Promethean role say I was sorry. "Unless he does," said the foolish Miss P———, "he does not remain in my class." So father took the rebel out of Horace Mann and placed me in public school which could not refuse him. I was happy with the change; the new boys' toughness warmed me.

This is my exact memory of the little drama: I can add nothing, take nothing away. Is it too pat a symbol: the young Prometheus uprising alone against Jove, god of things as they are? It's a think-able thing that happened. But why, if that's all there was to it, do I find myself reminded of the dark, deep library in my father's house? The bookshelves were ponderous mahogany, and above them, against the brown walls, were the pictures of my father's heroes: large portraits of Washington and Lincoln, Napoleon and Beethoven—each in his last phase of pain. What is the associative character that binds these disparate men together, in unbreakable closeness? It is the ego; it is the will of the ego. Washington ex-posed his at Valley Forge, the ego-will of the American to be free of England. Lincoln revealed his, when, to hold the Union to-gether, he willed to be dictator and to devastate the whole South in order to bind what had burst asunder. Napoleon's imperial ego willed to equate Europe (and tomorrow Asia, Africa, and America) with the beat of his own pulse. And the ageing Beethoven, maniacally tortured by the need to hold his nephew against his nephew's mother, willed the revelation of joy within the tragic substances of the Ninth Symphony and the last quartets. Poor Waldo with these giants of will looking down upon him! . . .

The principal of the old public school on Amsterdam Avenue to which I went when Horace Mann School expelled me was named Boyer, and this is no joke. He was indeed a man of boys, most of whom loved him, including the toughs. I can still see his gentle face, intelligence tinctured into sadness. He spoke softly and acted slowly. The automobiles, appearing now with ever swifter frequency in the avenues west to the river—soon to be mass-produced—were going to abolish the Boyers. But nobody seemed to know this. His teachers represented him. With especial fond-ness I recall Mr. Daniels, a short, stocky, testy man with upstand-ing grey hair, explosive and humorous. His black alpaca coat was always daubed with chalk, and his way of getting the attention of a pupil was to shoot a bit of chalk at him, as one shoots a marble. He must have been good at marbles. I progressed to DeWitt

Clinton High School which, the year before I left, entered its magnificent new building on Tenth Avenue and 59th Street . . . north of Hells Kitchen from which the Irish toughs strayed to make life hellish for gangless youngsters. Public school in New York at the century's turn was a dynamo of power. The classes, not too large, were people—*the* people, with none of the electronic attractions, radio, movie, and TV yet drawing their pristine energy away. The teachers were individuals, some of them queer ones. In none of my future contacts with school and college was I to meet so alive a group. There was, for example, Mr. Doty who taught Juvenal and Martial as if they had just come out; and Mr. Berry, forever cracking nuts and cracking algebraic problems as if they were nuts.

I loved Clinton, but trouble was brewing for me again, more precisely *because* I loved it. It was my last year. There were two school publications: "The Magpie," a monthly affair that printed my first writings in prose, and "The Clintonian," the yearbook which each senior class brought forth. I was one of the editors of both. We had an editorial room of our own, where the staffs worked or loafed, ate a sandwich or smoked a cigarette. One of the English teachers, a Miss Maud Frank, taught Shakespeare trope by trope. I objected to this method of Shakespearean exegesis. Head of the department of English was Miss Helen Garrigues, and, I suspect, I was in love with her—short, matronly, with great dark eyes under her black hair. The arrogant boy announced that he knew Shakespeare better than Miss Frank and was not going to spoil what I had. I therefore cut my English class and took sanctuary in the "Magpie-Clintonian" office. I say that I was in love with Miss Garrigues, but how could I *make* love to her? By bedevilment, by defiance? Miss Garrigues tried to root me out. If I did not attend class at once, she warned, she would flunk me, and I would lose my school diploma. I refused to be frightened, and finally the principal, Mr. Buchanan, was called in to decide the contest. He ruled that "The Magpie" and "The Clintonian" office room belonged to the editors; Miss Garrigues could not enter it and could extract no one from it. He ruled further that of course Miss Garrigues could flunk any student that did not attend classes. My memory of Mr. Buchanan is doubtless romantic. He must have had his faults and limitations; but surely I cannot be expected to invent them for realism's sake. I still see him clearly: the large head covered with a silken down like a fledgling bird; the relaxed twinkling eyes, the graceful walk as if the old man (as he was to me) might be an excellent dancer. The assistant principal was a brilliant, ambitious, soured Jew named Wolfson (he soon left education and became a man of business, making—I trust—a fortune). Dr. Wolfson and I were too much alike, in some respects, not to clash. One day, I was called down to the office for some breach of the rules. Wolfson clenched his fist and said:

"Frank! If I struck you, it would cost me a month's salary—and be worth it. You are the most insolent . . . the most arrogant . . . the most————."

Mr. Buchanan from his end of the room broke in: "Frank," he smiled, "Dr. Wolfson is using the superlative, I think, in the *Latin* sense. He means very————"

I sympathized with Dr. Wolfson. I was arrogant, insolent, inconsiderate. Without charm, I would have been impossible. Miss Garrigues was hurt, and I did not get my diploma. Did I guess the key to my defiance? that I had no other way to touch her?

I have run ahead of my subject—not that it matters, since I am not writing a chronology. "The Magpie" began my publications but I was composing long before that. When I went to Europe with my mother and sisters in 1901 (*aetat.* eleven), I filled a crimson-leather-bound blank book stamped in gold letters: *My Trip Abroad.* And even earlier my grandmother, whose pet I was, gave me a blue notebook which I filled with platitudinous precepts that reveal my anxious earnest life. The book has vanished, but I remember it. It revealed a surprising intimacy with God whom I was going to help run the world. On the front page, I wrote: "For Mama. Not to be shown to anyone." And when she opened it and read it, she must have felt a certain discomfort, for she said: "This is beautiful, dear. But don't forget that God wants you to obey your mother and your father. That is the way to please God."

I took the notebook back, and tore each page and crumpled the torn pages. My mother was distressed. "Oh, Waldo, why did you do that?"

I could not explain. Nor could I explain why I hated mother's calling me in to be exhibited to her ladies who spoke to me as if I were a precocious monkey.

Meanwhile, the outside world broadened and came in. In 1896, when I was six, a monster named Bryan threatened to ruin the country. If he was elected president, I learned from talk at table, grass would grow in the streets and every dollar would be cut in two. One day in the park, I saw a big man wearing on his lapel a big Bryan button. I looked at the man: he had a kind face . . . seemed a good man. Yet he was going to vote for Bryan! I could not understand and carried my trouble home. Two years later, I saw pictures of starving Cuban children. They kept me awake at night. I wanted to help them and pinned on the wall of my fourth floor room newspaper pictures of General Miles and Commodores Dewey, Schley, and Sampson—all of whom were out to help the starving Cubans. But father frowned on the war. It was politics, he said, unnecessary. I disapproved of my father. Vaguely, the naked Cubans, young or old, fitted in the picture of the slums at both ends of the block with our house at the center! How events within me crowded and jostled!

An old college friend of father's, now a judge in a Pennsylvania city, remarked on the little fellow's "composure." "Phlegmatic, isn't he?" observed Judge Strauss. Waldo's phlegm was the tumult of contradictory exposures. Out of it burst temper and tantrum. My father was by nature warm and tender, but by conviction he was a Roman stoic. His way of helping me get over my twitching nose and eyelids was to twitch his own and say, "Bunny." I lay in bed—it seemed for hours, doubtless it was minutes—trying to control my face. And when I failed, which was always, I felt guilty.

Another college mate of father's played a strange role in my sense of guilt. Henry Leipziger was a dry man with a beard very black against his ashen cheek. He looked (this I did not know) like Svengali. He was in charge of the city's program of free adult education. This consisted chiefly of lectures: Greek sculpture with slides, Brazilian rivers with maps, astronomy with enlarged photographs. When Dr. Leipziger dropped in on father of an evening and cast his baleful eyes on me, I felt guilty.

Guilty of what?

It was a rule when father came home from the office about six for the children to come down from their floor, greet him with "Good, today," if they conscientiously could say it, or, if they had erred, to report the misdemeanor. Dr. Leipziger had nothing to do with this, of course. True, there were little facts in my life that I divulged to no one. With a leap of the heart I had discovered, for instance, a lighted room in the row of houses visible from my back window where a woman undressed without pulling down the shade. And it became my habit to sit in the dark after I was supposed to be asleep seeking illicit glimpses. The rewards were slight. Sometimes, a bare back of promise turned out to be a man's! Sometimes a woman, as if suddenly aware of my hungry eyes, after starting to disrobe pulled down the shade or vanished. And there were other guilts: a lie, a forbidden book, a stolen candy.

All this had nothing to do with Dr. Leipziger. Simply, his bleak and baleful eyes made me guilty. What was *he* thinking? Perhaps he wanted to come close to me or got some satisfaction out of making me uncomfortable. Perhaps he was a mere refrain of father's lesson that play must improve, that fun must nourish, and that nothing must be wasted—despite the seeming waste of motions in the gulls circling sometimes in from the river. Perhaps Dr. Leipziger envied me; he was a lonely man, and few attended his lectures.

The fact was, of course, that my father was a self-contradictory stoic—and to a rationalist the paradox of antithesis means guilt. He taught himself to play the piano and the organ. He liked and knew good wines and took delicious food for granted. He was a constant student and an expert swimmer (having as a youth saved several lives from drowning in the downtown East River). Moral rectitude was the premise of all his dealings, and the friend that was caught in a lie was deleted from his favor.

Yet when I was fifteen, this exemplary man was almost lost in an intrigue with a woman of the breed then called "adventuress." While the spell lasted my father suffered a complete amnesia both factual and moral. Mother and the two girls were abroad. Joseph (I believe) was at Cornell. Only the cook remained, and when this woman came into the house cook left in loyalty to her mistress. The woman, who was pretty as a southern belle, faded at thirty, tried to seduce me; and I escaped only because my fear and sense of outrage was stronger than my awakening lust. Not knowing where to turn, I ran away.

My pennies took me to Long Island; my last nickel bought me a lunch of *zuzus* (ginger crackers). Hungry, I landed a job as time-keeper of a road-gang of Italian immigrants, but it was Saturday and the work would not start until Monday. I crashed a trolley back to Manhattan (well aware that the conductor was aware of me) and sat in Madison Square Park on a bench listening to the men and women discuss Harry Thaw's sensational murder of the architect, Stanford White, in the roof restaurant of Madison Square Garden.

A man sitting beside me guessed my condition and invited me to a meal of ham and three fried eggs which made me know for the first time the ecstasy in food when one is truly hungry. Ecstasy assuaged, the warm evening returned, the soft and brooding city. We went back to our bench in the park. The man (I believe he said he was a printer), as night mantled the town, opened my fly.

But I did not respond except to turn away, and the gentle pervert sublimated his need by getting my story and giving fatherly advice.

"Your mama's in Europe. Think of the state she'll be in, when she learns you've run away. The spunky thing for you to do is to go home. When? Right now. I'll take you to the door."

Forty minutes later, I appeared before my father, in the library, where he was sitting with the woman. "Take off your clothes," he said, "take a hot bath, and go to bed."

In the morning, the woman was not there. My father was gentle but firm, as if I were ill. Nothing was asked or said between us. I had changed my clothes, and father seemed pleased. "I've got you a job," he said. "You'll handle the switchboard at ——————," he named the company owned by my mother's brothers, and the weekly wage. It was a gruelling week, and I have admired ever since the cool poise of telephone girls. After about ten days, I became ill. The nervous strain of the work was too strong for my weak nerves. My father shipped me to Maine to join a couple of friends, and I passed the rest of the summer swimming, camping, reading in wet weather, and peering in hunger at the girls who gathered at the post office and general store. Meanwhile father's brothers, Alfred and Jerome, had hired a detective to shadow Mrs. X. And they soon got incriminating evidence against her, sufficient to persuade her to shift her operations to another city. Her brother turned out to be her pimp, and she was not pregnant as she had claimed to be. Poor Mrs. X! She had a pretty face, a willowy body with large delicious breasts, but her brains were slighter than her body which reminded me—to my chagrin and shame—of my mother's body. The scandal was averted; the home with its romantic music and stern stoical regime went on. The whole family, that autumn, took a trip to Europe. And father never gave a sign, until the day of his death, of having memory of what had happened. His amnesia seemed perfect. I began consciously to love my father, and even to admit that I loved him.

Before I was sixteen, I had greatly broadened my knowledge of the city. I discovered the Bowery with its human wreckage sluicing south to Chatham Square where harp houses and saloons stank like swill and garbage in the sun. William Randolph Hearst, whom I would get to know decades later at the home of Marion Davies in Santa Monica, was running for mayor (1905) against both Tammany and the "silk socks" Republicans, and I was for him. Hearst's yellow journals were not allowed in the house but I smuggled them in. Hearst was for municipal ownership of rapid transit lines, and I on the high school debating team had argued in favor of this mild socialism and won. I did not question father's judgment that Hearst was a demagogue concerned exclusively with winning power. I accepted father's verdict that Hearst had practically staged the war on Spain. Hearst's portrait, plastered all over town on billboards, fascinated me: the jutting male jaw, the bland girl brow. I went to a meeting where Hearst's lawyer, Clarence Shearn, a shrewd and slippery Irishman, called for Hearst watchers at the polls. "They're going to try to steal the election from us. Only watchers at every poll can stop them." Despite my agreement with my father about Hearst there was I, not yet sixteen, a political volunteer with a ribbon badge on my coat lapel. I received instructions on what to do if I found fraud. And on election day I found it, and fear in my heart. In one voting place, a stationery and cigar store, the curtain covering the shelves suddenly flared into flame, and under cover of dragging the curtain down I saw the boxes with the votes vanish to be replaced by others. In another station where I was posted, I saw the regular Tammany organization man hide a stub of pencil in his hand under two fingers which with a stroke invalidated the ballots for Hearst. I was afraid. I looked at the policeman and knew where the "law" stood. No help for me there. Had I protested, I would at best be laughed at and called a little liar; at worst be thrown out with my head bashed open. So I quailed, and accepted that I was a coward. Finally I went to the Hearst headquarters and saw my watcher colleagues with bloody noses and gashed scalps. Hearst lost the election officially by 3,000 votes. I was sure that Hearst had really won, and the taste of practical politics revolted me. I had seen the hard hostile men who looked me over only to sneer and shove me aside. Was I a coward? Perhaps. Perhaps the boy who cried before he was hurt was still not far away. But if life was going to beat me up—of this I was sure —it must be for the sake of something better than the politics of Hearst.

Courage for the sake of poetry, for instance?

I had begun to attend summer camps. The one I remember best (there were at least three) was on an island of a large New Hampshire lake. By now I was writing much verse, amalgams of Tennyson, Swinburne, and the pre-Raphaelites. This summer I was at work on a long poem in blank verse, called *Lauraea*, and I guarded it fearfully under the mattress of my tent-cot. No one, I was sure, knew of its existence.

One night I was awakened from sleep by the most urgent need

to void my bowels. I sprang from my cot, out of the tent, and as I turned toward the privies, the diarrhea overwhelmed my sphincters. As in the times before Dr. Janeway! Next day the excrement was found just within the circle of tents, near the one I shared with two mates. The director, Mr. D———, fired questions at the boys. All denied that they were guilty. I felt guilty, but somehow the guilt was about the secret poem not the innocent crap. I stuck to my denial, and Mr. D——— to his suspicions.

A Sunday or two later it rained and the boys gathered as usual in the social hall, a spacious wooden structure for indoor meetings, games, talks. Mr. D——— got up to speak. He was a bull-necked middle-aged ex-pastor whose chief qualification, it appeared to me, for running a boys' camp was that he hated boys.

"Boys," he addressed the crowded rows of chairs—and when he spoke, his round face with bulgy eyes and a long slit for a mouth became a bullfrog's: "Boys," he repeated, putting jubilance in his croak, "we've made a great and happy discovery. Boys, we have a poet in our midst! A modest, shrinking poet, so that nobody knew until by good luck some of the immortal work fell into our hands. I've got it here, boys, and you're going to hear it." I knew before I saw the sheets of paper that it was *Lauraea*. And when Mr. D——— thundered forth the first lines and the boys whooped with laughter I knew they were right: the stuff was pretentious, awful, and empty. The boys roared. No one was looking at me. But I felt nakedly exposed, and also I felt challenged. I dreaded to show myself, I needed to show myself. I tore from my campchair, stumbling against the seats beside me. I crashed my way to the aisle. And now, 150 savages were aware of me as I raced to the door. They rose, one beast, and followed. Rain drenched the grass as I sped across the enclosure to the surrounding margin of trees and brush. Branches and brambles tore at my face. I plunged into the thicket. There was a path leading uphill to the ball ground; I ran clear of it but the boys followed the path and were soon beyond me up the hill. I crouched panting in the underbrush. I heard my shouted name. Then I heard the voice of Mr. D——— ordering the boys back. Long after, when I was cold and hungry, I returned to my own tent. And nothing was said about the matter. It was almost as if my guilt had gone to the others—above all to the director.

That last year, before the whole family went to Europe, I was already the author of a (never-published) novel. I remember it quite clearly. It was called *Builders in Sand* and every page of it pronounced the existence of a novelist named Tolstoi and of a novelist named Zola. I can see its bold rolling script on legal cap paper. It told the story of a youth and a girl in a village. The boy goes to New York and forgets the girl. She follows to New York, meets adversity, falls under the sinister spell of a floorwalker at the department store where she is working. I don't recall how it happens, but unknown to one another the boy and the girl meet in a room above a gaudy restaurant, and there, through the haze of alcohol and tobacco, recognize each other. More interesting than the banal tale is what happened to the book. My brother had a friend, long since dead, named Marion Elsberg who worked for Putnam's publishing house. The ponderous opus by a boy of fifteen entertained him, and he wanted to bring it out—to "circus" it, as he might have said a decade later. My father said No.

This trip to Europe was for the parents a mere "winter vacation," although unusual in those early years of the nineteen hundreds. To me, now sixteen, it was a catalytic, feeding the growth of traits which otherwise might have remained potential longer. The boat was German (my father was the American attorney of the Hamburg-Amerika Line, then the largest steamship company in the world). Its first port of call was Gibraltar. As the liner glided under the great Rock, it passed close by a group of British destroyers. I was standing on the promenade deck, next to two of the ship's officers, and I saw the glint of their proud German eyes as they took in the rival warships and then met in a pledge that almost spoke: "Der Tag!" Nothing was said. But for the first time, I sensed the ordered anarchy of Europe.

I did not look my age. I was stocky and short and strong: an excellent wrestler. My black hair was too thick for a comb to pass through, and no one seemed sure of the color of my eyes. The family had long called me Methuselah because I could be so solemn and sententious, but this Methuselah had violent bouts of temper. The turnover of governesses in the 78th Street house had been great, for the extremely proper ladies did not like to be bitten; and when they chastised the biting boy by shutting him up in the closet they did not approve of his coming out more rebellious than before.

Some of my pranks, Methuselah would hardly have approved. On my previous trip to Europe with my mother and sisters we had stayed at a hotel in Berchtesgaden (still innocent of Hitler). To celebrate the Fourth of July I played *The Star Spangled Banner* on the piano in the salon, accompanied by cannonades obtained by sitting on the bass end of the keyboard. The proprietor was furious, and mother appeased him by sending me to my room without supper. Then she relented and brought me a tray of food, which I dropped out of the window. The punishment, I said to myself, did not fit the crime. If I had played *Die Wacht am Rhein* with cannon accompaniment, the Bavarian would have been pleased and not worried about his old piano.

Now my sister Enid and I were placed in Lausanne: she at the school of Madame Heubi; I in the pensionnat of M. and Mme. Ami Simon. My roommate was a young six-foot John Bull, ruddy and round of face, immovable in his ideas which were fixed parts of the superiority of his immovable England. When I walked into the low-ceilinged top-floor room he was to share with me, the Britisher said: "I say! Do you sleep with the window open?" "Yes," I answered and all was well between us. The other boys were of Europe with the exception of a dark-complected Egyptian—probably an Arab—who seemed to me the smartest of them all. They were my age or younger: pre-college . . . and I felt them to be older than any college boy I knew, including my own brother. They were older in their pleasures—their experience of women for example; in their family attitudes; in their personal freedom. At night, in the common hall, they smoked and put rum in their tea without bravado. They were not bookish, but they all knew something vaguely of Tolstoi, Turgenev, and Nietzsche. The name of Marx, I believe, was never mentioned.

Whitman by now was in my blood, but the lucid logic of French prose guided my need of form. For this reason, some French authors whom I later rejected meant much to me at first: Paul Bourget, for instance, and Anatole France.

I was already, psychologically, a writer: what I mean is that I already had the habit of turning immediate experience into words. If I lay on a hillside looking down through vineyards to Lac Léman, I did not permit myself to relish what was before me by giving myself to it, but made words and tropes of it. If a glimpse of a girl's breast made me dizzy, I tried to understand the vertigo rather than enjoy it. I raced through the masters of French letters —from Rabelais and Villon forward; omitting no one—suffusing them all with my own consciousness and need to be articulate.

M. Simon was a cordial, sanguine Swiss whose tall, flexible body was always encased in the stiff black of his morning coat. His pink face beamed while he revealed the wonders of French idioms. His wife was his balance: homely, dark and acid, and, I suspect, a little stingy. At times, she invited a couple of the boys to join her and her husband in a game of whist in the Simon parlor, a room cluttered with ornate furniture and sun-excluding drapes. She did not like to lose, although they played for only a few *centimes*. The boys' gatherings in their hall were more fun. The preponderant talk was of girls, sports, and food. The rum or cognac bottle stood free on the table, next to the tea; and although no one supervised its use, no one abused it.

Lausanne was a honeycomb of schools. In the town's central square there was a spacious tearoom called *Old India* where the boys and girls met or sat at little tables staring at one another. It and the Saturday night dances at the *Hôtel Beauséjour* were headquarters for the first item: girls. The tennis courts and the boating at Ouchy (on the Lake below Lausanne) led the interest in sports. As to the third item: food, Madame Simon's cuisine was nothing to boast of. Therefore, every Sunday morning, three or four of my friends skipped the dull continental breakfast and went to the *Hôtel Gibbon*, not far away. I can still see the venerable dining room, the brown wallpaper above the brown wood panels, and the venerable waiters. The *Gibbon* of course was named for the great historian who had lived there and brought there the grandeurs, the follies, and the rot of Rome. I can still taste those *oeufs sur le plat* of Sunday mornings, served in hot brown pottery plates, and the rapturous strong coffee.

Less than a decade away were the world wars that gave the *coup de grâce* to the brief hegemony of Western European culture. It was hard to foresee in the international relations of the citizens of the Pensionnat Simon. They had their arguments: Arab, Briton, German, American Jew. But they never took the shape of politics or economics. The death of millions, the death and birth of nations, the basic dislocation of the masses and of races . . . hard to foresee. The worlds distilled in their cognac and their rum: the boys took for granted and assumed would last forever. . . .

Many years later, while we were walking together the streets of Parisian Ménilmontant and Belleville, Jules Romains said to me: "The normal man falls in love with every woman he meets, if she has the normal feminine graces. Usually, the instant flickers out for want of opportunity, leaving no trace. Only if it is fed does it flame." In Lausanne, I may be said to have learned—modestly—to know love. But I had always, so it seemed to me, been in love with someone. There was the ethereal first grade teacher at Horace Mann, an emanation in dim colors of fairyland. There was the honeymoon bride of the first trip to Europe who inspired my adoration and loved to be adored by this odd child, letting me sit in her cabin while her new husband played shuffleboard on deck. There was the dark Anita, of the summer I camped in Maine, who so absorbed me that my role in the camp play was spoken solely for her. On one of my first visits to my sister in Madame Heubi's school, I saw Lucy-Jane and was lost in love, I was sure forever.

I learned the hour the girls took their regular walks, lined up in a column, and watched for her to pass. I frequented *Old India* where Lucy-Jane often sat at a long table, biting into little cakes and giggling. She was a black-haired beauty from Alabama; and her favorite swain was an American boy, very blond and trimly dressed with a neatness I could never achieve, much taller than I, whose sox and pants were always rumpled. She danced with him at the hotel dances and I was outclassed. My plight was so palpable and poignant that Lucy-Jane's mother took pity on me. At one party she placed her daughter with me at a table for two. But it did not work: Lucy-Jane sat silent, longing for her crush and resenting my interfering presence.

Through Lucy-Jane, I learned strange truths about true love. I learned that, full of lusts, I felt no lust for Lucy-Jane; my love for *her* was "pure," like my love for my mother. (Freud was already among the very living, but I would not know of him for years.) I wrote letters to Lucy-Jane when we both left Lausanne, and Lucy-Jane's replies were obviously just enough of a tease to keep me captive. A year later she returned from Europe, and in high excitement I went to meet her at the dock. She greeted me with surprising warmth (evidently the blond swain had faded), and I looked aghast at this vain, gushing girl of beauty who had no contact with the dream to which I had been writing letters. I writhed with pain at feeling nothing, not even direct pain: this was a little death. (Lucy-Jane, a couple of years later, married a West Point lieutenant; I have masked her name and state lest her offspring be embarrassed by knowing her brief touch with the author of these pages.)

Enjoying and a little suffering in Lausanne, I had not perceived the relation between the city above Lac Léman and the world of West 78th Street. I felt at home, but it would have surprised me to hear that these were the same world—the brownstone and red brick house in a row of identical houses in New York and the Swiss city full of students from all the parts of Europe. I was an organic part, although humble, of a whole, and I expressed my unity with it by tensions felt at oppositions. I was sure I was transcending West 78th Street and thereby respecting it, whereas in truth Lausanne was simply another phase of the same cultural order. The boy from New York going to the Swiss international town and loving Europe had not budged an inch!

But I was nearly seventeen, time to think of college. I knew French; I knew German. Why not go to one of the great institutions of these domains? That would mean the fulfillment of what I was experiencing in Lausanne and the final burial of West 78th Street! I do not recall why I chose Heidelberg rather than the Sorbonne or one of the great universities of England. Perhaps my ruddy-faced roommate at Lausanne had cooled for me the attractions of Oxford and Cambridge. Perhaps the romantic appeal of Heidelberg or the strong prestige of German scholarship swayed me. I wrote to the university on the south bank of the Neckar in my most studied German; gave my qualifications, and was soon answered. There was no objection to my attending lectures at Heidelberg. I wrote to both my father and my brother to announce my choice.

Julius Joseph Frank, we have seen, was a man of passionate antitheses. He was a democrat of Jefferson's school who wielded an aristocrat's hand in his home. There were strict rules of conduct, and they were obeyed: rules about food, about study and entertainment, about saving electricity, and phone calls . . . about the hours and the minutes. But in his children's deeper choices of life and thought, the home stood for freedom and an almost rigid refusal to interfere or to intervene. Moreover, Julius Joseph Frank enormously admired Germany, including its flamboyant Kaiser. The father wrote back to the son: if he wanted to go to Heidelberg, there were no paternal objections.

My brother Joseph reacted differently. When the summer vacation permitted, he left Cornell, where he had just obtained an instructorship in Chemistry, and went to Europe. We met in Paris.

"No!" was the elder's emphatic judgment. "You are *not* going to Heidelberg."

He paced up and down the drab little top-story room (father wanted his sons to travel, but cheaply) with its mansard window overlooking the rue de Rivoli and its arcaded buildings. "You're an American, aren't you? You've got to get trained to live in America. You're not a European. You're remote enough as it is from your own country. The years of German university life would finish you forever. Your queerness, I mean. You're coming back home." He was eloquent and he was (which is more remarkable) convincing.

"All right," I said at last, "I'll go to Harvard." I had already taken the entrance examinations and been admitted.

"No!" brother Joseph said again. "Harvard would be almost as bad for you as Heidelberg. Harvard is full of anarchists and aesthetes. They're 'above' America, which is even worse than to be out of it." Joseph made himself clear: "I want you to go to a college which believes in America, not just New England, and loves America. Which models citizens to be and to act American. What about Yale? Have you ever thought of Yale? The good Yale man puts poets in their place. Believes in success. . . ."

If I did not go to Heidelberg or make the round of hoary European institutions, I did not care much where I went. Since for some never articulated reason, I *had* to go somewhere, let it be Yale. I cancelled my reservation of a room at Harvard, wrote the necessary letters (Oh! how treacherously easy in those days it was to go to college—provided of course the bills and fees were paid).

My memory of this talk with my brother is certain, although of course not *verbatim* . . . and I trust no one will accuse me of writing that bastard: biographical fiction! But the *site* of the talk, as my memory has it, worries me. When Bolívar (about whom at the time I knew exactly nothing*) was in Paris before his decision to return to his America and to free it, he stayed in a room overlooking the rue de Rivoli; and there he and his friend and tutor, Simón Rodríguez, witnessed the induction of the emperor Napoleon—a ceremony he had refused to attend formally since he disapproved Napoleon's taking the crown. Has my memory played me a trick, placing myself in what was really Bolívar's room in order to suggest (in the way of dreams) some analogy between Bolívar's American work and (in other terms of course) my own? This is, to be sure, a presumptuous comparison, but part of the auto-examination here being written.

I see the two years before the evening of September 1907, when I took train for Yale, as a complex of many forces, choices, courses. They do not make a linear progression; they are all there together, and often they replace each other. The faithful way to record them therefore is not to cabin and confine them into an ordered experience but to depict them as a simmering and brewing of strains whose flavors become too mixed to identify. The strange crisis in the life of that upright man, Julius J. Frank, had deep effects on me, his son. My father seems to have got by his

* On reading, I find that this is not quite true. I knew the equestrian statue of Bolívar topping the high ground of the park, near Central Park West and 82nd Street. A carriage road led up to it and circled the statue (which was later moved). This circle was where I learned to ride a bicycle, helped by my cousin Lucille. But about Bolívar beyond the fact that he was a great soldier, therefore deserved a statue, I knew nothing.

syndrome; the rest of his life was as unitary and transparent as its beginnings. My crisis never ended.

In my last year at DeWitt Clinton High School (which refused me my diploma because of outrageous truancy from English class) I made a friend, a man named Beck, who owned a store for artificial limbs, trusses for hernia, and the like, who was a persuasive Catholic, and who did his best to convert me. He introduced me to Thomas Aquinas and Francis of Assisi, keeping me away from the banal priests of the neighborhood, and prepared me to read the language . . . cosmic and personal . . . of the Gothic cathedrals. Beck (in his mid twenties) was a short man, clad in trim black with a pale bland face—as if a priest, himself. He may, I see now, have been a homosexual, but at the time the word to me meant merely the unimaginable case of Oscar Wilde. It is fair to say that Beck loved the stormy boy I was and dreamed of glories for me, managing to get *his* satisfaction from the dream. I came near to succumbing to the Church by sheer empathy. My other, dissident traits "saved" me. I could still wait hours at my darkened bedroom window for a glimpse in the downtown row of houses of a woman's naked breast. And to counter the ornate intellectual apparatus of the Roman Church I became a devout Tolstoian.

One evening, I took a pad of foolscap paper and wrote Tolstoi a long letter. It is surely lost, but I can still see the round, black, sprawled script, the letters rolling along like empty barrels in a heady stream. I poured out my heart to the great Russian Prometheus. I told him that New York was a sink of corruptions, typified by the saloons of Chatham Square where derelict men drank themselves into stupor a few blocks from the elegant Government buildings. I spoke about my home, with slums around each corner. I never sent the letter, although I kept it for some time. Long years later, I told of it to my friend, Romain Rolland, who at the time lived in Villeneuve near Lausanne. Rolland said: "What a pity you did not send that letter! Tolstoi would have answered it. Oh, surely!" And Rolland told me how he had written such a letter to Tolstoi, and Tolstoi had answered! (My friendship with Rolland began with a letter which Rolland answered, in the first year of the war.)

More inconsistencies: Tolstoi was a vegetarian, I loved the excellent meats of my mother's table. Tolstoi condemned most modern art and letters, which I loved. By the hour I could improvise on my cello, making a music subtle as the winds of a still summer eve which Tolstoi would have condemned. Tolstoi's altar was naked as the word of Christ; and his word of Christ was action.

I accepted his anarchist revolution and at the same time enjoyed the bourgeois 78th Street, my permissive "ethical culture" 78th Street. When I returned to New York after the year of Europe, I began to know the basic common ground between the family brownstone house and Lausanne and Europe.

My readings revealed incongruities. I still loved the massive Balzac (a framed photograph of Rodin's statue of Balzac half-emerged from the rock stood on my desk and remained there throughout college), but had discovered with delight the intricate narcissisms of Gide. Blake was unknown to me but the disciple of Walt Whitman enjoyed the hothouse tropes of Swinburne. You could have all Dickens, Eliot, Thackeray, with Fielding thrown in for good measure (but reserving Smollett), if you left me the works of Meredith, whose subtleties however did not spoil me for the miracle of Swift's love of life emerging intact from his despair and hatred.

Going away to college, I carried a confusion wider and deeper beyond modern Europe. I knew a little about the Schoolmen, whose grammar was the Gothic church. I knew a very little about India, the *Upanishads,* the *Dialogues of Buddha.* But I was a Jew by birth, and had no Hebrew. I had never set foot in a synagogue. My Old Testament readings were less than scant. My Talmud was zero, as was my Marx, and I had never read Spinoza. I was an American—a typically ignorant American college man and had never been west of eastern Pennsylvania; never south of New Jersey. A Jew without Judaism, an American without America . . .

I sat in the old day coach with its worn red plush seats, and such intellectual paradoxes did not trouble me at all. I was on my own now; I was leaving my mother, and I knew that the feeling of liquefaction in my body was fear. Home had always enclosed me, even in Lausanne. Now I was really going *away* into a future open as a parabola. I sat in the day coach alone. The lights in the car were fitful, like the lights outside, barely pointing the dark. I heard the tattoo of the wheels over the rails and ties. I saw the other passengers (the car was half empty) and knew I was not on the same track: whatever took them on their journey was outside me. I was filled with a longing emptiness that has a name: my mother.

This was a birth, not to be avoided. Yet my whole body and mind wailed to avoid it. What were my thoughts? The kindly pederast in the park had awakened me to my mother whom I was hurting by running away in rebellion from my father. Now, there was no one to lead me back to her. I could not go back to her. The train became a loom weaving the warp and woof of distance from her . . . *my* distance from her who was my past home, my past journeys—my everything that I could never be again, riding to a new life of which I could know nothing.

Even mother was not simple; she included *her* mother (now two years dead), as I sat feeling her presence in the train. For the past decade she had been the blind old lady in black, with a white lace cap on her head, the very person of gentleness. Yet in her aura there was no doubt, no problem, and upon *this* rested her gentleness. For every circumstance of life there was an exact answer, one right, all others wrong. Grandmother was soft, but beyond her softness was the panoplied might of an orderly society where the disposition of everything that counted—the rich, the poor, the learned, and the evil—was sustained by weapons ready for war if they were threatened. My grandmother was in my mother, but my mother's complexities went farther.

It was dark night outside, and the car's jerky motions made its lights fitful. And I, the stocky little fellow whose black eyebrows met and whose chin bespoke sensitivity more than strength, knew I was afraid.

As I regard this vivid memory of a journey I surely made, I wonder if it is a symbol imagined and not real. Why should a youngster freshman going to matriculate at Yale have taken a night train? Perhaps, if he came from the South or the West, he might naturally have arrived by night in New Haven. But starting the bare two hours' trip from New York would it not have been more probable that he would take an earlier train so as to find offices open and his reserved room on York Street ready to receive him? Was the "dark" he moved through a psychological image? an image stronger and in a sense more real than the ordinary sunlight outside the car window?

If I had dared, I would have got off the train at the next station and run back to my mother who had never insisted that her precious boy go to Yale lest he be "too different" from all the other boys. *Of course*, he was different, she might say, and always would be different. If she had known her older boy's reasons for "rubbing Waldo down" to normal, she never would have approved. And yet she wanted me to enjoy all the privileges of commonplace and convention. But is there not something strange in the singularity of what I remember? I do not see myself saying farewell to my mother. I do not see myself getting to the station. Nor do I see myself announcing my arrival at the offices of dean or bursar; nor at my room, where I was to sleep and study an entire year. All I see of that room is, over the desk, the photograph of Rodin's Balzac.

And why afraid? I have travelled quite a bit in Europe—full of excitement, with no fear. I can explain it only as a situation of change or of the need of change. Lausanne over 78th Street had not been a change, but variation.

And I was afraid because I knew, darkly, that I was going into a struggle. Joseph had been half right; Yale would work upon me; but I would fight for myself. I was going to confront; I was going to overcome! And what *I* became was going to be America! The infantile god of Waldea was still living.

2

Bright College Years

Yale in 1907 had become an aristocracy of business (management and politics), represented by the young men, smooth and facile, who stood symbolically, if not always physically, half a head higher than I.[3] My position was contrapuntal. I was striving to get in, and I was striving to get out and beyond this culture. For the first year the impulse to conform ruled me; by the fourth year it had so weakened that my class activities were minor; I was trying to get out.

Within a few days of arrival, when the boys were not yet coalesced into the freshman class of the college, a rush came to spontaneous birth. The newcomers sallied forth from the campus to meet the sophomores. The sophomores did not show, and the freshmen marched on, distilling adrenalin and joyous animal spirits that soared as they met no opposition. I was about halfway in a column of shouting youths, most of whom did not yet know each other. The ones from prep schools, since they did know each other, formed clusters of leadership within the mass. With no sophomores there to fulfill the traditional role of enemy, they had to hit something. They were beyond the built-up city, approaching the tracks of the New Haven Railroad, when some natural leader shouted: "A bonfire under the tracks," the mass not knowing that this too was a Yale tradition. Just ahead, was a small culvert making a bridge of wood ties for the rails. The men up front quickly prepared the coming conflagration which would have held up the main line between New York and Boston. But the police knew the tradition, and charged; the rush turned full around, back toward college. The police lost the leaders who were the first to scatter. Presumably, to prove their vigilance, they needed a few specimens as trophies. A half dozen lads were therefore pinched and marched to the waiting station wagon, I among them.

At the police station, we were thrust into a grey room with

barred windows, but released almost at once into the hands of bondsmen who underwrote our bail on our assured appearance in court next morning. We were handled gently; after all, we were gentlemen and good, every one, for a mere five-hundred dollar bond. This tribute to class, of course, did not occur to any of us, who could not know how bums or arsonists, not enrolled at Yale, would have been treated by the police. I slept in my own bed that night. What did I think about? I had followed the mob who were classmates wanting to see the fun but above all wanting to *belong*. If I belonged, I instinctively figured, I must somehow through that fact have *participated*. This was the truth for me, even though the fire under the rails never got a start, and the few who actually moved a piece of wood into place were not among the arrested.

Next morning, we were all arraigned together. Each boy pleaded not guilty as he faced the magistrate: he was there, each said, "watching," nothing more. Had he helped build the fire? Certainly not! Had he intended to help build it? Oh, no! I took the stand and was sworn to tell the truth, the whole truth . . . The magistrate asked me: "Did you help to make the fire?"

"No, I was pretty far back."

"Was that the reason you didn't help? because you were pretty far back?"

"I guess so."

The magistrate frowned, pondered and smiled. "Do you mean to say that if you'd been up front, close to the culvert, you might have helped build the fire?"

"I don't know."

"Try to think."

"Maybe."

A murmur in the courtroom.

"Step down." The judge shuffled his papers and studied the boys. One by one, he named us, found us guilty and fined each one $25. Me he came to last. "Ten dollars," said the magistrate. "I fine you less, because you alone have been—frank."

The courtroom laughed. Next morning the papers fed by the Associated Press had a two or three stick story over a headline: "Frank the Frank." This was, I think my induction into the public prints.

I was pleased. Quite a few of the freshman smiled as they passed me on the campus. I had wanted to belong; so had most of the others, but they confronted less barriers and were less anxious. Moreover, I took the judge seriously and tried to tell the truth, whereas the other boys wanted simply to get out of trouble. Trouble, for me was not to be avoided; in fact, as my life grew, I often seemed to seek it. The world of West 78th Street with its enormous comforts taught escape from trouble by obedience to what it called basic laws. I refused the laws, or meant to learn how to refuse them in order to get free of the world of West 78th Street.

The little episode did not overcome my loneliness. Yale was a stranger. I came from no prep school, had no single friend at first among my classmates. The boys in Lausanne seemed closer. This new alma mater of mine was cool and remote for a mother. And I constantly reminded myself that I was a Jew, a little Jew, for my height was below the average. The boys were tested in those early days of the first term at the college gym on Elm Street: strength of wrist, handclasp, arm, leg, back, etc., were clocked and recorded on machines. Despite my small stature I found that I was among the strongest in the class of over three hundred. I was proud of it. I never forgot this pre-eminence of muscle. I was a fair tennis player (shrewd rather than brilliant) and resolved to go out for the team. But afternoons devoted to tennis, I learned, would prevent taking on the history of Europe a course that sounded good. I chose the course, which disqualified the tennis. This, perhaps, was a mistake; the course taught me little but platitudes and falsehoods. The tennis might have strengthened my self-knowledge.

From my father I had learned the habit of long tramps through the country and the city. When we children went to Horace Mann School, father walked with us (weather permitting) up Broadway (the Boulevard) from 78th to 120th Streets. Frequently on Sundays, Doctor Putzel, a college friend of father's and the family physician, appeared at the house, a sweater under his coat, a blackthorn in his hand, ready for a hike along the Palisades across the Hudson. In Europe, I had learned to absorb the spirit of a town by walking its streets. When I grew up, the method would become conscious and produced finally my "portraits" of towns; *Our America* and *Virgin Spain* were the issue of countless miles of walking along through cities.

In Yale, that first year, I walked alone. I might take a trolley to the outskirts of New Haven, out across fields, climb hills. One autumn afternoon, that first year, I clambered to the summit of a rock and stopped short. At my feet was a lime-kiln sullenly steaming in its natural stone bed. I stepped back, shuddering. I might have stumbled in and knew that I was frightened of myself; I could not bear my own fear. I forced my eyes to measure the kiln. Its opposite end was lower; a good jump, my eyes told me, would clear me safely. I winced and knew I must leap. My feet landed on the uneven shelf of stone and turf and I threw myself forward. One of my ankles hurt, but I had done it! Done what? Risked death for nothing? I could not name what I had done, but I knew it was not nothing. In good spirits, I limped back to the trolley.

There are other instances of sheer physical foolhardiness in my young life, which we may come to later. What do they mean? Was I a physical coward, fighting my cowardice? That is part of it, I surmise. A deeper part is best approached in an experience of childhood which I described in *The Rediscovery of Man*. Let me quote from it: *

> One late winter afternoon when this man was a boy of about
> ten remained with him. . . . The wet windless snow was falling;
> the street's sparse gas lamps burned holes in the dusk and
> the chill on his face pleasantly stressed his warmth within his
> wool coat . . . He reached the lamp post before his house, and
> saw on the first step of the stoop a small black cat with a
> white patch on its face. He stopped to look at it, while the snow,
> muffling the white street, welded together the houses patched
> with lights, his body and the little beast. His mind framed
> a question: *What would it be to be this kitten?* And an
> immediate answer overwhelmed him: *Nothing would be
> changed.* With the instantaneousness of touch, he knew this.
> The kitten peering at him, he looking down at the kitten, within
> the silent moving street, would be as they were! Then, the cat
> ran, the boy climbed the stoop, the door of his boy life opened
> and absorbed him.

Having no technique, no methodology, no tradition to inform and to instate this inward sense of the whole, as I would have had if I had been Hindu or orthodox Jew, I sought wholeness violently by swimming in a stormy sea (that nearly destroyed me)[4] or jumping a lethal lime-kiln.

Of course, there was violence in the air. World war was only seven years ahead, although Yale did not dream of war, awake or asleep. There was a panic in Wall Street—and doubtless Arthur Twining Hadley, President of Yale, with all his bills to pay worried about it and thanked Messrs. J. P. Morgan and J. D. Rockefeller for bolstering the banks with their gold. But the boys had

---

*p. 256. IX: Relation as Knowledge.

to provide their own pretexts for violence: bonfires, rushes, beer nights at Mory's . . .

As I look back on Yale there is a symmetry in my selection of friends. They fulfilled my need to resist the conventional Yale man, without failing in the overall imperative of each man to "make good." The regular pattern was to be popular, to make a team and one's letter or an editorship, to join a fraternity and to be tapped on tap-day of junior year for one of the senior societies. Any of these goals was hard for a Jew to achieve at Yale, although not impossible. I was too proud to try. From the start I elected to be of the minority who chose *not* to run for the *right* goals. But I needed a warm and cozy relaxation to take the place of family. I found it in "Hans" Stix and Robert Goldman, both from Cincinnati's cultured and completely secular community of Jews. Hans, witty and charming, thought he loved books (his favorite author was Mark Twain). Bob was serious almost to solemnity, plodding, the very substance of conventional integrity. Hans became a manufacturer of shoes; Bob, a lawyer in a leading firm of Cincinnati and a community leader. When the war came and I put myself outside the pale by registering as an objector the deep differences between us hardened into a permanent intellectual breach. But my affection never faded. Hans and Bob were a way left open back to family.

Howard Tallmadge Foulkes of Milwaukee and Joseph Wickliff Beach of Worcester, my second symmetrical pair of friends, were deeply interested in religion. Foulkes became a lawyer but was prominent throughout his life in his Episcopal Church. Joseph Beach, whom his friends called Sandy Beach because of the color of his hair, was the son of a minister whose missionary gospel led him all over the Near East, close on the tracks of Saint Paul. Sandy introduced me to his father, a Yale Divinity School man, hearty and bluff like the vicars in eighteenth-century English novels. Sandy followed his father as a chapel preacher, while with the years Howard became more and more high church. The creeds of both, distinct one from the other, differed radically from my homeless, mystical religiosity. With my Jewish friends, I discussed everything in the world except religion. With Sandy Beach and Howard Foulkes religion in the modern world was an urgent problem. There was a famous old synagogue in New Haven; it never occurred to me in my four New Haven years to enter it. The paradox of all this—the paradox of the paradox, was that its strangeness never occurred to me.

Already by sophomore year I was having contacts with the town of New Haven, beyond and to a degree *against* the college; and from this matrix came the third pair of friends, making the third triad with myself as the common factor. Ties with New York were of course not broken. The trains to New York were crowded with Yale men, particularly at the start of weekends. And in New York there was family, and there were girls; there were theaters and concerts. Mostly there were girls, distinct from the town-girls of New Haven.

My new friends were strictly of New Haven, not Yale men. Both had jobs and earned their living. Donald Lines Jacobus was a very pale, thin youth and a poet. I have not been able, to my regret, to find the pale, thin volume of verses which he had privately printed in New Haven. My memory of them may be inaccurate. I seem to recall a misty color, as in the murals of Puvis de Chavannes; a languor with precision as in Francis Thompson, with perhaps a seasoning of Swinburne. My memory of Donald Jacobus, the man, I am more sure of, although I may now see his intention in his poems rather than the poems themselves. I too was a poet (of prosy verse), and we walked the town together. Completing this triad, the third, was Lesley Mason: brash yet elegant, humorous, intelligent, and sly. Through Mason, I got to know a sporting element in New Haven: racy men in check suits, overdressed women who were dubious "ladies" and liked cocktails. They thrilled the cloudy boy to whom their sex was joy of living.

It was through this "crowd" that I landed my job, in senior year, as drama critic of the local morning *Courier-Journal.*

What did these "sports" like in me, sitting in the back room of Heublein's over their gin-and-bitters? I think it was my naiveté that drew them for a while away from horses and betting odds: an open candor both sensitive and aggressive. I was a virgin but not passive. I was ignorant of life but athrob with a life of my own. Mason worked for a promoter of shows: I seem to recall some development like Luna Park in Coney Island. There was a cloudiness in his eyes which could have been . . . or become . . . corruption. My college friends did not like Lesley Mason.

Everyone liked Freshman English, if he was lucky and had it under Chauncey Brewster Tinker. The course was compulsory, if I am not mistaken; therefore divided into several classes under several teachers. Tinker, still an instructor at thirty, soon to become an assistant professor, talked about books and love. There he stood, lean, very tall and taut, although his brilliant eyes and his animal-like mouth were relaxed, conveying to his class the excitement of his passion. The course was a loose survey allowing Tinker the freedom to digress and wander as he wished. He loved Ruskin, I remember. What he gave was himself, enhanced by his subject: always first, himself. In his famous course on the circle of Dr. Johnson, which nearly filled the largest lecture hall of the college, the crowd hushed like an audience in the theater as the curtain rises. The actors on the stage: Boswell, Garrick, Reynolds, Goldsmith, and always, of course, the ubiquitous Doctor Johnson came alive through Tinker and became Tinker's substance.

The most widely known literary man at Yale was William Lyon Phelps, pet of the lecture programs of the Women's Clubs and the nation's annual discoverer of a Great American play or novel. Two of "Billy's" courses were even more popular than Tinker's: Tennyson and Browning, known on the campus as "T-B," and Contemporary Drama, rechristened "Contemptible Drama." Each week, an author and one of his plays was discussed: Shaw and Pinero; Becque, Rostand, and Brieux; Hauptmann, Sudermann, and Wedekind; Ibsen and Bjoernsen; D'Annunzio, Benavente, and Clyde Fitch were seeped into the consciousness of a couple of hundred students each year; and through them the mysteries of drama dimly stirred the provinces of the country.

My first year, I submitted an essay for the prize contest of the *Lit.* In accord with the rules, it was signed by a *nom de plume,* accompanied by a sealed envelope holding the true name of the author. My essay was on Zola, and its theme that the founder of "scientific naturalism" in the novel was the most lurid romantic poet of them all. It was, I suppose, not a bad essay, but "Billy" Phelps was enthusiastic about it in his customary generous way. He looked for the author, going through the lists of seniors, juniors, sophomores in that order. Having found Frank at last among the freshmen he sent a note in his bold running script, inviting me to tea. And I learned how gracious New England could be. Mrs. Phelps was childless (one felt her deep deprival) and mothered both her exuberant husband and the students. Professor Phelps was the big brother, bursting with questions, bubbling with satisfactions. The large library of the colonial style mansion, where I was received and plied with nonalcoholic drinks, had books *en marche* to the ceiling, in corners, on the tops of tables and chairs. On the shelves there were double ranks of books and piles of magazines: American, British, Continental. Professor Phelps, out of his great security, was cordial. Yet where, in all this plenty was there room for me?

Many years later when I was regularly writing "Profiles" for the

New Yorker,[5] I published one on Phelps which was unjust—and I make amends for it now. Its title was "A Kind Man." Its theme: that Phelps's kindness to young authors made him over-eager to boast and moved him often to praise paltry works or to level what he said to the taste of the *Ladies' Home Journal.* Phelps was not a critic. He was a big protective brother, an announcer. This too has its function, which the young zealot from New York failed to understand although he himself with his Zola piece had already profited by it.

Phelps reminds one of Theodore Roosevelt, and indeed the two were friends and often played tennis or went on rides together. The professor's bluff, cordially overflowing sap resembled T.R.'s. The ex-president's mind in social political matters and in political ethics was qualitatively on a par with the professor's literary judgment. They were both quantitative men, rather than qualitative leaders. T.R. expressed dramatically a turn of the American road toward democracy, and Phelps helped prepare the way for the renascence of American letters which in another decade was to find voice in such beginners as Frost and Dreiser, Masters and Sandburg, Amy Lowell and Vachel Lindsay. In more than one of these writers the circus barker is not distant, and Phelps exemplifies the danger. (Professor Phelps was deeply wounded by the *New Yorker* "Profile" and never forgave me.)

Tinker too, on a far higher level, had the showman in him. He used to invite me of an evening to his rooms in Vanderbilt Hall and question me about the reactions of the students to his latest lecture. He lowered his professorial defenses (he was not yet a professor); the superfine New Englander, priest of eighteenth-century charm, and the small New Yorker, worshiper of Balzac and Tolstoi, became good friends.

But Yale in those days, had a presence of rarer vintage. Van Wyck Brooks in *New England: Indian Summer* names the epigoni of Emerson and Thoreau centered about Harvard and a few centered about Yale. Among these voices, fine if thin, he mentions Henry A. Beers. Beers was still teaching at Yale, and I came to know him—a man who had touched the world of Hawthorne! I was one of less than a dozen who took Beers' course on English Romanticism. In the small classroom, almost empty, he spoke with a voice so slight that it seemed he was speaking to himself . . . and the few faithful barely heard him.

He was a very little man, very gentle, with a head like a moustachioed turtle, which threatens every moment to retire into its timid shell. At the turn of the century he had written an Indian summer masterpiece, *The Ways of Yale*. To the boy emerging from 78th Street Beers brought a major thrill. The circuit from past to present was complete. *Beers had known Emerson in person!*

He and the young man became good friends. I told him of my aspirations, and the grave old man seemed to understand and to approve. This of itself was cause for wonder. There could be, of course, no literal translation of the youth's "proofs of God" into the terms of Beers' New England (it was too late for that by several generations.) And modern America was whirling too fast for the young man to find a base there for his vision. But the fact of a conduit between the spirit of Henry Beers' obsolescent forms and my yet formless spirit was proved. I might forget it in my need to kick free of the old forms hardened into shackles. The sense of the organic unity . . . the country's and the generation's . . . could not be lost. Whitman felt and sang it, because it was here.

In my senior year, Beers made me two gifts. He presented me with an inscribed copy of his famous book *The Ways of Yale;* more important, after reading some of my writings, he wrote me a long letter. Friends, even relatives, had expressed confidence in my future; Phelps and Tinker had found encouraging words; but the letter of Beers went deeper and meant more. . . .

Never for long did I forget my cello. At Yale I took lessons with Leo Schulz, chief cellist of the New York Philharmonic, who came up one day a week to New Haven. Through him, I met Professor Stanley Knight, head of the department of Music. He was a slight man, a sensitized wisp of a man, and a superb pianist although without the bravuro power of the virtuoso. Virtuosity did not interest Stanley Knight. He invited me to his house, together with a violinist whose name escapes me, and we played piano trios. Members of the faculty were welcome to drop in. An occasional guest was the president, Mr. Hadley: a comforting man to be administrator of an institution always in need of money and an expert on railroad economics and the relations between corporate and private funds. Mr. Hadley seemed to me to be as sensitive as an artist. His little body was slightly spastic and he had a defect of speech. Was Arthur Twining Hadley a typical Yale man? He seemed closer to nineteenth-century romantic music than to his own dismal subjects.

Professor Knight came to West 78th Street and accompanied my mother in songs they both knew and loved. He judged mother a true artist and came again. Then they discussed what they had played and sung, even argued a little, until the maid appeared with coffee and chocolate, richly embedded in whipped cream, and cakes as excellent as the music. Yale, through Stanley Knight, came to the world of 78th Street. I saw *my* Professor Knight at our piano, nodding, suggesting, criticizing . . . I was proud of this alliance in music. A victory for the Franks!

Part of the pleasure in these musical visits was the security they gave me. I knew that Mr. Knight was a superb musician; since he approved of mother's musicianship, she must be a good musician, not merely a good mother. Such security never suggested to me that I should hold to it: should build it up, strengthen it, base a life on it. The house and home must be abandoned! and the security. The language of Schubert and Brahms must be jettisoned. Yale must be discarded. It didn't make sense, this doom, and I did not ask that it make sense. What I *knew*—and this at least I knew—did not make sense, any more than my identity with a small cat on the snowing winter block made sense; yet was real. Nothing real made sense.

Back in my college room, I would sink into depression. I would throw myself on my bed; I would say half aloud: "I am weak. I am a weak, scared, miserable cat." In my mind was the black kitten of my first revelation. I did not call it a revelation. If I had, I might have wondered why it did not give me strength, security, and joy. Something was wrong, when knowledge that the Cosmos is within brought torment and fear.

It surprised me that my classmates . . . almost the whole student body, got along without a stir or tremor in search of life's meaning. As animals take their hungers, their milieux, even such untaught mysteries as birth and the nursing of their young for granted, the students accepted the college, the teachers, one another, and themselves. This had not been quite the case in Lausanne where there had been at least a tradition of search—if not research—into the nature of existence. But the teachers I have named (and the friends) most important to me were not the type who prevailed. These handed out fractions of information which, if the student could repeat them, landed him in the next higher class. At the top, a plateau, was graduation. On the way up was fun: sports, "heeling" for the college press, glee clubs, drama societies, beer at Mory's, whores in Bridgeport—although there was plenty of amateur sex right off the campus. (A few species of *demi-vierge* was already prevalent in New York for weekends: girls of good family, or at least rich, and the utterly wanton who went to any length until their maidenhead was threatened when they became hard and inflexible as a bank vault door. The words "petting," "necking," were I believe unknown, not their practice.)

The key word was success. It was assumed that students came to Yale to learn success. Not necessarily for money. You could be a minister or a professor on a small stipend, and if the crowds came to hear, you were a success.

But here was a glowing, intense little fellow who secretly faced failure. You made a contract with Mephisto for success; I had made a compact with a God who was a tougher bargainer than the devil!

What was the covenant? It seemed to me to have been always present (even in the nonsense of "Waldea"). But I had fully worked it out when I was only fifteen, in the 78th Street house. I was going to be an author. And authors had rewards. They made money (see Kipling). They made disciples (see Tolstoi). They won world fame (see Hardy, Meredith, and Shaw). I looked with hunger on these prizes. Well, *I was going to give them up*. Their loss would be my payment in the bargain. And what would God give in return? God promised exactly nothing of success on any level. He would simply and solely *keep open* for me while I lived the course of a *search* for truth, the course of an unceasing effort to put words together that summed to revelation of the truth, which was that *God is Present*. I might miss my aim; I might fail by any definition. What I compacted with God was to give up all the guerdons, not for the highest or deepest success but for the chance, while my life lived, to go on trying.

My classmates at Yale did not know of this lopsided contract. I hid it well lest I be laughed off the campus, as I had been howled off the grounds of the summer camp when Mr. D——— read my poem aloud. Yet they felt it in me, somehow. Even my friends had and heard no word for the covenant, therefore could not know directly it existed. But more important, and worse for my comfort, I myself was often to forget this treaty and to famish for fame, for rewards, like any aspirant of letters; to complain when I got what I had carefully paid for, *nothing;* and to cheat in my heart, hoping I would win both sides of the bargain. Constantly, I was to be thrown back on the realities of my compact, when I forgot it, by seeing that it *worked*. I won fame and influence only to lose them. Often in my striving to communicate the God I saw and knew as present in the phenomenal world, I experienced failure, and God went on exacting payment on his side of the bargain.

By senior year, then, the processes of "getting out" of Yale submerged the efforts to "get in." I had not "got in"; I was having a whale of a time "getting" and living "out." Was this year perhaps my happiest? I had completed, the year before, my work for the B.A. I was free of courses, except for one in which I wrote an interpretation of Shakespeare's *Troilus and Cressida* which Professor Charlton Lewis called "an original contribution." Fascinated by the metaphysical poets I studied Thomas Traherne (the vogue of Donne had not yet set in). For this work I got an M.A. synchronous with my B.A. I had free access to the stacks of the library and must have averaged a book a day. I played trio at Mr. Knight's and was drama critic of Colonel Osborn's *Courier-Journal*.

New Haven then was the principal tryout station for shows aimed at Broadway. Two great syndicates shared theatrical dominion: Klaw and Erlanger and the Shuberts. Half the new shows opened at the *Hyperion,* where I saw them and reviewed them with a freedom no New York critic claimed. I panned and praised as my arrogance dictated—for no man can make a deal with God however humbling, without an overweening arrogance like the saint's insolent display that he is humble.

Colonel Osborn, publisher of the *Courier-Journal,* in that whole year found fault with me just once. Mrs. Fiske came to town in *Becky Sharp,* and I praised it supporting the vogue of that over-mannered lady. The Colonel laughed at me. "What do you know, young man, about women? Mrs. Fiske is a fraud." The Shuberts opened a gorgeous spectacle, *The Balkan Princess,* and I panned it. Next day Mr. Shubert, small and concise, raged at me: "You're just a kid. Or you look like one. And you think you got the right to endanger our investment?" He named the figure, which I don't recall: it may have been $100,000. I resented the reference to my looks—I seemed younger than my years—and decided to grow a moustache.

All this *annus mirabilis* I kept going on fifteen cups of coffee per diem and five hours' sleep. (I will pay for it later.) I would rush from theater (sometimes a teacher, sometimes a friend, shared the seats) to Heublein's. There I would have what I called my "glass of sherry"—a half dozen or more oysters and four or six glasses of the wine—map out my column, and float with alcoholic ease to the newspaper office where what I had to say, already shaped, almost wrote itself. By one o'clock I would be in my room and read till three. At 7:45 A.M., I would slide away from sleep to the door outside where the paper waited. With ever fresh concern I would read what I had written—often surprised, pleasantly —and be ready for compulsory chapel at 8:10.

In that happy flowing year, I met some "successes." One was Clyde Fitch, leading American playwright of that era, who came to address Billy Phelps' "Contemptible Drama." I found him gaudy, vain, and shallow, but a good showman with an enviable sense of pace as he handled questions from the students as if he were writing a scene. Augustus Thomas, another "success," I found heavy as a leaden statue.

I asked him:

"Mr. Thomas, what do you think of Ibsen?"

"I've never read Ibsen, sir. I preserve my originality by staying away from the plays of my contemporaries."

I was shocked.

Near New Haven dwelt a poet, Ella Wheeler Wilcox, who had almost as many readers as William Randolph Hearst's *Journal* which regularly published her doggerel platitudes on its editorial page. She was, I believe, America's most read poet, and of course no poet at all. I visited her on occasional Sunday afternoons—and her businessman spouse. Mrs. Wilcox, on the proceeds of her verse, had traveled East and West, and wherever she went she brought back splendid native costumes, both male and female. She enjoyed dressing me in this finery, and the young man as a Turk, a Nipponese warrior, a Coptic priest, could be seen drinking tea and arguing with the other guests. One of them was a poet long since forgotten, Theodosia Garrison, who was enough of an admirer to give me a copy of her book, *The Joy of Life,* inscribed to me with an original poem.

What did I see in such collectors of the success I was barred from? I suspect I enjoyed the earthy heft of Ella Wheeler Wilcox, as a monk half starved with fasting, half mad with continence might enjoy the presence of a hearty peasant woman. I lacked contempt for such verse because I ignored it. I did not judge the poet, who was nonexistent, but I liked the crass woman.

Analogously, I was no gambler, no race-horse tout, no boozer; yet I loved being with Lesley Mason's sporting friends, as I liked composing my drama column in a haze of sherry. A few times, these years before and after graduation, after a football game or a bibulous New Year's Eve, I awoke in a New York hotel bedroom without a notion of how I got there. Then, suddenly, in my twenties, my tolerance for overloads of alcohol vanished. I found it was the loss of control of my autonomy I could not suffer. (For somewhat similar reasons, I quit smoking cigarettes, finding them a habit that became a tyrant rather than a pleasure.)

I never "heeled" for the *Lit.*, Yale's literary monthly; and, to go back still farther, when I was bounced from the respectable Horace Mann school I felt at home in a tough public school where the teacher smelt the breath of the big Irish and Negro boys to make sure they had not been drinking. Was I, among other traits, against culture? Was it Tolstoi's anticulture that appealed to me? There was at least one cultivated writer in my class, Thomas Beer. I hardly knew him at Yale, and we became friends only a decade later.

If, for whatever reason may emerge, I was anticultural in the sense that I rejected the culture of my college and my time, I was decidedly not anti-intellectual. I believed in thinking, the more rigorous the better. I had invented a phrase: *The good mind is one that knows its place.* That place was a prospect for beholding the mystery of life, but without presuming to encompass it. Whatever the view might yield, it would be no syllogism. It would be an *experience*, a full one, with its own measure. Yet only thought could free from the delusion that thought *explained.* Thought disposed of explanations, which were all false. Thought carried the mind to the living core of knowing which preceded thought and transcended thought.

I may be appending an interpretation of my attitudes, which jump ahead of my story. But, however dimly, I had felt (although not figured out) this *revelation.* There were two schools: those who nursed the quaint notion that the logical mind could account for reality (the rationalists); and those who, seeing the impotence of logic to explain its own premises, threw thought out altogether (the romanticists). I was at home in neither school. Did I delight in horse-racy men and women with sensual clothes because they at least knew what they were betting on? Was I declaring war on the minds all around that *did not know their place*?

But do not carry along with you, dear reader, the image of a young man of twenty wrestling forever with metaphysical and epistemological problems. He was much more likely of a spring day to be running through the woods like Pan and wrestling with a birch tree. I still had my habit of solitary hikes, although I jumped no more lime-kilns. Embracing a tree in a wood was connected in my mind with woman, but I did not often philosophize about it.

The same last year of Yale, I had begun work on a book, *The Spirit of Modern French Letters.* It was never published because it was never finished. My ideas and values kept on changing faster than I could bring the book to a conclusion. But in its incomplete form I submitted the manuscript to George Parmley Day, secretary of Yale and head of the University Press, who accepted it for publication.

So I had my B.A. *and my* M.A. and was an honorary fellow of the college (Professor Phelps was largely responsible for that, I suspect) and could wear my Phi Beta Kappa key as a mask of respectability over raging rebellions. Suddenly the scene shifts to the Rocky Mountains . . . to the real Wild West!

A classmate of mine had a cousin, Jack Rollinson by name, who had so hated the routines of success that he fled from Buffalo, his native town, to Wyoming where he acquired a small horse ranch and became a forest ranger. He invited me and two other classmates to spend the summer with him and his horses, in Wyoming, as paying guests. We three young Yale graduates went to Chicago and between trains visited the Everleigh Club, reputed to be the most luxurious brothel in the land. The stately halls were stuffed with Victorian furnishings, predominantly mauve gilt-framed pictures and bric-à-brac. The girls also seemed stuffed, and even the champagne we bought for them did not make them come alive. Legend had it that a famous millionaire had died in this house; whether by suicide or murder nobody knew, for the case was hushed up.

The dullness of the brothel and the women reminded me that most of the curriculum of college also had been dull. Few of the teachers had been exciting, as Beers, Tinker, and Billy Phelps had been exciting—each in his way. No wonder the beer flowed on Saturday nights; no wonder the men were forever hunting girls and finding girls and not finding in girls what they desired. Even the chippies had their rules of respectability . . . wanted something for a future that would probably not come, yet destroyed the present. Wasn't this what was wrong with success? Future-focused, it blotted and barred the present which was all we had. Feeling college already in some perspective, I realized that the "bright college years" had been a "sell." Extracurricular activities got all the votes: sport, a race for tap-day, "wine, women, and song"—no one was for study or research. But wasn't this a little mad? Millions of dollars and the best brains to make a university —and then to use it only as a springboard into the nonexistent?

The boys got to their midnight train, awash in liquor. The porter took our money, checked our accommodations, stuffed our change carefully in our pockets, and helped us get into the green trap of our berths. We were bound for Cody, Wyoming: a new world? a new old one?

My first impression as we walked from the Cody station to the hotel, lugging our bags, was of broad emptiness. The main street could have held two eastern towns with space left over. The houses were of two stories and their façades and sides were for the most part tin imitating bricks. The horses tethered outside saloons and stores looked like scrawny ponies. And even when they pulled a wagon or were mounted by a rider, they seemed to be stationary! Fixity, lack of movement, was my dominant impression. The dime novels and nickelodeon pictures from which I had learned of the "Wild West" were always crowded with motion: crisis and climax; this town . . . this real town of Cody was flat and asleep. Our hotel room with three iron cots, fly-spotted windows, two metal washstands, continued the void of the street. The pale sky made a megaphone of its enclosure, in which the plash of horse-hoof, the tap of high-heel boots, the swing of saloon doors across the street that let out snatches of men's voices, were enlarged. At a window of our room, I looked down on the hollowness of the street and up at the pale late afternoon sky; but I did not share the pallor. I felt strong. The huge T-bone steaks we were soon devouring in the hotel dining room vanished quickly within the furnace of our bodies. The air at that altitude gave resilience. After eating, we shopped—spurs, fancy riding boots with embroidered tops and red heels coquettishly tilted, waterproof ponchos, a shot of whiskey at the *Silver Dollar*—and studied the stocky half-wild horses we would be riding in the morning. Soon as we hit the hay, we plummeted into sleep; and at dawn Jack Rollinson on his Cayuse rolled in, rope-guiding three extra ponies. We boys finished our breakfast of sausages and hotcakes with sorghum syrup and were ready. Ahead was a sixty mile adventure, and except for a few polite rides with the English saddle I had no experience with horses.

Soon the road dwindled to trail under hills bare as boulders, and the trail melted. We went through hot badlands with deceptive pools of poisonous alkali water aghast in the sun. Suddenly, there were forests of pine straight as missiles; then the badlands returned. Properly standing in my saddle, I had no difficulty catching my pony's rhythm and falling in with it, so that quite literally we were making our way together. We forded streams; the mountains clad in evergreen moved closer. The air was a cold breath. Now we left the valley going straight up the flank of the Shoshone range. The horses knew how to take the rise and fall of the earth. They slid, jerked, jumped a fallen tree; they twisted and stopped, then leaped with their forelegs forward. I realized that my pony was solving a problem: getting ahead or (worse) getting down. The air, pneumatic and effervescent, warded off fatigue. The standing posture in the saddle saved buttocks and legs which with an English saddle would soon have rubbed sore. But I was fended from fatigue mostly by excitement. *This* was America! West 78th Street, Lausanne, Chatham Square, and Yale were as remote as if seen through the far end of a telescope. We levelled off into a new valley, and the horses of their own accord cantered across the waving grasses, knowing what lay ahead for them. The whole scene for me, from mountain pine to self, was a collaboration. I could have gone on riding forever, but the horses were braking their lope. And there it was: a ranch house of three low rooms on a straight line, a barnyard of barking dogs and fluttering chickens, and children; and a broad-beamed widow woman in a black city coat, standing next to her two sons beside the hooded well to welcome us.

We rolled out of our saddles; the boys took the horses away; we doused our heads in the sweet cold well water, and the woman led us into the kitchen whose long, laden table offered us sourbelly, beans, and spuds with sweet condensed milk (a luxury) for the boiled coffee. On the floor, at the table's end, stood a demijohn of whiskey. Jack Rollinson tilted it over his arm and poured it into his mouth like water. The woman took a draught almost as long. I declined, loving this intoxication of the ride over earth too well to change it for a lesser: this sense of earth and myself belonging to it.

In less than an hour, we rode again, gradually rising toward a notch of the Shoshone ("Stinking Water" in the Indian tongue), a door that would admit us into the long wide Sunlight Valley, its lush grasses bounded on both sides by immense black boulders and above all a sky clear as the blue eyes of a child. In this valley, separate each by a few miles from a neighbor, were a scatter of ranches, one of them Jack's. As we passed each property, corrals and log gates had to be opened to let us through. At one it was a tall woman in a leather jerkin who greeted Jack and stared suspiciously at the three city-slickers. At one it was an old bald man who walked stooped but swung the heavy gate with half a hand as if it had been made of matches. At one a colt sprang out and tried to kick the gate open and was followed by two youngsters who lifted the weighty log and then jumped aboard for a free ride as it swung. Many of the women, I was to learn, good respectable wives to the ranchers, came from Denver and even Chicago brothels. (Not one refused a spot of whiskey at any hour.)

Jack's home was like the others, but without a woman: a straight line of three long, narrow rooms, each with a door and little windows. The wood bunks had no springs, no mattresses; but I slept warm in a buffalo hide. Next to the house were the corrals, but the horses could wander up and down the open valley. Since its walls were bare, the horses kept to the green low land. If they went too far, a neighbor's gate was sure to stop them. Never a one was lost, except in winter if a horse strayed too far and got tired and was attacked by wolves.

We young easterners had a good time in Wyoming; more than a vacation it was a revelation. Neighbors dropped in, strangers, passers-by; cowboys looking for work, "bad men" who turned out to be Jack's friends and not so bad; an old-time Indian fighter whose speech had Indian phrases. Jack's job took him on long journeys, with us boys along: sometimes into Idaho and Montana.

Once I had to ride back to a ranch where I had left my pen. I found it and cantered forward again to join the others. We were going to pitch camp and night was gathering. I heard a call and answered it, then stopped my horse to hear better. The call came again, and I was about to answer again when I realized that it was the cry of wolves. I had answered the call of wolves. I shuddered, and the shudder became part of the darkening earth as the sun leaves it. I had been in communication with the wild: and it had entered me!

I found that I loved horses. Therefore I was good with horses. Jack's duty was chiefly the settlement of disputes between cow and sheep men in marginal lands where he was the sole viable law. Often we ate and slept in remote ranches where a dry ewe or hurt steer would be killed and served in our honor. Sometimes, I would venture alone along some dim-blazed trail through woodland. This time I found myself in a thick forest, and knew that I was lost. Then came a cloudburst. Through the sheets of water I guided my little Cayuse, but I knew I had lost my measures. The little mare tried to obey the directions I gave her but she floundered; she sank in mire to her knees; she whinnied and trembled and shook her drenched head. I began to fear we were in a swamp. Perhaps we would be stuck there until the last call of man and beast was absorbed in this vast, darkening drench. I threw down my useless reins on the mare's neck, so she would know what I was doing. "It's up to you," I said softly, and whispered her name. "Get us home, if you can." The little mare stopped, waited a moment as in thought, and turned clear around into what seemed to me the precise wrong direction. She began to pick her way, slow but deliberate and firm. After an hour or two in the black night we saw ahead the lights of the ranch through the tumultuous rain. No man could have done it.

Most of Jack's horses were Cayuse, the strong, intelligent, pedestrian offspring of the Caballo whom Spain modified from the original Arab. Slow at trot and canter, they were good walkers, and their knees stood the strain of precipitate slopes. But they were liable to panic, and the ranchers always carried a Colt revolver; less to use against bad men and desperadoes than to stop, if needed, a horse from plunging hysterically down a ravine, dragging others with it. One of Jack Rollinson's family of horses came from Kentucky: a high, black, nervous beast with eyes of fire. They called him Outlaw, because they could do nothing with him. He was stubborn, destructive with both tooth and hoof, and I felt must have been hurt in his dark Kentucky youth. Outlaw was unhappy; I asked for him, and Jack handed him over as "good riddance."

I proceeded to woo him. I caged him up alone in the corral and moved slowly toward him, holding an armful of savory alfalfa. Outlaw trembled, stepped forward, suddenly swung his head in a large loop and retreated. But the longing for the sweet grass (perhaps reminding him of the blue grass of Kentucky) was strong. After a week of tries, I got a halter on him. The saddle soon followed. There was to be no bit, no curb, only the rope halter, until the horse was gentled. (A bit in his present state would only have torn his tender mouth.) Now he was saddled, I opened the corral and the fence gate leading into the free valley. I knew what was going to happen. Slowly I moved . . . crept close to the horse who watched me, his ears flattened, his teeth bared. I leaped on Outlaw's already sweating back, leaning forward along the neck like a jockey; and the horse flashed like lightning. Gradually, as Outlaw shot past the corrals and along the valley bottom my pressure at the neck slanted him uphill on the valley wall. Outlaw's pace must slacken. Up . . . up . . . leaping over boulders, cutting his hoofs on the hard slope, the maddened beast sprang. The rider did not try to stop him; I merely by pressure on the neck aimed him upward. Suddenly Outlaw stopped, his flanks in lather. He shook his head and looked at his master.

Next day, he had forgotten all except his rebellion. But each day, the dash was shorter. In a week, came the full capitulation. But only I could feed Outlaw, only I could ride him. Outlaw became the swiftest walker on the ranch, and that meant much for the long hikes. I loved the horse and understood him. About his specific past I knew nothing. But it was plain that Outlaw needed the security of a master. The young man too was afraid and needed the security—if not of a master, of a purpose. More precisely, I needed the security of a *justification* of the fact that I lived. To live sentiently but meaninglessly in the spontaneous thralldom of nature was impossible for me. And this is weakness! I knew the weakness under the brilliance in Outlaw. I knew my own weakness. In this intimate relation with a horse I learned that much of what I had thought to be exclusively a man's trouble could also be a beast's. My world in this wilderness of Wyoming was wide enough to include the gentling of a horse and a reply to the call of wolves. In the same region, I lost this world. . . .

On one of our expeditions, Jack had to go to Gardiner, a small army post in Montana; and our best route was straight through Yellowstone Park. Here, I met, for the first time, the American tourist, who was soon to proliferate on wheels all over the country. At the hotels situated near the chief attractions I saw the midwest farmer, wielding his knife as he ate in bare sweaty suspenders, and the classier and richer eastern tourist gaping at the geysers. The visitors felt nothing . . . no silence . . . in a sapling or a flower, but Old Faithful gushing hot water thrilled them—for here was a column of it going up, instead of down.

I realized that my whole life must explore the silence within me.

A mile outside Gardiner we pitched our tents and tethered our spare horses. Jack went off alone to his business; Bayard, Jim, and I rode into town resolved to leave no saloon unvisited. By supper hour, Jim and I were hilarious and Bayard was lost. We decided we had no time for supper but that we would visit the dancehalls where the soldiers found their women. The biggest one, just off the road, had a mechanical piano blaring through the open door. Where Jim and I stood in our saddles we could see the wide dance floor and a number of doors leading to the bedrooms. We brought our horses close together and clasped hands and swore that neither would let the other go with a woman through one of those bedroom doors (the town had a bad name for venereal disease). Having repeated our protective oath and half fallen off our saddles in the embrace that sealed it, we rode into the dancehall and stood on our horses in the center of the floor. We were greeted with shouts of laughter. A half dozen of the girls scurried for lumps of sugar for the horses which were petted and then peaceably led away outside where they were tethered.

It was very warm in the large room. The mechanical piano, casting metal showers of sound against the harsh electric lights, made the room hot. Alcohol for me was always a soporific. Now I saw the place through a haze: the few men, the girls, and Jim bobbing up and down as he danced and joked, his head a cork. The haze around me was full of sleep. Dimly, through it, an awareness told me that something was wrong. At last I knew! My friend, Jim, was missing! I remembered our pact. What could I do? Half the bedroom doors were closed. To knock at one was the worst possible form and would cause trouble. The open rooms were of course the empty ones. I went to each shut door, and shouted: "Jim! Come out Jim! Remember our oath. Come out!" And got no answer. I had failed my friend. I had not saved Jim; I must not save myself! If misery lay before Jim, the least I could do was to take on misery for myself.

The room by now was a vortex. I became the vortex with the room whirling around me in heavy mineral waves. The electric lights were metal—and the music. Everything in the dizzying room was now the waves of metal. It was hard to hold to fixity within it. Next to the bar, on benches, sat a small group of women, who were still free. One of them, I noted. She wore a loose white blouse that revealed half her breasts. Only these breasts, of the whole room, were not metal! I wanted to touch them be- cause when I did the whole room with everyone and everything in it would partake of their tenderness, of the ecstasy of their fragrance.

She sat on the bench, sharply aloof from the others. Of course, my mind told me, this was nonsense; she was one of the whores, that's all! She had small sharp features, not in the least sensual. Her eyes were a little too small. She made me think of my mother; and I was not shocked, not shamed by this, because the whole world was a mineral vortex drawing everyone and everything to- gether; and only the touch of her breasts melted the metal into softness.

I navigated toward her and she waited for me. . . .

When I got to my horse tethered outside (having learned that my friend had left), I was sober and I felt well—as if I had slept. Had I really slept? In that woman's arms? I mounted and jogged slowly to camp.

It was dawn and a new melody of the world. The grasses sang it and the cool breeze and in a lower octave the trees. And highest of all the birds showered the same song of morning. Was this being sober? I said: "Yes!" I tried to be angry with myself, at the damned woman, at my friend who had failed me too. But within me was infinite well-being. I disapproved of what I had done; the well-being was beyond my dominion. Suddenly, pain pierced me, a pain that was fear. My hand had gone to my moneybelt next to my skin, and the belt was gone. Everything stopped, even the birds . . .

I turned Outlaw and spurred him, so that the horse, unused to this violence, made a leap forward into a swift trot. The whore house was a coagulation of stale lust. The Madame opened the sleeping door, and I brushed past her. At the woman's door I knocked.

She was lying on the bed, as if expecting me. Before I could speak, she pointed to a chair in the corner, where my belt lay with all its bills and silver dollars. As I strapped it on, I looked at her trying to hate her and failing. Her little face smiled.

"Thanks," I said; and her smile went on.

There was a silence. Into it, I said:

"If I catch a disease," I touched the revolver at my thigh, "I'll shoot myself."

She said at once: "No you won't. If you get sick, you'll go to a doctor."

There was a silence again, as I finished arranging my clothes, and I could live with it . . . live in it.

"Goodbye," I said. "Thanks, again."

She seemed hardly to notice as I opened the door.

This journey to Wyoming, just after graduation from Yale was part of my commencement.

3

Reporter in Baghdad

When I returned from the West at the close of summer, there was a job waiting for me as a reporter on the *Evening Post*. The editor was Oswald Garrison Villard, who had inherited it from his father Henry Villard, who had bought it from the famous Edwin Godkin. William Cullen Bryant, the poet, and Carl Schurz, most noted of the German *émigrés* after the unsuccessful revolution of 1848, also had been editors. The weekly *Nation* had its offices on the same floor of the Vesey Street building. Its editor was Paul Elmer More, author of the *Shelbourne Essays*, and chief champion, with Irving Babbitt at Harvard, of the classical resistance to romanticism and Rousseau. From the windows of the city room of the *Post,* I looked down on lower Broadway and on the Trinity Church gravestones at the head of Wall Street.

More and Babbitt held that for a culture the preservation of property rights was more important than the preservation of lives. The liberals on the *Post* did not agree; indeed the thought horrified them. Nevertheless, the *Post* was primarily an organ for gentlemen and the city room had the leisured aspect of a club. Rarely was more than one edition published. Carefully composed around noon, it reached the street about 3:30. I never felt at home on the *Evening Post,* as if I had somehow gotten into the wrong club. Years later I learned that my application for a job of cub reporter had been about to be turned down when my father, an old friend of Mr. Villard, offered to pay my salary of $12 per week. This angered and offended me because I felt, quite rightly, that I was in no need of nepotism. But much of my work on the *Evening Post* was never printed.

For example: my interview with the anarchist Emma Goldman. I found that I was good at interviews. I never showed pencil or notebook, figuring that they stopped the flow of words. I asked provocative questions which started the flow, and my aim was a portrait rather than an item of news. Emma Goldman was news because of a strike of women workers in a garment factory, which threatened violence under her uncompromising leadership. My piece described how I journeyed up Amsterdam Avenue to Miss Goldman's flat, how she took me into her kitchen and gave me coffee and a slice of *Kaffe Kuchen,* and explained to me that the girls were humans, with their own feelings. A woman emerged in lieu of the fire-breathing monster: homely, squat, matronly—a *mother* driven to ferocity by the threat to her children. Before the natural and ordinary woman, the anarchist vanished. But the interview did not appear. When I had waited long enough to be sure, I went to Mr. Villard for the reason.

"Young man," said Mr. Villard, "when we read this, we considered letting you go. Deem yourself lucky we did not let you go. . . ."

There was a scandal—one of the periodic scandals in the perpetual war of the reformers against Tammany Hall, the city's regular Democratic machine: a Judge was discovered to have paid a very large "campaign contribution"—really of course a bribe to get him on the ticket. I visited him in his chambers and got him talking about the legitimate uses of "publicity"; the voters' "need" of the full "data" to make an intelligent choice. And the gathering of data meant money. I let the man convict himself of his own sophistries, simply recording in my article what he said. Quite by chance, I learned that an exorbitant proportion of employees, who owed their posts to high grades in the Civil-Service examinations, lived in "the gas-house district" near Stuyvesant Square where the big boss himself resided in a brownstone mansion. Could this be chance, or did the air of 2nd Avenue and the square stimulate the intellects? On one pretext or another, I visited the flats of men with city jobs. The locations were humble enough, but above a butcher's or a saloon I stepped into ornate apartments cluttered with the most expensive products of Grand Rapids. How could a carpenter, a driver, a clerk on $1200 a year afford Tiffany glass electric fixtures? The district teemed with winners of examinations. My article laid out the facts. It was a little study of the sociology of Tammany, and the *Post* presumably hated the Hall. But neither of my articles was published.

I tried also to do a little work for the *Nation.* Reviewing Nietzsche's *Ecce Homo,* recently translated, I made the point that Nietzsche was a Christian *heretic,* not an outsider. Zarathustra, I wrote, was a variant of Jesus, not, as the German supposed, his destroyer. They had much in common. Mr. More did not like the idea and scolded me for it. Before I was eased out of these "wrong clubs," I switched to the *New York Times* where my wage rose. It began at $25 a week, and before long I was made a space-writer, earning at space-rates as much as $100 weekly.

Two reportorial adventures cast light on me, as a young man. An office building in Los Angeles, which housed a bitterly anti-labor newspaper, was dynamited. It was hinted that two labor leaders, the McNamara brothers, had a hand in the outrage. This Samuel Gompers, President of the American Federation of Labor, indignantly denied. Then the two brothers confessed, and Gompers' face was crimson. Gompers was said to be in town, and I was sent to get a statement from him. At the desk of the Hotel Breslin the reporters were told that Mr. Gompers had not registered, that he had left, that he was seeing no one . . . they might take their choice of refusals. The lobby soon emptied of reporters. Opposite the desk was the dining room, with its doors shut (breakfast hours were over). I pressed my shapeless slouch hat a little lower on my head and walked to the door, found it unlocked, and went in. The restaurant was empty, but in a far corner of the large high-ceilinged room Gompers sat alone at a table: a froglike figure, his hair upstanding, his black suit spotted with crumbs. I approached while Gompers stared speechless from his chair.

"Mr. Gompers," I said at once, "don't you think that perhaps your refusal to talk may be prejudicing the American public against you? Won't they think you aren't talking because you are too shocked . . . because you don't know what to say . . . because you're afraid. . . ."

Mr. Gompers' splutter burst into a shout that wiped out my concluding words. "What do you mean, young man? How dare you ————"; the shout leveled into a flow of words that became my exclusive story.

The second episode that tells something about the brash young reporter I was has for background ex-President Roosevelt's bolt from the Republican Party which had named Taft for President and the new Bull Moose party which was about to name Roosevelt. He was going to Chicago to guide the break. The reporters crowded the editorial office of the Colonel at the *Outlook*, a much read weekly of the time. They got no satisfaction. Mr. Roosevelt was not there. Was he going by train to Chicago? No one knew anything. So the journalists rushed down to Grand Central Station and learned nothing except that they were with special vigilance, barred from all Chicago trains. Roaming round the vast station, I noted a gate for a local train that was leaving at approximately the same time as the Lake Shore Limited. I bought a ticket for a local stop, walked to the head of the local train, jumped down to the tracks, and crossed them to the Chicago express. Unnoticed, I walked through the pullmans still I reached a private car. TR was sitting alone in a low chair, going through a batch of papers. He looked up: "How did *you* get in?" I explained what I had done and TR roared with laughter. I had an exclusive story.

One trait characterizes my behavior in these "beats"; the same trait that was revealed in my assumption that the *Post* would welcome my discovery that Emma Goldman was a motherly old woman. This trait is *naiveté*. It was naive to get to Roosevelt's train by the direct way—the only one not barred—of crossing the tracks. It was naive to guess that Gompers if he was hungry might hide and eat in a shut dining room. Naiveté can make a simpleton —and at times a good reporter. And naiveté lost me my job on the *Times*.

I had a cousin (long since dead), a young lawyer who wanted the glory of having his name in the paper. So he told me of a victory he had just won in the Municipal Court over an ambulance-chasing "shyster" lawyer; coloring his part to make him out a hero. Without verification (does one doubt the truthfulness of a cousin), I wrote the story as I got it; and it was published. The lawyer accused of being an ambulance-chaser sued the *Times* for libel. The case was settled out of court, with a retraction and a payment. And of course, I was dismissed.

Adolph Ochs called me to his office. The powerful proprietor of the *Times* was a smooth, dark, over-mellow little man with large hot eyes from behind which he seemed to look at you and appraise you. His mouth was mobile, while the appraisal went on, as if forever whispering a secret meant only for your ears. That this seemingly soft man was ruthlessly clear the shaft of the *Times* building seemed to suggest. Mr. Ochs waved aside my apologies. "Of course. Of course." But, of course, also, the *Times* had to let me go. "We hope you'll be back," said Mr. Ochs." "I hope we'll be having you back." I was made to feel that the *Times* liked me. What I carefully did not say to the great man was that I did not like the *Times* and did not wish to come back. It was probably the best newspaper in the world. But it lacked greatness of spirit.

I had learned good lessons as a reporter. I had seen all sorts of men and women, the rich and the poor, the miserable, the honored, and the doomed: alike in that publicity appealed to them all as somehow a fulfillment of their selves. Even the man accused of murder needed to feel alive in the social dimension he had maimed by killing a fellow human being. The great men of affairs,

I found, did not so much seek publicity as relax in it. Often they barred it and spoke "off the record" to a young nobody who became somebody by being a *Times* reporter. I found that subordinates were too busy or too careful to be good purveyors of "copy"; but the men on top had plenty of time for a chat, often for confidences, with the young one who symbolized the public. I got the feel of leadership from such entrepreneurs as J. P. Morgan, Jr., and Otto Kahn, such Maecenases of the American empire as Theodore Shonts and William McAdoo, and from such lawyers as Joseph Choate and the incredibly brilliant Max Steuer. But I talked with criminals also: for instance, with Police Lieutenant Becker, who ordered the death of Rosenthal when the gambler announced that he was going the next day to the district attorney with what he knew of the police control of organized vice over which Becker presided.

Until the very end, Becker could not realize what had happened to him. To collect thousands monthly from gambling and whore houses for police protection was as natural to Becker as the drop of a stone if you release it. That the stone should rise . . . that a big-shot gambler should "squeal," was the mystery . . . the malignant miracle. That he, Lieutenant Becker, should be found guilty of murder and sentenced to die was a bad dream; he could not believe it. Yet he could not overcome the dream. At the end he said, half to himself: *"What can I do?"* as if he were trying to wake up. In this haze of two conditions, an unbearable waking and dream, he walked the "last mile."[6]

The family still occupied the house on 78th Street, but, with a paying job, I left home and lived in a succession of lodging house rooms in Greenwich Village. The one that held me longest was at 75 Washington Place, a step from Washington Square Park. I had a large room on the third floor, and I paid $5 per week, with no kitchen and no private bath. In these old rooms, once parts of a living household, I recall myself chiefly as lying on the couch (at night, it was bed) fighting a deep depression; not because my experience of the day was gloom but because—when I got home by myself—I failed to make an organic connection between the glamor I had enjoyed and my inward reality.

These were the years of what might have been called "the consulship" of O. Henry (who had died in 1910). I did not admire him as a writer; his prose was brittle and thin, his effects were contrived, and he shrank when measured against a Maupassant or a Chekhov. But O. Henry's view of New York as a magical Baghdad—to be explored, exploited, above all to be enjoyed and wondered at—was the fresh vision of that hour. Manhattan was the home of Harun Al-Raschid and the Arabian Nights. New York was fabulous and a fable. As I recall, the flimsy texture of the O. Henry stories worried me. Was this a meaning: that the splendor of New York was conveyed by such thin and such cheap substance? But my debt and that of my friends was conscious. Every week or fortnight we met for dinner at one of the Italian tables-d'hôte of the Village and northward, (the charge was usually sixty cents with a bottle of wine), and we called ourselves the Baghdad Club,[7] surely a tribute to O. Henry. The Baghdadians talked books and music, never politics. I recall one member who was insane about Wagner and never missed a performance at the Metropolitan (he bought standing-room). Half the men were sure they would write the Great American Novel. One of the most modest was Sinclair Lewis, at the time an editorial drudge in one of the big publishing houses. Later, Lewis was to turn down my novel, *The Unwelcome Man,* with a warming, generous letter that predicted for me a career as Dionysian as Rolland's Jean-Christophe.

The Baghdad Club lacked the cohesion of Yeat's Rhymer Club in London, the authority of the *tertulias* in Madrid (all still unknown to us); but we were aware of stirrings: Reedy's *Mirror* in St. Louis was publishing parts of *Spoon River* by E. L. Masters; Dreiser had written a suppressed *Sister Carrie,* and Robert Frost, wandering from New England to Old England, via San Francisco, was preparing to sing "The Death of the Hired Man." I was trying —and failing—to conclude my book on modern French letters and already experimenting with short-stories that remained unpublished but led toward *City Block.*

One member of the club should perhaps have been listed with my friends at Yale, except that what followed after Yale was more important. Edward Curtis Wheeler loved good books—or hated them. Anarchists like Tolstoi, mystics such as Whitman were the targets of his withering rage. We two young men wrangled and abused and liked each other. Wheeler was an avowed militarist, a proto-fascist before the name; and my Jew's preference for ploughshares over swords earned his contempt. While still at college, Wheeler joined the Connecticut National Guard, and he did not wait for the draft to join the Army. Transferred to the Air Force, he was killed in a crash in 1927. The last meeting between us took place in the Plattsburg Officers' Training Corps. I, on my way home from a visit with Sherwood Anderson near Plattsburg, dropped by at the camp to see my brother who was in training there. Looking for Joseph, I ran into Curtis Wheeler who asked me what I was doing in the war. I told him—other fledgling officers were present—I was registered as a conscientious objector. Wheeler said to me: "You deserve the firing squad. I hope we shoot you. I hope I'm in command of the firing squad that shoots you." We shook hands warmly, and I went on looking for my brother.

The earth is a globe, and man is its mere surface shared with the animals and the innumerable flora. The fauna and the flora are content with this surface; they live in it, and it bounds them. Only man needs to pierce it, upward, downward, and within a new dimension of profundity which comes upon him at first as awareness of the surface. The unsatisfying surface. He knows he is not a mere flat viscid scum of the earth's face, by becoming aware of the scum. He knows his depth that takes in the whole earth like a globule of gas by knowing that he lacks the depth . . . needs the depth to be himself . . . needs terribly to know it. When this knowledge takes a specific form, there is a human culture. The form changes and dies and is displaced by another. This is the major process of our time. In a few years I was to begin describing it in what I called "The Revolution of the Arts" which first took shape as a series of lectures in the Rand School (the New York Socialist center) and then in the New School for Social Research. The depth psychologies of Freud and Jung, of course, belonged to this process (although their creators were not immediately aware of their discoveries' metaphysical implications), as did, more directly, the new forms in the arts: the new poetry and prose, the new painting, the new music. As at the birth of earlier cultures, lines of vision and deed were being drawn on the earth's surface which took their meaning only by consciousness *beyond* the lines and beyond the surface.

In a small gallery at 291 Fifth Avenue (which was to become world renowned) a restless and ruthless man named Alfred Stieglitz—with hair-tufts in his ears like a faun and a face like Socrates—knew this revolution and passionately, monomaniacally served it. I've tried so many times to write an estimate of Stieglitz —in *The Rediscovery of America;* in the symposium, *America and Alfred Stieglitz,* in articles and portraits published by the *New Yorker, McCalls,* and other magazines—that I cannot again go over the old ground.[8] Suffice it to say that I became one of the frequenters of "291" and listened by the hour to Stieglitz's descriptions of this revolution (the vocabulary of course is mine), and how it impinged on the behavior and the work of every sensitive person: on the paintings on the walls but even more on conduct and ethic.

Stieglitz, of course, had an art of his own; although he absolutely refused to call it "art," to call it anything but photography. Without tricks (he abominated the touched-up negative) his work revealed—in a cloud, in a face, in a hand, in the testicles of an old horse harnessed to a horsecar—the being of depth beyond the surfaces of space and time, whose experience by a people is their culture. America, he and we were sure, was in travail of a culture.

But music was my "second art;" perhaps because of my mother's radiant song that had suffused the childhood house, music was my primeval language. Yet I was nothing but an amateur cellist and a musical illiterate, knowing no harmony, no counterpoint, no grammar of orchestration. I did have a keen intuitive perception of tone structure, as an illiterate peasant, if sensitive, might have true responses to a spoken story. It was a significant day for me when I heard the Flonzaleys play Arnold Schoenberg's First Quartet. The audience laughed, shrieked, shouted; ladies huddled in their muffs and ran away. I did not understand much, but I knew without fully understanding the statement of the "Real" I was hearing.

Once a week, on the average, I toted my magnificent Testori cello (recently bought at a bargain price from Leo Schulz who had acquired a Guarnerius) to the Central Park West apartment of Claire Raphael. The entrance, a stone semicircular driveway for cars, made the place a fortress; and I got a thrill like a revolutionist's beholding the enemy's stronghold from within. Claire played the piano with a hard, unsentimental brilliance. The violinist was Walter Kramer, already a well-known musicographer and critic (he once with more warmth than justice called me the best amateur cellist in town). We played the classical trios and the moderns. When tired we turned to the table in the corner, laden with delicious sandwiches and coffee cake and beer. (This weekly feast on the margin of music plus the weekly Baghdad dinner and the occasional dropping-in at 78th Street for a sumptuous meal kept me in good shape and balanced my cheap feeds in the Village.) Munching the good rye bread and the leberwurst, we would talk and talk (sometimes Claire's sister Alice was there, or an old friend). Talk of what? Of the revolution, of the arts . . . of the exploding circumference of life revealing the real as opposed to the merely realistic. (Of course the language is mine . . . of *my* "Winter" regarding *that* "Spring.")

One Saturday afternoon, Claire took me to a private recital at the home of Bertha Feiring Tapper, a distinguished teacher of piano and theory. Her young star pupil, Leo Ornstein, just back from overseas successes—principally Paris, which he had had to leave because of the war—was going to play; and perhaps he would include some of his own pieces.

The long room with a façade of windows giving on the Hudson was astir like a convention of birds with the elegant gentlemen and ladies perched on their camp stools, and facing their twitter stood the silent black Steinway grand. Now a youth, not much over five foot, in his late teens, sidled past the rows of seats; and as he came close to the piano his head seemed to sink into his shoulders. He crouched rather than sat on the piano stool and placed his large, beautiful hands on the keyboard. The noise lessened. His long head rose, and his body straightened; he seemed suddenly a foot taller. With a single finger he struck a single note; and as if it were a signal, the silence became perfect.

He played a Debussy Prelude, making the music an overtone of his own strong seclusion. The music died, the applause burst, and the pianist took it as an almost unbearable invasion of the music. As if to stop it, he touched the keys again and played a piece by Ravel, whose wavery arabesques he hardened into springs of steel. When the applause came now, he faced it, turning his head barely, his body not at all, and continued at once with a composition by Albéniz.

Mrs. Tapper stood up and announced to her guests that Leo would now play some of his own music. Leo responded with a voluminous, cacophonous broadside of chords that seemed about to blow the instrument in the air and break the windows. Chaos spoke. Ladies laughed hysterically. The music growled like a beast, clanged like metal on metal, smouldered before it burst again, and suddenly subsided. Leo drooped over the keys, like a spent male after coitus, his head down as if he were praying. The audience shot to their feet, unconsciously determined perhaps that the ordeal be over and they need hear no more horrors. Claire and I shouldered through the throng to the piano which might have been a guillotine. I noted that there was blood on the keys. I looked close at the small ghetto-bred body (Leo, born in the Ukraine, had been brought up on the lower East Side), the strong masculine head, and threw my arms about Leo Ornstein, loving him at once because I loved the music.

I have not heard it in years. I suspect it might now seem the raw material of music—like some Bartok without the Hungarian's folk-music base—too direct to be integrated into live organic form. Whether this finality has been achieved by Ornstein in his later work, I do not know. Of this, I'm sure: much of the pattern-making music of late years wants the chaos of that outburst—without which chaos no new worlds are created. The encounter and the friendship which followed were of importance to this Baghdad reporter.

My love of music was not more intense than my love of the theater. There was theater in New York at this time, but it was not on Broadway. Theater, except for architecture, is the most social art. It must feed a public that endures beyond the life of any play. It must employ a comprehensible public language. It must reveal, and share with its public, passions, ideas, implicit myths of the culture. The consummation and concatenation of all the elements of theater—the audience, the dramatist, the director, the actor—occur seldom. For each achieved theater—the Athenian, the Medieval Mystery under the Cathedral Porch, the Elizabethan, the Spanish of Lope de Vega, the French of Corneille, Racine, and Molière, the recent Irish—there have been a score of periods without theater. America's theater, when I began to write plays, was not the claptrap of Broadway whose chief purveyors were such carpenters as Augustus Thomas, Clyde Fitch, Charles Klein, and the Pinero-Jones imports from London. Perhaps the closest to a theater on Broadway in those days was the musical comedy of George M. Cohan whose song-and-dance met a responsive and quite permanent taste in the public. American vaudeville—the country-wide circuits of the Orpheum, Proctor's, Albee's—were proto-theater. And the Yiddish houses on lower Second Avenue, where a faithful public might see Jacob Adler in a Jewish *King Lear* and next night a comedy by Scholem Aleichem, certainly gave the substance of full theater. The most respectable group in town was the German Irving Place Theater, where a stock of more than competent actors and directors sustained a repertoire that ranged from Sophocles to Hauptmann.

When the group around George Cram Cook, Eugene O'Neill, Susan Glaspell, Mary Heaton Vorse, and other fugitives from bourgeois America opened on a Provincetown wharf, there was a proto-theater in the American language (one not destined to mature); but I did not know them until later.

Cook wanted to produce two of my one-act plays. But I was not satisfied with them and took them back. As with the book on French letters, my focus was forever shifting and invalidating my previous conclusions. These plays, like the early stories, were never published; although there was a solicitous market for them later.

The Boni brothers, Albert and Charles, who had an avant garde bookshop on MacDougal Street called a meeting there to discuss the founding of a theater. Edward Goodman, who became director, was there; Philip Moeller, compound of English aestheticism and American bounce; Lawrence Langner, patent lawyer with a passion for the business of theater; Lee Simonson a scenic artist with a coruscating wit, agile as it was arrogant; the sober businesswoman, Teresa Helburn; and the tragic, beautiful Helen Westley, "nympholeptic of some fond despair." From these and a few others came the Washington Square Players; later the Theater Guild; even farther in the future the Group Theater, led by Harold Clurman, Lee Strasberg, Cheryl Crawford, and a lyrical young genius, Clifford Odets. Of these more later.

Now the scene is the bookshop and these young men and women conspiring to start a theater. They were all steeped in the *fin de siècle* drama of Europe: Maeterlinck, Andreyev, Lord Dunsany, Lady Gregory enthralled them. And the towering Shaw. I listened to them in silence and grew pale. For all I heard was alien to what I wanted in the theater. They were talking like *importers*. "This is all wrong," I wanted to cry out. These plays of Europe have their roots in their own soil. Their own climate suns them and waters them. I do not say: Never produce them. But they are not our main business which is to grow *our* flowers in the loam and rains and mulch of our own fields. I was not afraid to speak, but I was sick of heart. For I knew that this dissent was deep and enduring. I could not work with these men. "I do not belong." I said it to myself; I knew it was true. Yet I blamed myself.

I had sent my stories to the magazines. Printed rejection slips came back accompanied quite often by open and confiding personal notes from editors saying the text pleased them but was not quite what would please that mythic customer, the average reader. "Write us the sort of thing *we* want with *your* talent," they were saying. Which I was beginning to suspect was as sensible as to ask a hen to lay duck eggs.

I was also trying to write full length plays which I showed to such intellectual theater men as Winthrop Ames, director of the *recherché* Little Theater. And they were interested and encouraged me to go ahead. But as my plays grew less bad, the managers' interest waned. I discerned a difference: I was trying to write a *good* play with a living subject. *They* wanted a successful Broadway production.

I left the bookshop meeting depressed. I did not fit. And I blamed myself. Could I not adjust myself? Could I not pitch in and work with men on differing levels? I lay on my grey lodging-room couch and knew that the creator and the importer of fashions cannot work together. At each moment there will be dissent and distance. I also knew, so anxious was I to share, that I was wrong, that my reason for not working with these men was less living than the nonrational impulse simply to go along with them.

So I blamed myself. This was to be perhaps a key sin of my life: the arrogance and egoism of self-blame.

Such was the matrix-mood in which *The Unwelcome Man* was conceived.

If I had accepted what seemed to me the limitations of my potential colleagues, I would have jumped in, pressed my ideas so far as I could, and felt that I "belonged." If I had accepted a basic difference and resolved to live in it, I would have found a "communion of saints" to which I "belonged." I did neither. I tried to live in two incompatible worlds, whence an exacerbation that made life hard but kept it, without balance, always at the quick of living.

Nietzsche's *amor fati* was frequently in my mind. My adolescent vow with God was seldom consciously recalled, but it tinctured my life, as did my devotion to Tolstoi's anarchist refusal of the current civilization.

Yet at that time, on my work table I kept a framed picture of Anatole France, in a grey cloak and a red hat that suggested a Cardinal. Anatole France, the archetypal man of letters! But there can be no man of letters without a functioning and corresponding public, and I might have known that this element was vanishing in the West. Anatole France knew it and destroyed his own image of a man of letters. When war broke out in 1914, aged 70, he tried to join the Army, to shoulder a gun—as if to say, the function of the man of letters is past. Tolstoi too destroyed himself as a man of letters, dragging down literature with him. Whitman knew better; he strove for disciples, not a public. In me, already, there was a tension of opposites to make me what I became.

Among the diners of the Baghdad Club was a man named Barney who became my dearest friend. Barney was a southerner, a short, slim, lithe man with something of the bird and something of the serpent, and a prolific writer. New York was for him indeed the Arabian Nights. He had a room on West 8th Street in an Italian boarding house, and he introduced me to the broad-breasted, broad-hipped Signora who presided at the table and whose huge pot of minestrone, forever replenished, never touched bottom. The boarders at the long table illumined with unlabelled bottles of red wine were genuine O. Henry "Baghdad." There was the unavoidable Italian count, penniless and picaresque; the plain-clothes police detective; a pickpocket or two; the Sicilian *bel homme* who lived off aging women; the marble cutter who should —with a little luck—have become a sculptor; and a miscellany of women married and unmarried, bright and dull, fat and lean. This became my place of daily bread. With each to hear and to applaud the other, Barney and I together mapped out a literary America, with plenty of room for ourselves. We knew everything needed about this world except that it was to vanish, *spurlos versenkt*, in the next decade.

Barney wrote profusely about his South and about his Baghdad. His plots had glamor; his insights into character were sharp. But his prose was flat. A few of the pulp monthlys published him, never the magazines he aimed at. The man was brilliant, gen-erous, quickened; why did none of the glow, none of the incan-descence get into his pages? In Barney's room, on a niche nailed to the wall, on a blue silk altar cloth, sat a Buddha, Barney's true god. Perhaps this explained his failure as a writer; he was perhaps too detached from what he wrote to give it of his blood.

The end of Barney was sad. Making more money than I needed at the *Times*, I gave him $1,000 to go to Europe and bring back the Great American Novel. Perhaps in Paris the mass of Balzac's world was too much for him. The novel was not born. Barney ventured and capitulated, becoming a prosperous "interior decora-tor." He died soon of a malignant encephalitis.

So, through excessive naiveté of one sort or another, I lost a second newspaper job. I was fed up anyway with the daily grind of reporting and with the cynicism of the reporters. I had some money saved, and my father had offered to help me out. It was time to sail to Europe and have a try at uninterrupted writing.

March 1913: off season, so that the first-class cabin to myself on the *Kaiserin Augusta Victoriá* cost about $65. I had sailed to Europe before and was already a lover of this form of travel. Does this reveal something about me? Order and comfort on the boat are perfect; service is perfect. This makes for pleasure and secur-ity; *yet the ship swims through the dark and secret chaos of the Sea*. On deck or in one's berth, sea clamors ever close; the deadly sea that is alive, beneath one's feet with myriad forms of being farther from man than the at least visible planets. Both death and cosmos are present, infinitude with the most intimate creature pleasures.

All the great lines know this—German, British, French, Swedish, Dutch, Italian—and exploit this sacrament of antitheses: only the rational Americans ignore it.

The fat German vessel was almost empty. I remember two passengers . . . the famous pugilist's name I have forgotten; but I can see him, boyish and large, clumsy in his new well-tailored clothes. I hardly ever spoke with him, forever surrounded by his entourage, his manager, his sparring partners. His simple face was open, his eyes were baby blue, and his head round as a bowl. Early morning, he trotted the promenade deck in his sweatshirt or sampled the machines in the ship gym. Dull evenings he drank German beer and quietly gossiped with his men, doubtless about other fighters. The flavor of the man was his sweetness, aloof as a well-fed herbivorous beast's. The other man I recall, with whom I spent many hours of thrilling talk, was Captain McKern-Keston of the British Army, an Oxford man, short, dark and voluble. He might have been Welsh; he might have been an Arab or a Turk. He called himself a convert to Mohammedanism, and he had all the fervor of the convert. The key to his talk, and later to his voluminous letters, was the decadence of Europe and the rising strength of Islam. He had a Moslem name, Achmed Abdulla, under which he tried, in the years to come, to be an author. But his unsolved problem was the same as Barney's: lack of a true language. He spoke and he wrote correct English; he was well-read, if not learned, in literature, in history, in metaphysics. But there was no integration of his faculties into a living texture. He was at least ten years older than I, and his years seemed to have carried him around the globe. But the variety of his experience remained formless. The fact that I was never certain if he was British-born or of the Near East and never trusted his evasive statements about his origins, typifies the man's protean or inchoate nature.

Is it a trick of the mind that of that voyage there remains the memory of these two archetypes alone: the simple, boyish slugger and the over-complex cosmopolite? Does my memory *make* this pattern of extremes from interest? Doubtless I spoke to others on the boat—and forgot them. My memory is selective? A handy memory to have, but historically suspect. I can imagine myself as a young novelist *inventing* these two symbols of the world: the primitive slugger supplying the public need of violence in viable commercial form, and the cloudy sophisticate quoting the Koran

with Oxford accent. But although I feel no distinction of substance between the imagined and the remembered, I know these
men were real. On sunny days, my thrilling friend and I sought
a spot on the hurricane deck and talked and talked. Evenings, in
the smoking room, over the recommended cognac (none of your
mediocre Hennessey or Courvoisier), we went on blithely talking.
For several years the talk became long letters. What would they
amount to if reread today? How comes it that the silence of the
pugilist seems more substantial than the words of the articulate
Captain?

It was Shrove Tuesday . . . Mardi Gras . . . when I got to Paris.
The ripe town was dancing and singing, as a ripe fruit gives forth
flavors. All Paris was in motion, its buildings and its bridges and
its humans; it was an open fruit giving its mellow liquor. I aimed
straight at the *Rive Gauche*, my Paris. On the boulevards, the
papier-maché floats rang and careened; the cavorting girls and
the virile men might in plain view have coupled without harm to
the carnival spirit; the lilt of the *Maxiche* fusing with the buildings. I took a room for the night at the Hôtel Lutètia, and next
morning after the *croissants,* tender and crisp, and the aroma'd
café au lait I went forth to find my home in Paris.

I do not recall my precise route. I seem to have drifted down to
St. Germain des Prés and to have touched the lush streets of
food: rue de l'Ancienne Comédie and rue de Buci; then to have
worked up from the Boulevard St. Michel perhaps by the rue
Racine to the Odéon, as rich in books—from the classics, costing
a few centîmes, to de luxe editions—as the other streets in cheeses
and fresh greens. Looking perhaps into the dark, damp hotels of
the rue M. le Prince, finding the hotels near the rue de Médici and
the Luxembourg Gardens too expensive. In a street of the same
name I found at last the Hôtel Corneille. In the vestibule (no
lobby) the concierge said: "Yes, we have a room. On the top floor.
Fifty francs *au mois*, payable in advance. Does Monsieur like to
see it?" He unhooked a big key from the key-rack and handed it to
me, inviting me to look for myself.

The room was about twice the size of the double bed beneath
the single *mansarde* window. Farther along the wall of magenta
paper was a table for working, an armchair with torn crimson
brocade, a table for washing: water pitcher, towel rack with one
towel worn threadbare, and a slopjar.

This was my home for months. Long after I had left it, I
learned that the Hôtel Corneille had been the Paris home of

Synge; also for a while William Yeats had stopped there. This thrilled me, a young American for whom Synge had always been the greatest—certainly the truest—of the Irish writers. Long years later, after World War II, I was in Paris with my wife. To show her the hotel where Synge created, I led her up the rue Corneille. The hotel was gone, and where it had stood there was a vacant lot, completely cleared, making a gap in the block like a lost tooth. I learned the story later. The hotel had been a focus of the Résistance; its proprietor one of the leaders. The Germans surprised a meeting of the group; and they were lined up along the wall of the hotel court and machine gunned. This wasn't enough for the Nazi who felt he had been forced to search too long. He ordered the hotel razed to the ground as a warning to the neighborhood. The luminous words of Synge had long since flown away.

On that prewar visit I met no writers, although there were many painters among my friends. This was good luck. For when, on later journeys, I knew the literary leaders, I already had a common sense of the city and the land to counteract the distorting glamor of an Anatole France, an André Gide, a Dadaist. . . . I could "see Paris plain. . . ."

I had very little money. I learned that Paris was a city arranged for artists, poets, scholars, who had very little money and only a secondary impulse to make more. My room cost $10 a month. I lunched for one franc fifty (thirty cents) with a carafe of wine and feasted for dinner at 2 francs. With my student's tickets I paid half fare for buses, theaters. . . . Even the problems of sex were psychologically and economically handled by this greatest work of art among the modern cities of the world. There were young women who wanted to cook for one as well as sleep with one. There were women of high caste who found it a thrill to leave their chic apartment near the Étoile to visit a "genius" in his humble hotel bedroom. Paris was an integrated organism—with a stupendous variety of parts and each related to all others.

For example, among my friends was a man approaching forty, a Polish count with a diminutive income who was going one by one through the several faculties of the University of Paris. He already had his doctorate in mathematics, now he was getting his doctorate in medicine. Next would come the law. He was a rather flabby gentleman with down, not hair on his head, and the watery eyes of a too sedentary life. And he was not a "freak"; his detachment and gratuitous activity, free of "usefulness," was a major element of the city and affected thousands who would never hear of him. I learned, delightfully, through him that the American compulsion "to get there and make something of it" was not the universal rule.

There was another Polish count (they were legion) taking the life classes in the art schools of Montparnasse, whose impulse was mystical; he had visions and needed to put them on canvas; and he was an integer of the city along with the rationalist grace of the architects of the Louvre.

American students of art abounded, of course; and I got in with groups whose masters, Hawthorne and Richard Miller, left me cold. Their great god was Velazquez, who impressed me but whom I did not accept. Only later when I knew Spain and El Greco was I aware of why. Meanwhile the Frenchmen, Braque and Fernand Léger, the Spaniards, Picasso and Juan Gris, were already painting cubist pictures in Paris; and someone steered me toward the galleries of the rue de la Béotie where their early products could be seen. To say I did not understand them would be an understatement. But I was excited by them and knew they had a value not shared by a Richard Miller picture of a girl in a lovely frock seated at a window with sun and breeze caressing her blond hair —or even by a Whistler! Already I linked what I saw in the new paintings with what I heard in the new atonal music.

One evening, at the Comédie Champs-Elysées, the Diaghilev Ballet performed *Le Sacre du Printemps* by Igor Stravinsky, a young Russian. My seat was in the balcony. When the curtain rose, there rose with it from stalls throughout the parquet hisses, shouts, and catcalls. I saw on the stage the groups of dancers move through their harsh, stylized figures, but could hear nothing of what the orchestra was saying. When the outraged majority cried of silence, their shouted anger was met with more shouts. The music was utterly erased; the dancing bodies on the stage, strictly controlled, were partially barred from the music whose function was to join these bodies to the audience, who themselves were split into those who came to hear and the clique who clamored to destroy the music. The isolated dance, without the communication of the music seemed a stylization of the orgasm. The ballet of course had fecundity for its theme; the sap of tumescence rising from groin and breast. Here it was harsh and stark as an animal copulation. The final result of the attack upon *The Rites of Spring* was to eliminate the human and to reveal spring's naked structure. I was to hear and see this masterwork many times, but never so triumphantly as this first time when I could not hear it. I felt a relation, of course, between this stript art and the reductions of cubism.

Two generations before Paris, which always takes its arts in passionate seriousness, had similarly battled over the opening of Victor Hugo's *Ruy Blas* which blew away the three "unities" of the French classical drama. Formed by my childhood to rebellion, I was all for revolution. But I took pleasure also in the conventional French drama. The two national theaters, the Comédie-Française and the Odéon were hidebound in those days, and I went there seldom, although my half-price student ticket was cheap. But I respected the artifice of the boulevard "well-made play": Brieux and Hervieu whose plays were formulae for reforms; Henry Becque whose two great plays, *La Parisienne* and *Les Corbeaux* were syllogisms; Capus and Porto-Riche, whose plays were delectable nonsense written like a palimpsest over the solemnities of the social order (Capus' satire of business success, *La Viene*, is a masterpiece); Mirbeau and Bernstein, who built up climaxes of passion that exploded like bombs. Brilliance sometimes marred or hid the excellence of the boulevard confections. Of course, more significant were the men of Antoine's naturalistic theater and of Copeau's Théâtre du Vieux Colombier. But Antoine was gone, and Copeau was unknown to me until later. My acquaintance with the *Nouvelle Revue Française* was of the future, where war brooded. Meantime, I was at ease in Paris.

I got to know Paris. When, years later, my literary friends . . . Jules Romains, Charles Vildrac, and others . . . walked with me through the distinctive neighborhood organisms of the Ville Lumière—Belleville, Menilmontant, Buttes Chaumont—they were surprised at my familiarity with Paris.

Finally, I left the Hôtel Corneille. With two American painter friends I moved into a large proletarian flat near the Place Denfert-Rochereau in the Orléans district. From the teeming rue Daguerre, named after the pioneer photographer, we entered the court where a fishmonger, a carpenter, a cobbler had booths and an old woman sold flowers. The concierge had a daughter who swept and cleaned for us after a fashion; she was memorably, indeed monumentally, ugly; and she fell in love with one of the American painters. Every morning, he found a fresh flower on his pillow or in a glass on his table. There was never a word between them. But she accepted her life; and when they passed each other, the face of the American did not change but hers changed. Without loss of her ugliness, indeed within it, she became beautiful.

A variety of entrancing individuals dropped in at the rue Da-guerre: such as the two *ci-devant* Vicomtes de Soissons. Their father, the count, had never accepted the Republic and lived in voluntary exile and near penury in London. From the window of a third-class car, as the train swept them by, they had shown me the vast estates between Soissons and Château-Thierry which once belonged to their family. They showed the land without bit-terness and also without humor, as if it were still theirs and their distance from it an accident which would vanish. Charles was studying architecture at the Beaux-Arts; Pierre, less adjusted, dabbled with writing. He was a confirmed monarchist, still dream-ing of impossible revivals. "You'll see," he said. "Everything must go wrong in a republic. And a democratic one ————!" he threw up his arms in lordly deprecation. The quality of these nobles showed best in the court of the rue Daguerre where they were on the best terms with the people who loved to address them—a caress in their voices—as Messieurs les Vicomtes.

With spring came expeditions. A favorite spot was Petit An-delys, in Normandy on the Seine. There was a hotel beside the river, where for five francs—a dollar—one had breakfast (sweet-buttered *tartines* of bread and coffee laced with calvados), two delicious meals with all the wine or cider one wanted, and a spot-less room with a huge scarlet *édredon* smothering the wood frame of the bed. The *femme de chambre* expressed her amaze when she saw the Americans drink water. Had she never tasted water? *Crédieu que non!* Water was for washing. She was a large-limbed young Norman, six foot tall with a round small head and braided locks like a little girl's. The Americans pounced on her one day, lashed her to a chair, forced her mouth open by stopping her nose, and poured a jug of the cold clear spring water down her throat. She struggled and cried, as if she were being raped, and giggled and choked. Pierre Soissons saved the situation by assuring the landlord, who was getting angry, that she had not been poisoned. The girl acquired a taste for water! Associating it perhaps with pleasantly rough young male hands on her breasts which were as firm as apples.

I felt the classic temptation of the American artist to remain in Europe. There was even a girl who wanted me to stay and could not understand why I must leave since everything I loved was in Europe, and I could earn a modest living in Europe by writing home about it. Nevertheless, I knew that I was going home. The "pact" somehow called for it—as Walt Whitman knew.

When summer came, I bicycled with Middleton Chambers (an

artist whose home was in Virginia) from Paris to the Bavarian Alps. When we reached the frontier cities, Nancy and Verdun, we found ourselves submerged in war manoeuvres. We knew, of course, that the European nations had great armies. It was to them a kind of hereditary disease bound to die out soon, as it already had in the United States. On my arrival in Paris early in 1913, one of my first experiences had been the rioting students on the Boul' Mich', protesting against the new law that increased military service from two years to three. Anatole France himself had urged the students on, while the reactionary leaders, Barrès, Maurras, Action Française, screamed treason. War itself? Middleton Chambers who had a dry wit and a high sense of the ridiculous scoffed at war. "War's for tin soldiers." (He was to die a few years later not far from where we bicycled.) Another kind of war concerned me. War of two factions at *The Rites of Spring;* war of Picasso against the *pompiers* of the Salons. . . .

As we wheeled onward, we came to roads that were shut off; camions studded with armed troops thundered past us; the verdant fields of Verdun rose into hidden batteries: steel within green bulwarks. We felt a mood of dark resolution in these French which displaced our jests about the child's game of tin soldiers. We crossed the border into German Alsace and Lorraine, and now the mood was arrogance. From one *gemuethlich* village to the next, the rigid German discipline prevailed. We forgot our joking about war; now in turn we forgot our serious mood and insight that this *was* war . . . war of a kind already. We were young men having a time. And the German beer was good. . . .

I don't recall how my friend and I happened upon Reit im Winkel. It was a Bavarian village five or six kilometers from Koessen within the Austrian Tyrol. In Koessen the coffee was good; in Reit im Winkel the beer was better; and many a day we made the brief journey from one to the other, according to our thirst. No sooner were we settled, each in his Bauer house, than it began to rain. It rained for a month, and the town dared not bring in its harvest. This meant confinement; and confinement, heating the deep desires and discords in the folk, was to reveal much.

The villagers learned that I played the cello. Two fiddlers, a violist, and a pianist were soon found; and the quartets and trios began. Long afternoons grew shorter with the music. Nights, there were dancing competitions with teams from neighbor villages dropping in and then relaxing over their beer and wine. The dinner table which I shared was, I presumed, typical: at the center in a round wooden dish was the *Maelspeise;* each member of the family had a long wooden spoon with which he helped himself from the one dish. The "civilization" of this folk was primitive. There was a hardly a machine in the house, except the elaborate old clock which struck the hour and half hour in a circular procession of wooden functionaries in black robes with gold chains. Yet these "primitives" could play Schubert! Not well (technique was wanting) but with understanding.

At the end of the month, I was in trouble again . . . or helping to make trouble. The village had a school, of course, and a schoolmaster who resented us Americans for acting, he said to himself, as if we owned the place. To me, short, nervous, articulate, and self-assertive, went most of his odium, not to Chambers, the tall drawling southron, whose sole passion was painting.

One night, the *Schuhplaetteln* had been particularly good with a team from a neighbor town; but the visitors did not wish to go. At last, with the dawn near and much witty wine consumed and a few from our village along, we took the road toward home. At each house where there was a couple we broke in, lifted the man from his warm bed and wife, and dumped him outdoors in the rain (it was still raining). We were getting bored, I decided; and while we waited for the rain to stop, I began to teach the villagers the new American dances. I was no expert but could manage, so could Chambers. In less than a week the whole village was dancing, after a fashion, the Charleston and the one-step. The teacher came, saw, and was scandalized. Unconsciously he had been looking for a pretext. He went to the policeman of the village and told him that their good, docile, Catholic flock was being taught lascivious dances. With his adjutant, the constable marched onto the hall floor where Chambers and I were giving lessons and placed us under arrest. The Americans were only two, but we had plenty of allies. The new dances were popular. This gave me the courage to ask: "Why? On what charge are we arrested?" And the officer thought it best to tell us.

"What!" shouted I. "Lewd and obscene dances? Do you realize who dances these dances? In the White House? In the Congress? the president. President Wilson of the Vereinigten Staaten. So our president is being accused of dancing obscene dances."

The two officers wilted. Luckily for him, the teacher was not there. It was *lèse majesté* to accuse the chief of a friendly power . . . international incident. . . . All the German servility and fear came out, as the policemen urged that nothing should be said. *Ein Irrtum.* The two Americans were, of course, free and entirely wel-

come to remain in Reit im Winkel so long as they obeyed the laws
—as they had done, had done. . . . But perhaps it would be best if
they soon said *adieu* to Reit im Winkel?

When late next summer the armies mobilized and war opened
its bloody blooms all over Europe, the young woman I was to
marry was with me in a village near Cape Cod on the Massachusetts coast. I read of the bombing of Rheims Cathedral and in
the violence of my reaction learned that I loved France and
wanted to help France. I rushed to New York, leaving a note for
Margaret.[9] The French consul's offices were packed with noisy
and sweaty Frenchmen—waiters, coiffeurs, businessmen—clamoring for immediate passage back to join their army cadres. I
awaited my turn on the long line and when it came told the man
at the desk that I wanted to be shipped to France as a soldier. The
hamster-like little man patiently listened and went to an inner
office for instructions. He came back shaking his head; President
Wilson had just issued his Neutrality Proclamation; the con-
sulate did not know how this would affect volunteer Americans
abroad: "So for the present, Monsieur, we can do nothing. . . . Of
course, if Monsieur went over of his own accord ———:" The
man meant "paying his own way."

For two weeks I tried to borrow a few hundred dollars from
friends and family who suddenly became ungenerous. Margaret,
too, had rushed to New York and was warning everybody that I
had suddenly developed a mania to be killed by a German *obus* in
defense of Rheims Cathedral and that they must all fight a delay-
ing action against me. I did not even have a passport. (In prewar
Europe, passports had been almost obsolete.) The ships were
crammed. Now "the pale cast of thought" began to "sickly o'er"
my will to be a soldier. Was it my destiny to defend Gothic
churches or to build my own stately mansions? As the weeks de-
layed me, France refused to ship me; and my friends refused to
finance me; one fact became clear: I was no longer clear. With
the first fine fervor gone, I was behaving, I began to see, like an
extremely ignorant young man. A period of clarification started:
a little war with Margaret conducting the offensive. She warned
me bluntly. If I bounced over to France and somehow managed
to get in the war (there were plenty of ways, it soon developed, for
Americans to get in), she was finished with me. Let my sympathies be with France; nevertheless, this was not *my* war. France,
the second largest empire in the world, was part of a capitalist
system which made for war and had made this one. If she had

fallen in love with a romantic sentimentalist aching to die for Jeanne d'Arc, she would fall out again. To love a man was to live with a man, not let him gratuitously die. Gradually the impetus to act blunted; the impetus to wait and to weigh sharpened.

This was all a complex business, and it was going to take a couple of years before I grasped it: years of testing myself and my equilibrium in the mad whirling war. For example, I soon learned that there were good times to be had in war, and I knew plenty of men and women who were having them. I learned also that I was afraid of war; my imaginings of bodies maimed and blinded and torn in cities burned and broken were vivid for making fear. Even more fearful was the abdication of my freedom that a uniform meant. What I had to learn was whether my fears begot my convictions. Perhaps I was a mere coward, rationalizing my unwillingness to die. Or was the true coward the accepter of war with open eyes, who knew war's sterility and madness?

France, in the first two years carried on an active cultural propaganda in America. The Théâtre du Vieux Colombier, which I had missed in Paris, crossed the sea and began to give performances in the old Garrick Theater off Broadway. On their first visit I got to know Jacques Copeau, director of the theater and of the *Nouvelle Revue Française;* Gaston Gallimard, the publisher of the *NRF.* Now the company followed: Louis Jouvet, Charles Dullin, Valentine Tessier, Suzanne Bing—the entire group. And it was they who purged me of any last vestige of romanticism about the war.

The cathedrals, they said in effect, were gone long before the war started: their spirit, their social and intellectual forms no longer valid. The war was a hideous shambles, they said—some of them fresh from the trenches. Peace must be made; peace without victory, before the marrow of all Europe festered. Many of them —Copeau, Jouvet, Gallimard among others—came regularly to Margaret's and my flat on East 30th Street, where they felt at home and their language was understood. Their straight talk revealed the sickening meaninglessness of the fratricidal war toward which America was careening. They hated war. They had no hate for Germans. They had respect only for those who fought against the war or—unable to fight it directly—at least tried to save themselves. Death in this war was no patriot's deed, said these good and greatly gifted Frenchmen, these distinguished heirs of France's art; it was surrender to idiocy. They spoke with desperate sympathy of the soldiers (growing in numbers) who lopped off a hand or infected themselves with syphilis in order to escape the worse maiming and infections of the trenches.

In the meantime, from his place of refuge in Swiss Villeneuve on Lake Geneva, Romain Rolland fired his *Audessus de la mêlée,* a brave word by a brave Frenchman against the suicide of Europe. The people of the Vieux Colombier and the *NRF* had no use for Rolland as a writer. They rejected his *Jean-Christophe,* a novel about a German composer who becomes the symbol of dionysian Europe. But in their own terms, they harmonized with Rolland. I had been in touch with Rolland before Copeau and his troupe came to New York. In the dark early days of the war, when I was still living alone on Washington Place, I had written to Rolland; and, unlike my letter to Tolstoi, this letter was mailed. Weeks passed; my mind was full of other phases of my problem of survival. Returning to my room one afternoon, I passed as usual through the basement where mail for all the lodgers lay always waiting on a table. The dim basement light was just enough to read an address. I held in my hand a thick envelope with my name written in the graceful soaring script of Romain Rolland.

It began: "Dear Friend." After such a letter I can only say: We are friends.

On May 7, 1915, a German U-boat sank the *Lusitania;* and more than 1100 men and women perished. The great British liner was loaded with guns and ammunition destined to kill Germans. That evening I went to Luchow's on East 14th Street. The crowded restaurant rang with the exultant Germans' *Hoche!* as they downed their seidels of beer and saluted Germany's showing America her invincible might. Around the corner from where I lived there was a delicatessen run by a bristling German and his gentler father. They explained to me, patiently and proudly, why no one could beat the Kaiser. America was "all right" (although it had too many Jews), but of course the world's leadership was and must be German. How could my French friends with their delicate insights meet this megalomaniac German menace? How could capitalism explain this war? Rather it was (so I thought) the egoism of the people which explained both capitalism and the war.

I was groping, more than a decade before *The Rediscovery of America* and more than four decades before *The Rediscovery of Man,* toward my own ideas about the self with its ego, its social and its cosmic dimensions: its ego that could never be destroyed or transcended (here I differed from Platonists and Brahmans) but could be *transfigured* by the growth in the self of the self's social and cosmic dimensions, as inherent to the self as the ego. It was this emphasis that barred me from being a moralist or a political writer and that made me—so I surmised—primarily a poet.

Meanwhile, German U-boats sank innocent ships, and thousands of young men died in the trenches. It was hard for me not to be lost in hate of Germany and dislike of arrogant Germans— with the acceptance of war to put Germany down.

President Wilson called for the draft; the country was drawn to war as by a mighty magnet. I registered as an "objector to this war," expressly dividing myself from the conscientious objectors who would fight in no war because of their literal Christian creed. I was no pacifist; and perhaps there were "just" wars. *This one,* I had become convinced, must be fought by refusing to fight in it —inevitable product, I was sure, of the normal "peace" of the contemporary nations.

With this clear, I was still not clear in my own conscience. "Am I opposed to this war, not only because of its capitalist-imperialist origins and its certain capitalist-imperialist end, whatever power 'wins' it, but also because I am afraid to die?" This, I had to *find* out, and it seemed possible. I was registered, but the selective draft was not yet in operation. Therefore I could not know what would be done to objectors without benefit of a recognized religion, such as Jehovah's Witnesses. In France, friends told me, I would be stood up against a wall and shot. Let me assume the same procedure in the American Army. That made it simple. My conviction is that the war on both sides is unmitigated evil from which nothing can issue except evil (how right I was!). So I refuse to join. So I am stood up against a wall; a firing squad of six men face me and fire. Am I ready for that? Can I go through with it because of my conviction? Then the coward-motive for refusing to fight is overcome—even if it is there.

The common soldier faces death in company; and since the company and the country live, he does not die. I faced death alone; and after I had died, I repeated the experience the next night. I went to bed. When I was quiet I stood against the wall; I lined up the squad of six men with their rifles aimed. They fired. I beheld my mind crumpled into blankness, my body collapsing. I had died for my refusal to fight an idiotic war. Next night, to make sure I meant it, the scene was repeated. In a sense, I died nightly. In a month, my nerves showed the strain. I became ill. . . .

My father returned from Washington, where legal business had taken him. He had a proposition to offer me, backed by a high authority. They needed interpreters, and my proficiency in both French and German could be helpful. I would be classified as non-combatant for the alleviation of my conscience. I was tempted. After all, why not? I would not be fighting a war I hated. Yet I would be helping *the people* who were fighting, and after all I wanted *the people* to survive. It did not work; I could not stomach it. Whatever one said, such an arrangement meant that I would be in a safe task that depended upon others less safe; and the whole a participation, a collaboration, in the war. I couldn't do it. I refused the job and remained jobless . . . positive in self-exclusion from the war.

I expected prison, at best—and went on working at my second novel: *The Dark Mother*.

4

The Tragedy of the <u>Seven Arts</u>

I met James Oppenheim in the winter of 1915–1916; it must have been at some small gathering or party.[10] Oppenheim was a well-established writer of stories about New York immigrants, for which he was paid fabulous sums by the mass magazines. He was also known as a poet. He was a short, soft-bodied man in his mid-thirties: humorless, soft-spoken, with a flavor of fatherly tenderness to his smile like a devout orthodox Rabbi's. Also his homely homespun handsomeness reminded one of Lincoln.

Probably I had read none of his stories, convinced they could not be good because of where they appeared. But I found myself talking to a listener who inspired me to pour out heart and mind. I bewailed the literary status of the country; rushing toward war it was eyeless and voiceless. There were a few fitful foci of light, I said: *Reedy's Mirror* in Saint Louis published Masters and Dreiser; in New York, the *Masses* and the *New Republic* had something to say, but it was almost always political when it was good; the deep loam of the imaginative and the creative was not there. Meanwhile, the supposed organs of culture: the *Atlantic Monthly, Century, Scribner's,* and *Harper's* had been marooned on a desert isle by tides they did not even know existed. Whitman, I said, was underground; the true Mark Twain was repressed by the curb bit of the Richard Watson Gilders. We need a magazine, said I, thinking of my unpublished stories and unwritten diagnostics of what was wrong, and why.

I was so enamored of my own outpourings that the quiet responsiveness of the older who appeared to be sizing up the younger one seemed nothing but natural. Oppenheim listened; Oppenheim asked leading questions, and I flowed on. "Yes," said Oppenheim; and "We must go into that." He saw the boyish face, younger than his years, not yet marked by its intensity, the thick black hair no comb could tame; the rounded chin, receptive rather than aggressive; the passion and flame of the young man for the good and true in writing.

"We must study all this," Oppenheim got ready to move on.

"Oh, but the money!" I keened. "All this is all very well. But the money! How can it be done . . . how can it be *begun* . . . without the money?"

Oppenheim's face crinkled with a smile, purposively cryptic, as he finally said: "Don't worry about the money."

Soon, in that grim winter of approaching war, I learned the fact: the radiant fact: there *was* the money. And while I was feeling sorry for myself and for the country with manufacturers and exploiters of the mediocre in every place of power, the money in Oppenheim's hand had been looking for a bright, young assistant.

Oppenheim had a friend, an intimate friend, Dr. Beatrice Hinkle, then the outstanding American disciple of Jung. She had translated Jung and found a good publisher for Jung's daring excavations into the paleontology of the unconscious. Moreover, Hinkle had a patient, a gentlewoman of means, Mrs. A. K. Rankine, who needed something to do with her surplus and her time. Dr. Hinkle had sounded her patient and learned that the idea of an American magazine, an organ of American culture, appealed to Mrs. Rankine. She had already brought her and Oppenheim together. He had informed her that she would have absolutely no authority as to the contents of the magazine. But she would be the company's president, and her lawyer its secretary-treasurer. This satisfied Mr. Meek, the lawyer, who knew the powers of money. As editor, Oppenheim would have unchallenged sway over the magazine's policy. And Oppenheim already knew who would constitute his board of advisory editors. Among them were Robert Frost; Robert Edmond Jones; Louis Untermeyer; David Mannes, the musician. What he lacked was a dynamic young assistant with the right ideas. When he heard me speak, that night of a chance meeting, it seemed that the young man knew what Oppenheim was seeking and was answering a cue. The evening seemed inspired. And this was just the sort of "mystery" to please both Oppenheim and me.

A contract for the first year was signed. Mrs. Rankine paid the bills unless there was a favorable balance of earnings (which no one expected). Oppenheim was editor with a salary of $5,000, and the magazine became his property. I was engaged as associate editor and my wage of $35 per week began at once; for, as I saw it, the magazine was to be not the usual grab-bag of stuff more or less timely but an organism—an organism from birth, therefore before birth; for a living organism is not formed in a day.

Throughout that spring and summer, I breathed the business of the *Seven Arts*. And breathed the hot, rancid breath of approaching war. The *Lusitania's* going down a year before was the point of no return. Symbol of America's condition was the gay crowd before the lions of the public library whooping it up with oratory and brass band for money for war, for men for war. To all this I was in the books as an objector. Outside of this pandemonium which was unconscious of me, I knew that if *it* knew it would hate me. And feeling this hate against my thin small body, how could I keep from hate? from fear beneath hate? But why should a group of crass women and crude men rasping and thumping for America to get into the war seem to blot out the cosmos? I felt, rather than knew, these questions. If, as I thought, I loved America, why did it oppose me? Why was I so naked and thin against it? The intensity with which I threw myself into working toward the first issue of the *Seven Arts* (scheduled for November) derived from my fears of the hate that would brand me on the street if these passers-by knew my refusal of the war. Even my dreams were streaked with thoughts and worries of the *Seven Arts*. To the chill eye of today, this passion of the young man to let a word be collectively created—while America plunged into empire—seems almost unbelievable and absurd.

Of course, there were many details; and Oppenheim was usually too engrossed in the upper regions of strategy to come down to them. There was no "staff" except himself. An office was found in a charming old building at 132 Madison Avenue. A circulation manager was hired; but his mind, muffled in platitudes, did not rise to the occasion. Lists of potential authors were prepared, and a manifesto sent to them of the organ's purposes. America was alerted; also Europe—principally through my connections.

Contributions began: soon from a trickle to a flood. Well-known authors sent the piece that was too good for the general market. (Jack London wrote me a sad letter: "Too late," he said, "the lack of a market for what I might have written has meant that I never wrote it.") And the unknown authors appeared to be so numerous that the "great audiences" of Whitman might turn out to be an audience of poets. I had little to do with the poets, who were the department of Oppenheim and his friend, Louis Untermeyer. But even before the magazine was born, the prosemen and the artists in other media than words—music, painting, architecture—

tended to come into the hands of the associate editor. Even before the magazine existed, public response began. For example, the *Chicago Evening Post* ran an editorial: "There will soon be another magazine in America. . . .

Edna Kenton of the advisory board, our scout in Chicago, was probably responsible for this accolade; as she was certainly responsible for my writing to an unknown "bright Chicago advertising man," named Sherwood Anderson, who wrote stories and novels in his spare time. I asked for a chance to see them. Anderson sent them. Whence my article in the first issue: "Emerging Greatness."

Ever since Romain Rolland's first generous letter, which the reader recalls, I had been in epistolary touch with him. He was told of the magazine's expected birth and wrote me a welcoming letter. With his permission the personal part of this letter was deleted, it was titled "America and the Arts" and now our first issue had a central word, a total word.

The advisory board in its initial state lacked the name of Van Wyck Brooks. Its members were both established cultural figures and friends of the two editors and of Louis Untermeyer, who was as active as an editor. Robert Frost was Untermeyer's friend. Kahlil Gibran, the Syrian poet, was Oppenheim's. Paul Rosenfeld, who was my friend and extremely active, was not a member. At that time, he regarded himself as a budding novelist and literary critic. I assigned him to music and from the start he was more actively creative than most of the board members. Others, not formally connected with the magazine, lent advice and a hand; for example, Walter Lippmann, who wrote a confidential letter to Louis Untermeyer, which Untermeyer tactlessly showed to me. It was a warning against Frank, "who," said Walter Lippmann, "was a mystic!" Obviously, enough to bar me from any responsible position.

One of the magazine's true friends was Ben Hebsch who, in these jejune days, shared with Mitchell Kennerly the honor of publishing American books because they thought them good. Kennerly's assistant was a powerful man named Alfred Knopf. And one of Huebsch's authors was Van Wyck Brooks, whose *America's Coming of Age* Huebsch had recently brought out with no fanfare and few sales. Huebsch told to Oppenheim, "Get in touch with Brooks, get a copy of the book and give it to me." Oppenheim read it and passed it on to me who shared his enthusiasm for it. If Rolland's word was accolade, a trumpet calling for intellectual war, this was the very battle. The accolade gave heat, as did the program of the *Seven Arts*. But already there was light: Brooks' little volume was clear and luminous as flame—flame of sun at a dark clouded dawn.

Oppenheim and I wanted to see Van Wyck Brooks. We called together at the offices of the *Century*. We stood in a long room where a large number of men and women were bent over typewriters and figures. From this amorphous mass a little man separated himself and trotted toward us. He had hair like a black cap and a moustache like a small brush of tough bristles, and his eyes were warm and shrewd: a perilous combination for its possessor. Huebsch had forwarned him of the visit. He explained his low position at *Century* as tactical. He had to work to live, but he did not want to think about his work: the thinking he reserved for his writing. So he held a position of no authority which left him comparatively free. He accepted membership on the board; a few months later he was to become an associate editor like me. He introduced us to a man named Barry Benefield who, he said, wrote good stories; and in the first issue appeared "Simply Sugar Pie," a tale of the black peasants of the South, as deep as the best of Faulkner decades later.

The reader must not suppose that I clearly saw beforehand a pattern for the magazine. I felt what belonged, of what came in, and what did not belong—which included most of the offerings of the well known. The world plunged into war. Against its cold madness another world had to be created. Those whose work fitted often were opponents, but like the tensions of a healthy body. There was, for example, Edna Wahlert McCourt of St. Louis whose sense of woman was wildly potential; despite her trouble in finding a language to express her, she belonged—as did the precise Flaubertian prose of Frederick Booth and the luminous seeking prose of Anderson. (I found Booth in a lodging room on Bank Street—next to where Willa Cather lived; but soon Booth went south and vanished.) The shrill soprano of D. H. Lawrence fitted, and the still prose of J. D. Beresford, a superb English novelist now neglected. And what could be more apt than the counter-mysticism of John Dewey which turned out to be his insistence that his own mystical prehensions of life should speak a language free of theological rot and useful in an age of science? When a man spoke an idiom of a basic force, I went to him and asked him to write. So, Dewey wrote for us, "In a Time of National Hesitation" which admirably expressed American doubts as the nation fell to war. When his pragmatism made Dewey accept the war, Randolph Bourne was there to reject Dewey's pragmatical acceptance. Dreiser also fitted: another organic tension. He had been mired in the bumbling censorship of Anthony Comstock. I got to know him well, wanted his anguish in the magazine; and the result was his long piece, "Life, Art and America"—a schoolboy's inordinate title and a creative man's confession of what it is to be an American artist.

Dreiser's poetic play, *The Dreamer,* related the man's fantasy with his worship of accumulated facts; and this too was much of America. Meanwhile the critics . . . Leo Stein, Mencken, Willard Huntington Wright . . . brought muscle and tone to the monthly structure. The mails bulged with stories that tried to reveal the world's dawning sense of death and transfiguration. Most were sent back, but never (if they showed signs of life) without an editor's personal appreciation. Artists of other forms were encouraged to put their credos into words: Ernest Bloch among the musicians; Marsden Hartley, the painter; and Lee Simonson, the scenic artist, writing of circuses and museums. A mystic ranger of the seas, Kaj Klitgaard, turned the waves into song. A Yankee from down-east Maine, Wallace Gould, answered the polished verse of Khalil Gibran, the modulated eighteenth-century verse of Robert Frost which contained anarchism and sedition as Whitman contained multitudes.

One inner grouping of the magazine, which grew of itself, began when Seichi Narusé, a soft-voiced Japanese, came silent footed to the office with a letter of introduction from Romain Rolland. Narusé wrote "Young Japan"; John Butler Yeats, father of the poet, visited the office, and "Young Ireland" and "Youngest Ireland" by Padriac Colum followed. A youth named John Dos Passos, with the eyes of a colt looking at the world for the first time after being dropped by his mother, reported on "Young Spain." "Young India" followed. "Peter Minuit" was invented, a mask behind which anyone could write when he had something mischievous to say. For instance, John Klaber, an architect, wrote of the "Masqueraders"—the imitation French châteaux and Gothic chapels along Fifth Avenue—and I forget who wrote the scathing report of the college class reunion. (Perhaps it was Paul Rosenfeld?)

The materials were variegated enough to fit the counters of a rummage sale in a New York department store? Nothing could be less true. They made the body of a breathing work with the editors not knowing, as they rejected, suggested, selected, what was coming alive. I was no longer alone! I belonged to America and America belonged to me. There was no demarkation between my contacts as an editor and as a man. For instance, I saw John Dewey not only at his office at Columbia University but in his New York apartment and his humble house in Long Island. So modest was he, he seemed actually pleased when this cub, not yet thirty, wanted to see him and wanted to print his homely words all stiff at the joints. He confided; yes, he wrote poetry of a sort. Oh, no! it was not to be seen. He surrounded his silence with the noise of children; and as if his own and his schools' were not enough, he adopted a lad from Italy; and, lest he forget him in his long sieges of work and absorption, he had the boy share his bedroom.

Dreiser had come east from Chicago and lived in a large flat in Greenwich Village. This was childlike America, this strapping Hoosier folding and unfolding his body at the little kidney-shaped desk where he wrote and wrote in the upright hand of a schoolgirl. When he was idle he kept shaping a handkerchief in accordion folds, and there was some connection between the handkerchief, the handwriting, and the cumulative details of his stories. "If my name were Dreiserevski what a success I would be!"—he was perpetually wounded and perpetually licking his wounds. But like a schoolboy, he shouted at his own jokes. When his girl (he was separated from his wife), after an evening of talk with friends, brought a chocolate cake from the kitchen he couldn't wait; he had to be served first. Colossus with tender feet, he bestrode America. His brother, who called himself Paul Dresser, had written the popular song "On the Banks of the Wabash," a mere trickle by Dreiser's measure; and his heroines, Sister Carrie and Jennie Gerhardt, partook of his own size and became giants of feminine softness.

There were others who fitted the *Seven Arts* as if it were made for them: Marden Hartley, equally at home in the studios of Paris and Berlin and in the forests of Maine where he unearthed Wallace Gould; Leo Ornstein, whom I already knew; Paul Rosenfeld, who became America's most sensitized of listeners for new voices. And already there was dissidence from the mystical tincture of the magazine, now within the group but soon to become open dissent: Edgar Lee Masters, for instance, whose spirit died when he denied the spirit of Lincoln; Vachel Lindsay who tried in vain to naturalize Congo rhythms into the sidewalks of New York and the kitchens of Midwest farmers; and Mencken with his progeny who made a song with clashing cymbals of his discovery that America was a nation of yokels.

Ernest Bloch, the Swiss composer, like the Japanese Narusé, came to the *Seven Arts* with a letter from Romain Rolland. He had left Geneva, where he had worked in his mother's souvenir shop and had lectured at the University of Flaubert, to tour America as orchestral conductor for Maud Allan, an American dancer. The tour folded in a small Alleghany town, and Bloch had to beat his way to New York. Answering a telephone call in the lobby of the Hotel Astor, he left his coat on a chair and returned to find it stolen. He was penniless and the winter was cold. But in a month his music would fill Carnegie Hall. There is a photograph of Bloch, Narusé, and me, all staring together into the future. Bloch's eyes are rods of intellectual power. Less than a decade later, I will dine with Narusé and his wife in a rich Paris apartment overlooking the Seine near Cour la Reine and find him changed utterly . . . hidden from his old American friend, doubtless a recruit of Japan's already preparing bid for power. All this, still to come. . . . The present was hope and confidence. In the May issue appeared a prose poem, *Holy Russia*. Written by me, it was unsigned because it expressed the editorial faith.

There was a lunch I recall because it seems typical of that hour. At one table of the Harvard Club sit Max Eastman, editor of the *Masses;* John Reed, fresh from the Mexican Revolution and Pancho Villa; and I. Close at another table sits Theodore Roosevelt with two powerful leaders of the movement to get America in to the war. The ex-president smiles with his teeth at Reed and Eastman, gloating over the day when such traitors will face a jury, and the two flaming radicals smile back, as much as to say: "Your grave is ready."

The men of the *Seven Arts* did not forget that it had promised to be "an expression of artists for the community"; but a prophet might have discerned in us, already, the trend of the arts toward politics, a natural course when the society is menaced for causes exterior or internal.

The monthly editorial, written by Oppenheim, became a problem. It was hortatory and, as the war neared, progressively grandiose. Sometimes it was addressed to Lincoln. America, it said, longs to be "a great nation." And it discovered that war was getting in the way of its high destiny. Brooks did not agree with the editorials. He was to say later that a literary magazine should keep out of politics, particularly the politics of war. In the office, he was likely to keep silent, to close the door and write his luminous chapters of the book to be: *Letters and Leadership.* I agreed, more articulately and warmly, with the sentiments of Oppenheim's editorials. But they were all sentiment; that was the trouble with them. They added nothing to the substantial, explicit stuff of the stories, essays, poems. They lapsed into free verse which uncomfortably revealed the superiority of Whitman's. (About this time Oppenheim published two volumes: *Songs for the New Age* and *War and Laughter:* verse in the Whitman idiom with a tincture of analytical psychology by Jung.) But the body of the magazine was itself *substance:* solid, versatile, nutritious. Worse than mere dilutions, the editorials militated against the sober body of the magazine. Oppenheim would call Brooks and me to his office and read aloud the editorial he had just written. Squirming invisibly, Brooks would make objections which Oppenheim accepted gracefully. Next morning he would show up with a new version, which merely variated what we had not liked in the first. For we were against the idea of a sermon. As the war drew close, the editorials became entirely free verse. And I got the uncomfortable feeling that Oppenheim thought he was Lincoln—a Lincoln reading to his Cabinet and, of course, always by one dimension *beyond* his Cabinet.

The editorials certainly did not kill the magazine, whose circulation soared. Indeed, as I see now, the sermons in dithyramb may have pleased many readers, as on a lower and dishonest level the sermon-editorials of Arthur Brisbane pleased his millions of readers in Hearst's *Journal*. Oppenheim had proven by his stories that he knew how to reach a public. What he certainly did not see was that his editorials were making a rift between him and his two associates and also between him and certain members of the advisory board: Frost, Amy Lowell, Sherwood Anderson, Robert Edmond Jones. The poetry continued to be edited by Oppenheim and Untermeyer, but the magazine was preponderantly prose; the selection of stories, essays, plays, with the ordering of specific essays, became chiefly the work of the two associates. It was Brooks who brought in Randolph Bourne. And very soon Bourne, from his analyses of American culture, drew conclusions about the war which jeopardized the magazine.

Brooks, except intellectually, was a timid man. His tendency when the others shouted in argument was to shrink back to his office and work on his pieces. So it soon came to be that I was the virtual managing editor. I did most of the legwork: visiting, suggesting contributions, such as, Dreiser's, Dewey's, Mencken's and Jack Reed's. I broadened my contacts with Europe, which included the *NRF* and Rolland's group; Bertrand Russell and D. H. Lawrence who distrusted a magazine "run by a couple of Jews"— yet still kept sending his welcome stories.

Oppenheim kept in close touch with Mrs. Rankine, whom the

associate editors seldom spoke to. The economics of the magazine took a good deal of Oppenheim's attention. Bourne's essays began with "The Puritan's Will to Power," a theme developed by Brooks and taken over later by me in *Our America*. In June appeared "The War and The Intellectuals" which made Bourne the conspicuous voice of the entire group—and at the same time separated him from the "hesitation" of John Dewey, Bourne's former teacher and master. In this essay and the subsequent ones—"Below the Battle," "A War Diary," "Collapse of American Strategy," which showed how by entering the fight America had tossed away the one chance to end it and to control the peace—there was no "hesitation." Bourne emerged as a hero, the banner bearer.

No one knew then what a symbol he was! He was a dwarfed hunchback; even his lips and one of his ears were twisted. A black cloak hid his sorrowful body as he walked, his spindle legs lifting him along like a crow. But his capacity to fly soon became evident. At first I could hardly look at him, lest my pain and horror be visible to Bourne. Then the deep intelligent eyes, the very light of reason, prevailed; the tortured body seemed to be transfigured. What had happened to this man when he was born? To the creator of the luminous word: *The health of the State is war?* Bourne's brave eyes were a truth; was his distorted form a symbol?

In the spring of 1917 when America declared war, the *Seven Arts* was long since committed to resist it and the country to wage it. Poor Mrs. Rankine, a gentlewoman of modest goals whose money had always cleared the surface pressure of her life confining her to the interior betrayals of her neurosis, suddenly found herself attacked by her relatives, her friends, the whole class in which her comforts grew and her life had been lived . . . attacked by incredible accusations she had not dreamed could ever touch her. She was supporting a "subversive periodical;" she was in the hands of "spies;" she was "pro-German;" in sum, she was a traitor!

Her friends began to cut her. Her family seriously considered her commitment to a sanitorium; she had better scramble to safety as quickly as she could. Ugly paragraphs appeared, even in proper papers, concerning the Madison Avenue nest of revolutionaries and pro-Germans. Odd individuals showed up at the offices; "poets" who had submitted contributions which, they claimed, had never been returned or acknowledged. And as they sat, facing the editor, they peered around with stealthy eyes at the files and asked strange questions. They were so plainly detectives that I was tempted to spoof them but refrained, dubious of the sense of humor of the United States Secret Service.

The unfortunate lady was incapable of a positive defense of what she had brought forth. Her conversion in spirit with these artists was real, but she could not express it, could not fight for it against the terrible charge that she was betraying her country. She made the one choice weakness could make. She announced, as her contract permitted, the withdrawal of her subsidy at the first year's end.

A few weeks later she committed suicide.

But it would, at this hour, have been false to say that the *Seven Arts* was dead. Friends with funds came forward: among them Scofield Thayer who with Doctor Watson a little later bought the *Dial* which they destined to be the *Seven Arts'* successor (in all but politics, of which there would be none). Other friends volunteered to find a new angel or a group of them. The offers for the most part came to Brooks and me; and there was a reason for this. It was felt generally that Oppenheim should remain as one of the editors but not as sole and titular master . . . as he had not been its sole maker. I declared openly that there should be three editors. Oppenheim, deeply injured in his ego by this, sacked me and invited Bourne to replace me. Bourne declined unless Brooks came in, which Brooks would not; he had had enough; a mistake had been made, fatal, as errors are likely to be in war. As a magazine of culture, said Brooks, war should be off-bounds. Meanwhile, some of my friends who knew what my role had been proposed that I head a new editorial staff. I declined, except on even terms with Brooks and Bourne—and Oppenheim, if he would come along. The premise of all these proposals was that if money could be found the magazine could live but only with changes in its legal structure. Oppenheim's formal position did not accord with his contribution; it rested largely on Mrs. Rankine's subsidy, which had been withdrawn.

In the last issue, there was a piece by Bertrand Russell: "Is Nationalism Moribund?" It foretold that the peoples must overcome their collective egoisms or tear themselves into maniacal and bloody shreds. Russell, in jail in England for resisting the war, got his manuscript into the plucky hands of Dora Russell (whom he later married); and she, as secretary to one of the British ministers on a mission to Washington, carried the text across the sea. She came one day to my office, a slight girlish figure, sat in the chair opposite me, opened her bag in her lap, and placed the Russell manuscript on the desk. It appeared in the last issue. In the same number, concordant with Russell, was Bourne's "Twilight of Idols." And the editorial, written in Whitmanese verse, was called "After a Stormy Twilight"; and one could hear the overtone: ". . . comes the stormier night." Egoism, individual and collective, was to rage, was to enlist the fury of dehumanized science and by means of it was finally to create the bomb that is the climax of the ego . . . of a civilization of the ego, where human madness joins with superhuman power.

Oppenheim had replied to my suggestion of an editorial triad by sacking me. The discharge came by letter. I was, said Oppenheim, despite my talents impossible to work with. Because of my egoism. There was anger and hurt in Oppenheim's letter. Also there was truth in it.

I loved the magazine, which for a year and a half I had lived . . . with others . . . to create. Even my dreams had lived it. This was to be no grab-bag periodical, no individual or narrow group expression, but a living organ articulate of America and of Cosmos: a proof indeed of God. And now its life was threatened. I agreed with our editorial position of refusing the war; but my egoism was too stunted of dimensions to let me see that more urgent than the magazine's program bluntly expressed was the survival of the born, living body I had helped to create, with a mother's wholeness. Now, unlike the mother, I was ready to sacrifice the creation. There is an egoism of the martyr, and there is a shrewdness of the saint. None of the protagonists of this masque of small egoism attained them. Like the old-world statesmen, who always end with war, bursting with their pride, pampering their blindness which they call vision, I and the others were quick to let our beloved die rather than forget ourselves—including our absolute standards and goals—and let it live. Oppenheim, in order not to lose his place of single authority, killed the *Seven Arts*. Brooks hated the quarrel and got out of it, neither compulsive like me nor messianic like Oppenheim. Coddling my conviction of justice and righteousness ("Since we made the magazine, we should have it all") and ready like any Quixote to liberate all men by striking off the shackles of a gang of convicts, I could not deepen or transcend my egoism—letting the body die rather than introducing in it the slightest impurity of compromise.

The extraordinary fact was that none of the editors really knew the quality of what had become a collective work of art. None of course had created it by himself. This I knew despite my legwork and my discovery of authors. We had all worked as a growing organism works: blindly. Who leads the genesis and proliferation of the cells that make the live fetus and the infant? The *Seven Arts* as a whole had made itself, as the embryo makes itself. If we editors had known our creation, perhaps we would have been inspired to transcend our egos, to study this storm of war, to learn how to survive it. Or was the finality of the twelve issues of the *Seven Arts* another symbol of what was happening to man?

The twelve issues should be reprinted as a single volume. For they are a remarkable work of collective literary art in our time of Western man; and their end is a monument to the destructive fate of the ego, individual and collective, in our perilous time. With the dislocating stress of war, impurities crept in. John Reed's "This Unpopular War," for instance, in the August issue is superficial prose, superficial thought; and work of the same calibre, months earlier, would have been rejected. Similarly, Bourne's "Collapse of American Strategy" was of the quality of a weekly journal of opinion rather than of the *Seven Arts*. In fact, the last three issues show an invasion of surface forces, too close to political persuasion. Yet on the whole, the month by month texture is firm. There is a remarkable symphony among the voices of young India, young America, young Japan; of composer, painter, writer prophesying a new world and its birth-danger.

The *Seven Arts* died, not because of money and not because of the war. It died because its leaders could not counterbalance their egoisms with the stronger social and cosmic elements of their selves.

Brooks said: "The time has come for us to write books." He collected his chapters from the *Seven Arts* into a volume and proceeded to *The Ordeal Of Mark Twain*.

Bourne, desolate with no intellectual home, worked on his book of *The State* . . . until the influenza, sweeping the world, caught him. With his book unfinished, within a year of the *Seven Arts'* death, he was dead.

I turned to the book *Our America;* my French friends of the *Nouvelle Revue Française* and the Théâtre du Vieux Colombier had commissioned me to write. . . .

5

From Our America to City Block and Holiday

The Unwelcome Man was turned down by about fifteen publishers before Alfred McIntyre of Boston's Little, Brown catapulted me into high heaven by accepting it. It appeared early in 1917 and was received far more cordially than it deserved to be. The influential Fanny Butcher hailed it in the *Chicago Tribune*. Clarence Day devoted a warm and generous page to it in the *Metropolitan Magazine*, calling it "one of the forerunners of a new style, a new note in fiction." And Van Wyck Brooks in the *Dial* drew a scholarly parallel between the Oblomovs of Czarist Russia who had values but no sociopolitical substance in which to enact them and my pathetic Quincy Burt who lived in a socioeconomic world of vast potential freedoms but had no values to pursue beyond the sterile one, success.*

Our America was a response to *The Unwelcome Man*. I had soon learned that I could write "a passable book for France about my country only if I wrote it *to* my country." The book was a success, although not a big best seller. It is safe to say that the liberals concerned with the problems of American civilization read it, from New York to California and from New England to England (where it appeared as *The New America* with a foreword by Hugh Walpole). The reviews were mixed but copious. The San Francisco *Chronicle* offered prizes for "the best answer to it"; and a worthy whose name I forget published a fat anti-Semitic pamphlet against it from Woodstock, New York, entitled "Our Jerusalem." Mary Austin, writer and champion of the Indian, more respectably de-

---

*Decades later, Gorham Munson who wrote the first book on me in 1924[11] published in *Forum* of the University of Houston an article on "Waldo Frank: Herald of the 1920s" which said, while criticizing the book severely (and correctly): "Possibly *The Unwelcome Man* should be described as the first psychoanalytic novel of our literature."

manded to know why *she* was omitted from the book—and how dared these New York aliens speak about America as if they owned it? Francis Hackett, in the *New Republic,* sneered; but Gilbert Cannan, the popular English novelist who had translated *Jean Christophe* by Romain Rolland, hailed the author in the Sunday *New York Times* as having "dramatized the country."

The translation by Hélène Boussinesq (who was to render many of my books into gracious French and who translated *Twelfth Night* for Jacques Copeau's Théâtre du Vieux Colombier) was published by the *NRF* with great *éclat* in Paris. And through this version the book was widely read in the entire "domain of Spanish" where the literate were likely to know French. At thirty, I had made a place in contemporary letters. Invitations to lecture at good prices and to write articles along the lines of the book became plentiful. All I needed was to exploit what I already had.

My response to these happy facts was perverse. I loved the resounding fame and rejected it, resenting its effect of vertigo upon me. I refused to exploit it and would have sorely missed it. I vanished from the city. This might have meant my going to other cities—Chicago, Boston, Paris—to gather up my laurels while they were still fresh. But I took the train to unknown Kansas. As a child, I had always puzzled my mother meeting my birthday in a black mood. Now I behaved as if it were my birthday! What did this mean? Masochism? The conviction that no fête could be adequate for so great an event as I? so that I preferred none at all! The malaise of my success, whatever its intricate components, was surely an effect of ego. But not entirely. There must be more —and better. . . .

Topeka in those days was a bland town, full of air and whiteness within the horizonless prairies. Its physical freedom was reflected in its relaxed and open social life; not for nothing was Kansas the foster home of displaced and seeking Yankees aspiring still, although vaguely, toward the rigorous ideals of the Zions-by-the-sea that had bred Roger Williams and Emerson and Thoreau.

Those were the halcyon days of the Non-Partisan League,[12] a true farmers' revolution—until Wall Street murdered it. I found the address I sought and left the silent street to enter a small room close with the cigar smoke of a half-dozen labor and League organizers. They had not read my book, but it was known to them by name and served for credentials. I told the men I wanted to work for the League. What could I do? I could learn to drive a Ford; I was an experienced reporter; I could write. . . .

They sent me to a farm town, Ellsworth, and to the prosperous local farmer who ran that branch of the League. Presumably, what I was after was an embrace with the heart of the America I envisioned. Well, down there I should find it: Ellsworth was the geographic center of the state and of the nation.

Did I know what *Our America* was really? Not an objective portrait of a real land, but an appeal to it *to be*? It was a recruiter. I needed an army; but it would come, I was sure, if there were captains; above all I was a captain in need of other captains. Why had I written those idealizing pages on Carl Sandburg, Robert Frost, Sherwood Anderson, Van Wyck Brooks? They, like me, were prospective captains of the army that must take over the country. The success of the book troubled me, for cause: it did not give me what I wanted. Sure, I wished to be famous; but deeper I wanted to be accepted, wanted my dream of America to be accepted. "The multitudes in Whitman," I had called the penultimate chapter of the book. By these multitudes the poet had not meant crowds, he had meant Cosmos. For the book's theme song, I quoted Whitman:

> None has begun to think how divine he himself is,
> and how certain the future is.
> I say that the real and permanent grandeur of
> These States must be their religion.

Not a trace of politics in all this. Sure, the Non-Partisan League was politics. It aimed at electing its own men to Congress, to state legislatures, to governors' seats. But for me, the politics was in the man; and it was the man who counted. I knew I was only a poet, a queer kind of metaphysical poet. I needed a great audience and was looking for it. But I knew also—and this was important to me—that I was basically closer to the men and women I would find on the farm and in the mines and mills than to the intellectuals whose cocktail parties (with palpable harm to my career) I had declined.

The Kansas episode with the Non-Partisan League is almost literally transposed into the western chapters of *The Death and Birth of David Markand*, which I did not begin to write until almost a decade later. But the name of the well-to-do farmer who welcomed me into his house is here disguised. Milton Sinclair was a child of the Puritans. Man's earth could become good, he was convinced, if only men were good; and men could be good if they obeyed God's rules. I knew the rules. The farmers needed to organize. Organization had an answer for every problem. Insurance against hail and wind was a problem? Organize state insurance away from the big eastern companies naturally concerned with their own profits. Prices for grain brought to market was a problem because the farmers were cheated? Organize a local institution among the producers to tabulate and price the varying grades. Mortgages, tenancies, foreclosures were a problem? Abolish the money control of Wall Street. Looking at my new friend Sinclair, I felt I had a clear view down the corridor of time to William Jennings Bryan, to the Populists—and to the Hebrew Prophets.

Mrs. Sinclair appeared to be rugged and steadfast as a mountain (she had never seen a mountain). Inside, she was a fiery furnace. But her children were grown and gone, and her husband was the one child left. Their house was a big one, half empty, with a summer porch and winter double windows. I lived with the Sinclairs. I learned to drive a Ford almost at once and went over the county with Sinclair, distributing League literature, collecting membership dues and subscriptions to the weekly paper.

The farmers we visited were like barbaric gods, like the ones Sherwood Anderson found in the fields of corn; Scandinavian, French, Italian. They held from the soil a security no city-dweller knows. Or they were poor exploited tenants, hardly more than serfs, loving what the League promised but not daring openly to support it.

Sinclair had bought the weekly county organ that printed all the legal notices. I went to school at this paper. I learned to linotype, to melt down the old lead. The owner-publisher made me editor, and I began writing little editorials that were as far as possible from the dithyrambs of Oppenheim but carried the same views. The farmers liked the editorials—never longer than a boxed stick or two. They came into the office and passed the time with this here fella from the East. Hard winter set in with the mercury at thirty below zero. We huddled round the kitchen stove together and walked through the icy halls to frozen bedrooms—despite the tight-shut double windows—stripping to our woolens and leaping into bed. The Sinclairs warmed each other; poor Waldo was alone.

Thanksgiving and Christmas were Gargantuan feasts: great turkeys and hams, home-baked bread, potatoes mellowed with margarine and sorghum—with the phonograph blaring from the parlor which was far too ornate and elegant to be sat in. By New Year, I knew the county like a neighborhood; and the neighborhood knew me. The Non-Partisan League convention was to take place in January in Saint Paul, Minnesota; and I went to it with Sinclair and a couple of others: without a vote, of course, but with all doors and voices open to me. The national leader Arthur Townley was a tall, sparse son of New England with cool eyes and a belligerent jaw. (He might have been an earlier Henry Wallace.) He was a marked man; the enemy was sworn to get him; and they did, sending him to jail on some trumpery charge. But Townley, who knew his peril, was relaxed and without suspicion. Indeed, I wondered at the unconcern with which I was admitted to important small committee meetings. Townley had talked casually with me, decided I was no spy, and accepted Sinclair's approval without reserve.

January in Saint Paul is a cold time. From the window of the room I shared with two others, I looked down on the locomotives of a railroad yard, whose steam froze as it rose. The streets' air was iron. And here in this inhuman element of cold were the warm-hearted men seeking their rights as citizens. I learned the tactics of our enemies. Stool pigeons got themselves elected to the legislature and then disgraced the League by proposing ridiculous bills. Salesmen knocked at kitchen doors and whispered to the housewives how the League intended to "nationalize" all women. Documents were replaced by forgeries, on the strength of which leaders were arrested. I remembered the New York mayorality election which I had been a watcher. But Townley was no Hearst, no demagogue. It seemed to me these were good men, brave men. And what they wanted was hardly more than what such countries as Denmark already had. But the newspapers were hostile, and dollars by the thousands poured in for weaving a web of lies against them.

After a long session, I would go into the streets of the rich stores and restaurants, of lawyers' offices and the other middlemen, as into another country. Half the delegates, when they got on their feet, talked hard figures and facts. But the other half talked like preachers, with a few Mormons among them. I did not see how the evangelists, ready to storm heaven, could get on common ground with the experts on the price of hogs and grain. Yet they had to get together! The rich and their law servants had long since got together!

One delegate who fascinated me was a small banker from a South Dakota town, who intended to enter the next Republican primaries for United States senator with the Sermon on the Mount as his platform. He invited me to visit him, all expenses paid, with a generous fee for my help in translating the words of Jesus into South Dakota language. He was of Norwegian descent, and he explained that the Norse were one of the Lost Tribes of Judah.

"You're a Jew, aren't you?" he said. "We belong together."

He must have been a fairly good banker, for he lived in an elegant house full of Tiffany glass and walnut paneled walls. His wife cooked, and his daughter waited on the table, and it was painful to feel the cowed spirit of his women: how they lived in fear and neglect while their master talked Scripture. Everyone in the country, it seemed to me, had a method for bringing health to human life, and none of the methods worked. I was not a politician, not an economist or preacher; I was a poet. My method was simply to tell stories that revealed—within the heartbreak, within the dark and terrible mystery of being born and of living—that joy which is the presence of God made known beyond knowledge.

I returned to home and wife, bearing America with me. I had for some years, whenever not otherwise occupied in lecturing or writing articles and essays, been at work on two novels. They were to be "proofs of God," who is revealed to every human being when he has the experience of love and calls it beauty. This sense of beauty is the sense of sharing Cosmos. *City Block* was to be a nexus of short stories, each revealing in humble and broken human lives the moment and the ecstasy of that true knowledge. The other novel, *Rahab*, extends one of the characters of *City Block*. I had already written tentative parts of *City Block* and published two in the *Seven Arts*. One of these, "Bread Crumbs," I rejected for the book; the other, called "Rudd," after magazine publication became "The Table" and is, for me, perhaps the most satisfactory of all my stories before "Not Heaven."

The two books grew together. The handling of the characters in these earliest of my mature works* points to the view of the nature of the individual which became premise and matrix of all my fiction. Unlike the assumption in "realism" that the individual is real—and until recently mortal, bound for hell or heaven, so that he may be portrayed analytically, historically, linearly—the premise for my work is that the individual is unreal and is transformed into truth, instantaneously, nonlinearly, *only* as the timeless and spaceless Presence speaks in him.

In the spring of the year, I received an interesting invitation from Jean Toomer.[13] This name may mean nothing to the younger reader, but in the early 1920s Jean Toomer was for many the great promise among Negro American writers. Toomer invited me to go

The Dark Mother appeared in 1920. Like *The Unwelcome Man* it is an experiment that failed, because no technique had been developed to express the book's specific form of vision.

south with him, which meant of course to live with him among Negroes as if I were a Negro.

I had been in the South before. I had seen the Jim Crow cars with conspicuously dirty floors and torn seats, as if to stress by deliberate insult the difference between white and colored. I had seen the benches in the parks, marked white and colored. In more than one town I had walked to where the paved streets, the electric lights, the neat brick schools ended and where the unpaved streets, the ramshackle cabins, the shanty schools marked the home of the dark race. I had looked, like all whites, from the outside. That, I took for granted, was the one angle from which a white in the South could see the exile of the Negro from American civilization.

I had been invited once to address the Tuskegee Institute in Alabama, the creation of Booker T. Washington, whose life story, *Up From Slavery*, I had read in the library of my father. I had had doubts about the good Negro educator's method for the rising of his race: it had seemed to me too docile and too slow. Now, approaching the famous school, I was amazed to find that I was in solid Negro country. The farmhouses were for the most part poor, set on posts so that the rain rushing down the red clay earth, would not carry the cabins with them. There were large farms, too, more prosperous . . . white; but the land seemed solid Negro as a farmland in France will seem solid France, with this difference: the French peasants largely own and run their land, whereas these Negro peasants of Alabama were exiles on their own soil, barred from its politics, its universities, held in subjection by the reigning culture.

Dr. Robert Russa Moton, the principal who succeeded Booker Washington, was a large black man whose gentleness subdued the bull-like vigor of his body. He was soft-spoken, and one felt that he could be both firm and giving. The huge hall was packed with boys and girls, standing (there would not have been room for enough chairs) with no noisy shifting of weight from one leg to the other. I spoke to them on a rather abstruse subject: Negro music and its relation to America; making it clear that I meant *ragtime*, the origin of jazz, not the spiritual whose source for the most part was neither African nor Negro. The boys and girls silently listened in unbroken attention, which was a marvel. There was no shuffle of feet. Did it show strength of mind or discipline, merely? And yet there was no rigidity; the boys and girls, with their eyes multiplied a thousandfold into a single eye of spirit, looking at the speaker saw beyond what he was seeing. This was the sharpest experience of that talk for me: that these boys and girls had a sure courtesy, as if they were aristocrats with a long heritage of command in their blood, while listening to the message of an envoy from a hostile neighboring country.

Dr. Moton with a few formal and flat words thanked the speaker and dismissed the multitude, who now noisily shuffled away with not a few cries and giggles. Then he conducted my wife and me to a screened-off area where we were to have a bite before we left. There were two tables: one set for a dozen or more; the other, two yards away, was set for two. Members of the faculty came up and took places at the long table, with the head place reserved for Dr. Moton; and it was clear to me that the small table was meant for Margaret and me; close enough to the long table for conversation with the principal and teachers, and yet "segregated."

Margaret and I protested. Dr. Moton explained the iron custom of the South (this was the 1920s), and still we would not have it. Dr. Moton explained that a breach of custom might have dire consequences. George Washington Carver, whose work with the peanut had made him world-renowned and whose grizzled face of an angel revealed why he was loved, solved the problem. He got up from beside Dr. Moton, taking his plate and coffee with him. Nobody sat. The supper became a buffet.

Toomer's invitation to me was of a different order. He was going first to Washington to see his aged grandmother, widow of the Reconstruction governor of Louisiana P. B. S. Pinchbeck, and from there to South Carolina where he would stay at the farms of colored folks proud to welcome "the professor" from the North and, of course, his friend too. No questions would be asked about my race; it would be quietly assumed that if I came with Toomer I must be a Negro. I had seen Negroes in the South more "white" than I: pale-skin men and women with blond hair (mine was black) whom a drop of Negro blood categorized as "colored" for ever. Toomer himself, tall, slender, lemon-colored, could easily have passed as white. His grandfather, Governor Pinchbeck, was part Indian, part Dutch, part English, and part African. What Toomer was offering me was a chance to see and feel the Negro from within the inside angle of the Negro.

We entered this world as soon as we sat down in the dirty, dusty Jim Crow car bound for Richmond, Virginia. We were deep in it when we got off at Spartanburg in northwestern South Carolina. I looked at the drugstore where I could buy medicines but not Coca-Cola, at the movie theater where I must sit only in the balcony for the colored, at the restaurant where I could serve but never sit. My place on earth had frighteningly shifted! Toomer carefully explained: "If you act white and anyone has seen you with me and other colored folk, you will be in trouble. Be careful!" It was painful to be careful. An old Ford with three of Toomer's friends bounced us along dirt roads into the dark world. I was welcomed as another "professor from the North." I was asked questions: What do you do for a living? In what city do you live? What is your church? Never: Are you a Negro?

Wherever we went, to welcome and honor us, turkeys and hogs were slaughtered, and the richest yams were smothered in brown sugar. The farther away from town, the more complete the Negro plasm, the more free the sweetness of this people. Of course, the two young guests were entertained by those economically placed to bring them the most comfort. But humbler neighbors dropped in, and I soon got a sense of the community. Those that worked at home or on a farm, the least touched by the white world, were the happiest; those who went to Spartanburg each day to make their living—lifters of heavy loads, barbers, servants, et cetera—were the most confused, resentful, and neurotic. I felt shame, as if I must confess the sins of my own fathers; I felt *with* the Negro. This empathy was startling. Lying in dark sleep I would dream I was a Negro, would spring from sleep reaching for my clothes on the chair beside the bed, to finger them, to smell them . . . in proof I was white and myself.

The adjustment of this folk to the grinding white world could never reach a balance, for resentment broke it. The black resented that the white had made their dark skin a curse. The white resented that the black could sing and laugh and be happy, as the whites were not.

I saw with wonder what their church meant. The blacks were Christians because they had to be, lest hate and frustration overwhelm them. It was not a matter of will or even of good will; they feared to hate because hate threatened to consume them. Their laughter was to cover their hate; their Christian charity for their oppressors (whose sickness they knew) was self-preservation.

And I knew that these children of Africa were a potent people. The white world that crushed them from all sides failed to crush them; they sidled in, notwithstanding. This, I saw, was the meaning of their dance and music. They crooned, they twisted, they slid sidewise in escape from a cold world—and they survived! The machine did not devour them; it only stamped and molded them, made them more flexible. They knew the machine to be the cold, white will of the master race. But they knew how to run the machine for their own purposes. And all the troubles dimmed in the deep dark country lands Toomer and I visited together. The whites, if only a few miles away, were forgotten; the blacks were happy.

The church deep in the pines was their citadel, their school, their theater. It gave birth, it weaned, it wed, and it buried them. It relaxed and it empowered them. It spread a needed strength. Above and under all, it saved them. It was the wondrous place where God's word, which few of them could read, became flesh of the preacher's singing and dancing. When a distinguished visitor from abroad (and all beyond Spartanburg was "abroad" and all that wore a white collar were "distinguished") was to be honored, he was asked to speak at church. This honor came also to me.

On a warm, fragrant morning with the sap of the tumescent pines simmering upward from the earth, I had my little say before several hundred colored men, women, and children. I told them of the change in attitude of *scientists* toward religion. The great men of science, I said, had always found God within and beyond the laws of nature; but in the last century it had been thought that science might replace religion. This might still be true of the little scientists, the shallow men. The great in science did not agree. For them, the logic of mathematics, the laws of physics, led up to the mystery of God. The audience, filling the broad wood church in the clearance of the pines, listened in rapt silence, even the children on their uncomfortable benches. And when the speaker stopped, they all burst into applause. I was pleased with my success. But as I walked away with Toomer, I was troubled by his silence. I wanted praise . . . corroboration.

"It went well, didn't it? They liked it, didn't they?"

Toomer merely nodded, and said: "Yes. Sure."

"What's wrong, Jean?" I said at last.

"Well," Toomer stumbled a bit, "you see . . . these—ah—people . . . they ah . . . they don't know what the word *science* means."

All the talk had brought was the warmth of a stranger. My good will toward them. This had been enough.

On the way North we stopped for a few days in Washington, and I got the feel of what was then (perhaps it still is) the most conscious community of American Negroes: the poets, the intellectuals, the scholars of such institutions as Howard University, the bureaucrats with Government jobs. They were aware of their ghetto and their awareness corroded their instinctual relation with the Negro peasant and with the earth of the South. They were intelligent, sensitive, neurotic. To be born colored was a trauma they all suffered together.

I went home (we were living in Darien, Connecticut, with our infant son Thomas) and wrote *Holiday*. The first draft poured forth in a month; and it could not have been written at all without the Southern journey. The year *Holiday* was published (1923) Jean Toomer gathered his verse and prose into a volume, *Cane*, which Liveright brought out with an introduction by Waldo Frank. It said:

> A poet has arisen among our American Youth who has known how to turn the essences and materials of his southland into the essences and materials of literature . . . who writes, not as a southerner, not as a rebel against southerners, not as a Negro, not as apologist or priest or critic: who writes as a *poet*. . . .
> For Toomer, the Southland is not a problem to be solved; it is a field of loveliness to be sung: the Georgia Negro is not a downtrodden soul to be uplifted; he is material for gorgeous painting; the segregated, self-conscious, brown belt of Washington is not a subject to be discussed and exposed; it is a subject of beauty and of drama. . . .

I was right about Toomer's lush genius; I was wrong about Toomer's ability to write not primarily as a Negro but as a human being. The foreword continued:

> The gifted Negro has been too often thwarted from becoming a poet because his world was forever forcing him to recollect that he was a Negro. . . . The English poet is not forever protesting and recalling that he is English. It is so natural and easy for him to be English that he can sing as a man. . . .

Toomer's trauma was deeper than the others'. In his need to forget he was Negro, he joined the transcendental pseudo-Hindu cult of Gurdjieff,[14] whose psychological techniques aimed at obliterating in the catachumen the condition of being a man. *Cane*, a chaotic beginning, became Toomer's only publication. As a poet, and as a natural leader of his folk, he vanished.

Only long later could I fit the disappearance of Toomer into the pattern of other defeats, such as the end of the *Seven Arts*. In the early 1920s, everywhere in the United States the promises of deep cultural creation were to founder because the candidates were not mature enough to know how to mature—how to avoid the current designs for maturity, false because partial; the Marxist design, the Freudian, the theosophist design, the masochist surrender to despair and to life as Wasteland with the one way out perhaps the Church of England—were not mature enough, not maturely enough taught, to plumb down straight into the self, into the cosmos within the American self, sung by Thoreau and Walt Whitman.

I was restless; my itinerary shows it. I had been all over the country in the years since the *Seven Arts* died of the editor's immaturity in a perilous world. I had been to New Mexico and Colorado with their traces of non-European cultures, Indian and Hispanic, to Chicago where Sandburg's grass grew under rusted and abandoned machines, to the South of Toomer, and to Robert Frost's *North of Boston* where mad women glared through wooden bars in garrets, and to Anderson's Ohio where a sex-starved young woman walked naked through the corn. I knew what I did not want; not what I wanted.

Having written a book about America, I was ready to "find out" what America was. Having written three novels with an aesthetic form of their own to incarnate my sense of man, I was ready to break the mould and start another, more wide, more deep.

I gave a series of lectures on "The Revolution in the Arts" at the Rand School, New York's Socialist center. My main point was that the significant artist seeks *sound* materials for his art. By materials, I meant not only the pigment of the painter, the sounds of the composer, the words of the poet but also their accepted meanings and values in the economy and culture. When Giotto painted a woman, the prevailing mystic sense of woman derived from the Virgin was sound material for his portrait. Already with Raphael and Titian the fleshly, the sentimental, the decorative prevailed and became the dominant *sound* substance for the art. In Cézanne woman's cultural role is weak and the artist, drawn to dynamic materials, discards it: woman is now the biological creature, the functional female. With the cubism of Braque and Picasso, even this is gone. What remains that is sound and sure is the cylinders and spheres of mass. Woman herself has vanished. In the surrealists, the rational is gone and only the dream is valid. The process of elimination of *un*sound materials precedes the use of the sound stuffs, physical and ideological. Of course there are still painters of Madonnas and of sex-charms. But the strong creators, in deep touch with their age—even if it rejects them or ignores them—refuse the obsolescent. This, I said in those early 1920s, was "the deep revolution." I followed the same process in the other arts: the atonal music (for tonality is a cultural rule no longer valid) and the use of dissonance to indicate the rejection of the accepted harmonies of the culture; the novels that are "anti-novels," attacks on the linear concepts of the individual which still reigns although the culture which created this "man" is doomed and disappearing.

Later, I shifted to the New School for Social Research and my long lecture tours began. Throughout the country into Canada, I spoke at colleges and businessmen's lunches, at church and Jewish forums, at teachers' conventions and women's clubs. I was a good performer, holding my public, although many, doubtless, like the church in the South Carolina pines did not know what I was talking about. I considered the lecture a bastard intellectual art, related to vaudeville. I was scared each time I faced an audience. I had no studied method. Almost crippled with stage fright, I got control by making myself realize that this was a captive group come to see and hear me *because they wanted to*. It was an audience willing to be amused (in the true sense of the word) and to be led—unless I lost it. One of my simple rules was always to give something authentic, even on the women's club level. I figured out that at most six percent of a large audience was genuinely concerned. So I woo'd the ninety-four percent and fed the six. Aside from the good money it paid, my talks were experiments in communication. All the ideas that were developed in my books I tried out first in lectures.

These were the wild inflation years when literary and artistic America, broadening the trails of Whistler and Henry James, crowded into Europe, led by such *mauvais bergers* as T. S. Eliot and Ezra Pound. Living was cheap on the Continent if you had a dollar. The cost of beans at home in Kalamazoo paid for a dinner with vintage *Rheinwein* at the Adlon in Berlin. But this was only half the attraction. The American intelligentsia liked Europe because it was *not* America and because you had it for nothing. After all, if you loved America you must do something about it, which cost some effort. But what could the uprooted Yankee do about Paris, except enjoy it? Enjoy the surfaces, of course, for nothing deeper was known or touched. This was the age of Mencken's cynicism about Main Street, which came cheap abroad like the drinks at La Rotonda.

So everyone kept going to Europe.

One day it occurred to me: "Europe for me means England, France, Germany, Italy . . . *why not Spain?*" The Hispanic in the American Southwest had moved me; I had acknowledged it in *Our*

America; I had not looked to understand why I was moved. *Why not go to Spain?* Even now, I unconsciously resisted a serious strain in my casual interest. I'd like to see Spain; I'd write a few picturesque pieces about Spain for magazines to defray the expenses. I made satisfactory arrangements with the editors of several well-paying periodicals—*castanets, get ready.*

My wife and I boarded an old Fabre liner that would let us off at Lisbon on its way to Marseilles. It was a long delightful journey. The captain, an intelligent, indolent, pig-eyed son of Rabelais, navigated equally well on the high seas and among bottles of Bordeaux. The ship's doctor, a Norman tall as de Maupassant, might have stepped out of one of his tales. Margaret and I were at the captain's and the doctor's table where each night at dinner a winey haze lay between us and the sea's sober salt. Days the sea was passive and sun-scented; after dinner it became alcoholic.

Our first call was San Miguel of the Azores, where the streets were paved with gemlike varicolored pebbles and the volcano, rising sheer from the sea, formed an ominous background to the musical comedy city. The captain had told us where to find an authentic Portuguese dinner. We tasted the subtle, reticent, treacherous wines of Portugal and for the first time heard the keening *fados* . . . songs of the wives of the Portuguese seafarers who had gone to strange continents, a strange hemisphere, and might never return.

Beyond the provincial wines and the *fados,* I did not take to Portugal. Lisbon struck me as a stasis of mutually deleting parts. The populous market streets were lush and soft like spoiled fruits; the streets of business and the upper classes were cold, stiff, and sterile. The Portuguese, I knew, had held themselves free of Spain . . . surviving the violent Castile, the crafty Aragon, by alliances with Britain. In politics, they were superior to Spain and had paid for their clever self-saving aloofness with the loss of some deep element of the Hispanic nature.

From Lisbon, in that July, my wife and I took the train to the Spanish border, and there, at Badajoz on the Guadiana river, I saw my first Spaniard in their native home. They were a shipment of young soldiers, a score or two. They climbed out of a third-class car; they walked a hundred feet across the railroad yard and boarded another car. That was all. But it was enough. With dramatic sharpness I saw their abrupt difference from the Portuguese, next their deep difference from the human stock of western Europe. They had a tone of their own, a resonant *soundness* like a good violin but sheer and potent beyond the capacity of wood.

They had tension, their laughter was male, and they swung their bodies forward as if nothing could stop them. I knew nothing further. Indeed, I have put words for what I felt that exaggerate my consciousness, but not my experience. Something was in these men, something I had not felt before, and *something I must find out*, because in an unregistered way I knew it was important.

The second-class car waited in the Badajoz station, on the Spanish banks of the river, to be joined to the train that would take us to Seville. There was plenty of time. Still full of my experience with the Spanish soldiers, I walked up and down the station platform. I stopped to examine the books and papers displayed in the kiosk. The title of a volume intrigued me. It was by a writer I had never heard of, Luis Araquistáin, and it was called *El Peligro Yanqui: The Yankee Peril*. Partly to practice my Spanish and intrigued to know what a Spanish author meant by such a title a generation after the War of '98, I bought the volume and went back to our compartment. My own name caught my eye:

> ... one of the highest representatives of the new generation,
> Waldo Frank says in his book, *Our America*—a model of mental
> independence, of historical sagacity and of literary style—the
> following hard but exact words. . . .

I was not unknown in Spain! I could find friends in Spain! The thought came like a leap of the heart. I did not know that Luis Araquistáin was among Spain's strongest writers, and I forgot to seek what I had bought the book to find out: *What was the Yankee Peril?*

At once, arrived in Seville, I wrote to Araquistáin and in two or three days had an answer. Don Luis welcomed Waldo Frank and his Señora to Spain. Araquistáin was summering in cool San Sebastián on the Bay of Biscay and urged us to avoid the heat of Seville and Castile and to come north at once.

My Spanish was less than sketchy. A few weeks before sailing, I had bought a dictionary, a grammar, a novel of Valera, and *Idearium español* by Angel Ganivet, without knowing that the book was famous and that the controversy on Spain's nature raged around it, with José Ortega y Gasset leading the thesis that Spain was Europe and must be europeanized and Miguel de Unamuno insisting that Spain . . . part Europe, part Africa, part Semite (Arab and Jew) was *sui generis* and none of these. My French helped me to read; Latin helped me to pronounce. I could shape a question which the passer-by on the street understood; but when the answer came in flowing Andalusian, I could not recognize a word. In this condition Margaret and I went north. Araquistáin, who introduced me to his *tertulia,* spoke excellent English. But the others insisted on speaking Spanish and on bombarding me with questions which I had to answer with clumsy improvisations blended of all the Latin tongues.

In a week, I was acquainted with a vanguard of writers. Ortega y Gasset was there, bred in the German universities and possessed of a rare lucid style for argument and description. Pérez de Ayala was there, most urbane of Spain's novelists and interpreter of the aesthetics of *la corrida,* the bull fight, with whom I had a debate in the Madrid papers over American minorities. Pío Baroja was there, creator of a Spanish realism as ruthless as Ribera and other Spanish Renaissance painters. Azorín was there, whose superb portraits of Spain's varied regions had found their impulse in what was known as "the generation of '98"—the hours of Spain's humiliation from which a whole literature of self-analysis had bravely bloomed.[15] Blanco Fombana was there, picaresque story-teller from Venezuela. Don Miguel de Unamuno, rector of the University of Salamanca, was not there. The great poets Antonio Machado and Juan Ramón Jiménez were not there. But where was the note—pristine, spontaneous, age-mellowed, but tough—I had caught in those young soldiers at Badajoz?

Thus ended my first experience of Spain. The promised picturesque articles for the magazines were never written, never begun—at a serious sacrifice of needed money. I knew I was going back to Spain, not exploit it.

Margaret Naumburg returned to New York in time for the opening of the progressive Walden School she directed and had founded with Claire Raphael. I went to Paris and, in my room high up in the rue de l'Université with a balcony overlooking the city to the Seine, was absorbed again by my unfinished novel, *Rahab.* The impact of what I had felt in my first moment of encounter with Spain—the soldiers—seemed to be lost. . . .

6

Perturbed Lion in Paris

Our America at home had had a mixed reception; there were plenty of dissenters and refuters. In France, the reception was more than cordial. The closest to dissent, perhaps, was René Lalou, whose history of modern French letters had just appeared with great success. Lalou praised the book but insisted it was not American. "Read it," he wrote, "as a work within the tradition of the great Europeans, but do not read it as a guide to the American Fact." This disturbed me, perhaps because I feared it might be true. What really had I written? Why was it the book of the hour in Paris? The letter from Ernest Bloch had told me that my book was Hebrew: its style, its dramatization, its balanced figures and sentences. I had not been conscious as I wrote of my old "pact" with God. But if history was a mask of sacred meanings and if this interpretation of history was Jewish, were Blake and Whitman Jewish?

France, emerging from a war whose victory had exhausted it, saw its history as business, as political and military problems of survival, with such men as Georges Clemenceau, Poincaré, and Briand . . . hard-headed practical men . . . its archetypal figures. What did the cultivated Frenchmen who enthused over my book find in it?

In 1917, after his first visit to New York, Copeau was ordered by Clemenceau, premier of France, to reassemble his Théâtre du Vieux Colombier (some of its members had to be snatched from the trenches) and to set it up for a season in the Old Garrick Theater. One of the plays in the Copeau repertoire was by the premier. The aim of the venture of course was propaganda: to reveal to Americans the great culture of France. This immediate goal failed. The plays, after a gala start, were poorly attended. The rich who had bought season tickets (a new piece was produced every week) soon were giving them to their servants. Some students got exposed to the remarkable flowering of French creative energy at the old Garrick. But more important, I suspect, was the flowering itself than the public American response.

Already a friend of Copeau and Gallimard from their last visit, I became a part of the backstage, watching the direction, following the rehearsals. Gallimard asked me to write a brief book on *The Art of the Vieux Colombier,* and it was published by the *NRF* in the customary format. It was Copeau who suggested that the official propaganda on the historic friendship of the two nations— "Lafayette and all that"—be supplemented with a portrait of young America by young America, to be read by young France; and I accepted the engagement. Not only Copeau and Gallimard but as well those superb actors Louis Jouvet, Charles Dullin, Valentine Tessier, and Suzanne Bing made Margaret's and my apartment (we were married now) their retreat from the city whose rhythms lacerated them. They were full of questions. By way of answer *Our America* gradually shaped. (The term in Spanish, *Nuestra America,* had already been used by an Argentine named Bunge and by the great Cuban poet José Martí, but of this I was unaware.) The interrelation of French artist and statesman explains much.

Meanwhile my novel *The Unwelcome Man* appeared and was well received.

When I returned the following year, they welcomed me. Doors were opened. Nothing official: the doors that opened were the doors of homes, apartments in Paris, farm houses in the Midi. I was to receive in a few months a sample, remarkably complete, of the complex cultural life of the country. Only a few years before I had read these men of the *NRF* and been nourished by them, never dreaming that I would come to know them in person.

I cannot name all my hosts of that winter. In selecting some, one is tempted to name the well known—not for snobbish name-dropping reasons but quite simply because it is easier to introduce an individual already known, and with the well known it is easier to interest the reader. But the economy must be paid for; many a typical or archetypical friend is overlooked here because he is not famous.

Anatole France, to the men of the *NRF,* did not deserve his fame. In his renowned red *pantoufles* and *robe de chambre,* he sat beside his hearth tweaking his trimmed grey beard, his eyes a-twinkle. He represented a great tradition of his country: the pagan freedom of Rabelais, the social consciousness of Voltaire who was the skeptic of all religions. He was the sensuous, sensual man whose mouth—in Swinburne's phrase—was never twisted in prayer; the man who loved and caressed living; and he smiled at the young American. "In your book," he said, "you deplore the Puritans of your country; you fear they'll freeze or devour the land, but your worry is refuted by your women, I've seen photographs of them in your pictorial magazines. You can't tell me, Monsieur, that women with such admirable legs will ever let the Puritans win." (How right he was!) Strong through the centuries of France ran another parallel tradition: the Gothic. It had a spokesman as passionately intense as Anatole France was urbanely extensive. Paul Claudel's poetic dramas were suffused by fire and shaped by the aspiration of the great Gothic churches. There was rock in them, also. I had met Claudel in wartime New York at the Garrick Theater where Copeau and his company were rehearsing. He was en route from Rio de Janiero, where he had served as the French ambassador. The night I met him, Claudel was very drunk. He looked like a Roman emperor with too much fuel in him, yet retaining his imperial dignity. With him was one of the embassy's secretaries, the composer Darius Milhaud who for this night was in charge of Claudel. A third tradition was represented by Valéry Larbaud, in command of all the Western languages: English, German, Spanish, Portuguese. There was something hieratic yet warmly personal in his services to contemporary letters. He helped James Joyce with money and with critical support. He was both patron and interpreter of that vast field known by him as "the domain of Spanish." Larbaud's own creative writing was perhaps too soft spoken and too subtle to win a wide public.

Close, in Paris, to the traditionalists were the enemies and negators of tradition. Aloofness and detachment are the one position difficult for the French to sustain. The Dadaists were rampant and virulent in those postwar years. Dada's leader was a Roumanian Jew Tristan Tzara, long a resident of Paris. Tzara was a very good poet, whose forte was to be suave in destruction, urbane in outrage. Short, slender, dark, with great intelligent eyes, and a mouth forever flickering into paradox, Tzara made one think of a well-bred Jewish bourgeois boy nursing some bleeding trauma, some shattering psychosis . . . some one of the family of Leopold and Loeb, the boy murderers of Chicago. Tzara, of course, was in touch with Marinetti, the Italian Futurist. Less sensitive, less pure, Marinetti worshipped the secondary traits of the machine: clatter, speed, and force. Tzara, more the poet, accepted the machine's laceration of human flesh and nerve but voiced the human anguish.

The three most conspicuous French followers of Tzara were Louis Aragon, André Breton, and Phillippe Soupault. They were showmen. They held mass meetings on "Burn the Louvre!" "Burn the Bibliothèque Nationale!" Although I doubt if they yet knew Freud (perhaps Tzara did), their cult of the unconscious drew on both Zurich and Vienna. They were the forerunners of the irrational and spontaneous and became the present surrealists and abstract painters. Aragon was one of the most gifted of the young French prosemen. He was a handsome youth whose insolence became grace because of his natural aristocratic air. I once asked him: "I suppose your absolute rejection of French culture was born in the horror of the trenches?" Aragon was silent and then turned a withering eye on me. "Do you think the trenches were in any way worse this *this*? He swept his hand over Paris, over France, over the contemporary "peace."

Aragon, preceding Sartre, sought security in *le néant*, the nirvana of total annihilation. Not finding it, he became a Communist: not a romantic Communist like many of the French- and Spanish-language poets and painters but a precise, dogmatic functionary, finding his security in the function, carrying out Party orders, whether to edit a newspaper or to serve as host to detested bourgeois liberals at a congress for the Defense of Culture.

Of the same company, although tragically distinct, was Drieu La Rochelle, tall, lean, lordly, the poet of *Interrogation*, written in the trenches to voice his disgust for the filth and butchery of the war that was a continuous assault on common sense. Drieu in his political essays saw the future of Europe as an alternative between "Geneva or Moscow": a Western world league of nations or a Communism of the East. When the league failed, he replaced it with Berlin. When open war returned in 1939, he advocated French collaboration with Hitler as the sole salvation from Moscow. To his friends it looked like treason. What they did not see in Drieu's collaboration was the man's masochism, his despondency, his honesty, his bitter admiration for the sheer power of the Germans. When the Free French marched into Paris, Drieu shot himself.

Such, in the time of this visit to Paris, were the privateers of rebellion against all three traditions of France: the Gothic, the national, and the rationalists. But the most dangerous subversive, because the most wholly equipped with his country's culture, was André Gide. My first personal encounter with Gide was a parable. Gide invited me to lunch and was to pick me up at noon at the offices of *NRF*, then on the rue de Grenelle. Gide rushed in, a little late, wearing a wide slouch hat, a cape on his broad shoulders, and British brogans.

"Come," he grasped my arm, not my hand, "There's a big fire ... the *magasins du Printemps* are on fire. I have a police pass."

He pushed me into the waiting taxi, "Do you like fires? I never miss a fire."

I recalled an early book of Gide, *Souvenirs de la Cour d'Assises*. In 1912, Gide had done jury duty in a criminal court of Rouen. A case that intrigued him was of arson: a youth had set fire to a half-dozen houses. He insisted that he had "no motive"; indeed, he was on good terms with the owners, women who were relatives or friends. After the flames, he had felt *détente*, relief. Gide wondered if the experience were related to the orgasm but had not quite dared ask the question which would have shocked, or seemed absurd to, the stolid Normans of the jury.

We stood now within the police lines and watched the flames engarlanding the windows, weaving from the merchandise in the stalls on the street, and threatening the grey dignified buildings on the boulevard.

Suddenly, Gide had enough. Again, he clasped my arm. "For lunch," he said, "I thought I'd take you to England." We walked toward the Gare Saint Lazare where trains start for the English Channel. "England" turned out to be a British chop house. "Here," said Gide, "Huysmans used to come, when he was bored with the freedoms of France." It occurred to me later that the scene of the flames imperiling the city, the English ale and chops, and Gide's non-Gallic dress had a tonality of exhibitionism. Another episode tallies. . . .

I was having dinner with the family of Jacques Copeau; Gide was expected but did not appear. At last, when it was very late we all sat down around the long table and began to eat: Copeau, his wife, his two daughters, and Pascal, his son; also Louis Jouvet and his wife, a Dane as was Madame Copeau. The meal was more than half over when Gide burst in.

"Excuse me, excuse me," he cried, taking his seat. "I was walking up the Boulevard St. Michel, when I encountered a youth—of a beauty! of a loveliness! . . . I had to follow him. I'm sure you understand and pardon."

Gide's prose—easeful flowing, transparent, firm, and luminous —was an integration of qualities otherwise blended in Ronsard, Racine, La Fontaine, and Baudelaire. But the meaning of this classic prose is subversion and destruction of the classics. Substance in Gide assaults itself, turns into its contrary, plays games whose one rule is that all rules be broken. Like a Church plainsong opening to the Devil *Le Retour de l'Enfant Prodigue, Nourritures Terrestres, L' Immoraliste, Symphonie Pastorale* are all "Faux Monnayeurs." Passion with no heat, no light: the luminous decay (for Gide is always the moralist) that becomes penicillin.

Gide's general theme is the disintegration of the self, as the self has been regarded by the centuries of the Judaeo-Christian culture. It is still believed in, still defended. But the revealment that this self is doomed and no new form of the self yet emerged from our cultural chaos gave Gide timeliness and power.

There was a group antagonistic to Gide's although they did not deny Gide's gifts. Their most conspicuous member was Romain Rolland, "above the battle" in Villeneuve, Switzerland. Léon Bazalgette was of that company, the author of books on Thoreau and Whitman, whose poems he was the first partly to render into French. Larbaud, high in the gamut of the *NRF*, who also had made some translations of *Leaves of Grass*, slighted the work of Bazalgette; and the entire group had no use for Rolland's gigantic novel, *Jean Christophe*. One day I praised it in talk with Jouvet. "When did you read it?" he asked, and I had to admit that it had been several years ago. "I'll bet," Jouvet intoned, "if you tried now, you couldn't read it."

The Rolland-Bazalgette "axis" also had a magazine, *Europe*, and a publisher, Rieder. The editor of *Europe* was Benjamin Crémieux, a bearded, gentle Jew whose fathers had been driven centuries ago from Spain by Isabel and had founded strong centers of wealth and spirit in the South of France close to Spain's borders because they still loved Spain, the mother who had banished them. Crémieux was a lucid critic who had just written a definitive study of Proust, whose mother like Montaigne's was of the same blood and ethos as Crémieux. A few years later Crémieux was shot by Hitler.

The values of *Europe* were close to those of the *Seven Arts*. These were men socially conscious and militantly ready to renew their Continent by integrating politics and religion—inspired by Blake and Tolstoi. Some authors straddled the two camps. Thus Jean-Richard Bloch, with the face of an archangel, published his excellent novels in the *NRF* and brave social studies in *Europe* (later he was to be submersed by Moscow). Both camps (too various to be called groups) spoke freely with me as did Copeau's company in New York, for I was close to them in spirit yet free of their "family" frictions. Thus, Charles Vildrac whose luncheon table was a home for us all. My favorite was Léon Bazalgette ("Bazal" to his friends). He had written books on Whitman and

Thoreau (translated by Van Wyck Brooks) and was at home in the New England village whose white church steeple and clapboard or shingled homes he had actually never seen. His love of Whitman and Thoreau was so expansive it almost made a Yankee of him. Bazal was as emotional as a Yankee—but less repressed. Perhaps some alien nuance got into his prose, which the aesthetes of the *NRF* resented. America was his Zion and Zionists are not welcome in Paris. (In the writings of Bazalgette, the critical edge of *Our America* was missing.)

My welcome was not confined to writers. The *NRF*, led by Gide and Gallimard, had established itself as a cultural empire. It published, of course, serious novels and poems but also documentaries on economics, philosophy, and psychology . . . and a series of detective stories, largely "translated from the American." For a while it issued a monthly of Jewish culture, *La Revue Juive;* and the *Revue Musicale* sought order in the rich new chaos of tone. At the home of its director Henri Prunières, I met Stravinsky and a young Hungarian Bela Bartok. Here one night a youthful American was invited to play some of his music, for which he employed "clusters" of notes struck on the keyboard by the open palm or the entire forearm. He was Henry Cowell.

Charles Chaplin turned up for the first visit to France. He had revisited, for the first time since his fame, the East End slum of London where he had lived as a boy; and he had visited H. G. Wells. For a couple of years Chaplin carried around with him in his pocket a letter from Wells (also a Cockney son) praising his art and urging him to come to England. Having shown the letter to whomsoever he was with, Chaplin would say: "I must answer this!" and thrust it back in his pocket. The letter showed signs of wear; then it was in tatters—and still not answered. "I'll answer it in person," Chaplin said one day. "That'll be easier than a letter" —and at once was on his way from Hollywood to England.

France from the president down was waiting for Charlot. At the Cirque d'Hiver, one of the permanent one-ring circuses of Paris, the brothers Fratellini headed the bill. Jacques Copeau, induced by me, got seats; and after dining at a restaurant where a crowd gathered to catch a glimpse of their beloved Charlot, we arrived at the Cirque late and slipped quietly into seats close to the ring balustrade. The show went on normally. In the intermission we went to the Fratellini's dressing room, and Copeau introduced the classic clowns of Europe to the man who prided himself on belonging to the same tradition. The scene was moving; there were tears in the Fratellini brothers' eyes, and their hands trembled. Since they could not communicate in speech, Charlot and the brothers simply hugged each other. Then in perfect order came the last part of the show. It seemed that Charlot had not been recognized by the public. The final note sounded; the performers all retired. Suddenly, the whole arena poured down on the dapper little man roaring Charlot, and seeking to greet him, but endangering his life in a joy perilous as a panic. Copeau on one side, I on the other, we tried to protect Chaplin, rushing him to the door, fending the mob off, hopeful that if we reached the street we could get lost in the anonymous crowd. Somehow we managed; the Place Pigalle was before us; but it too was packed solid with shouting men and women—the whole wide square packed solid. Every man and woman needed to touch him; and Charlot, his collar crumpled, his coat ripped, allowed his friends to get him free before his was trampled. He kept saying aloud to himself: "*Nothing!* It all means *nothing.*" At last we found a cab and thrust Chaplin in head first, telling the chauffer to drive . . . drive.

Later that night, after Chaplin had changed his ruined clothes, Copeau brought us to the large back room of the Brasserie Lipp at Saint Germain des Prés where the actors of the Vieux-Colombier and many of France's authors waited to do him homage. Jouvet, Dullin, and the others showed a veneration for the master: a quiet and understanding reverence beyond any experience of Chaplin in America or England. There was selflessness, and there was simple sweetness. This authentic humility was new to Chaplin who saw the world of art as a jungle of egos—not the least of them his own. But I felt in a few of the writers envy toward Chaplin whose public was so much greater than their own. I felt it, for instance, in Jules Romains, whose unamistic art celebrated living groups but could command none, whereas Chaplin could gather the crowd of the Circus, of the Place Pigalle, of the remotest Chinese theater where a film of his was showing.

Was Chaplin right, muttering to himself, as the crowd roared its welcome: "It all means nothing!" meaning that publicity had done it? Chaplin was wrong. The crowd knew instinctively that the buffeted, helpless little man with oversize sore feet, weaving from humiliation to uproarious humiliation, was a mask for their own destiny. At the depth of Chaplin, anyone could love him. The most popular artist of our time was also the deepest.

I fell into a routine in Paris. My room was high up in the same

Waldo Frank, age nine months,
with his mother, Helene

Waldo Frank as an infant.
Frank mentions this photograph on p. 6.

Julius J. Frank, Waldo's father

Waldo Frank in his late teens

Graduation picture of Waldo Frank, Class Book, Yale 1911

成瀬正一.

Left to right: Waldo Frank, Ernest Bloch and Seichi Narusé at the period of the *Seven Arts* (1916–1917)

Waldo Frank, early 1920s;
frontispiece to Gorham Munson,
Waldo Frank, A Study (1923).
Photograph by Alfred Stieglitz.

Waldo Frank and Margaret Naumburg, early 1920s

Waldo Frank and son Thomas, about 1927

Waldo Frank and kitten, 1920s

Waldo Frank, 1920s. Photograph by Alfred Stieglitz.

Waldo Frank, 1920s. Photograph by Paul Strand.

Alfred Stieglitz, probably late 1920s.
Photograph by Paul Strand.

Jacques Copeau, 1918

André Gide. Photograph by Halsman.

Lewis Mumford, 1938.
Photograph by Eric Schaal.

Hart Crane, about 1930.
Photograph by Walker Evans.

Waldo Frank, seated center, in Argentina, 1929

Waldo Frank, fourth from left, in Argentina, 1929

Victoria Ocampo

Left to right: Waldo Frank, Kahlil Gibran
and Adolph Oko, probably early 1930s

Waldo Frank, 1930s

Waldo Frank and Adolph Oko, Cape Cod, 1930s

Waldo Frank, after being beaten up in Harlan County, Kentucky, February 1932.

Waldo Frank delivering the principal address at the opening of the Congress of Revolutionary Writers and Artists of Mexico, Mexico City, 1937

Waldo Frank with President Lázaro Cárdenas, Mexico, 1937

Waldo Frank having tea with his
wife, Alma Magoon Frank and daughters
Michal and Deborah in Hampstead,
London, 1938.
Photograph by his son Thomas Frank.

Waldo Frank visiting Romain Rolland
at his home in Vézelay, France,
late 1930s or early 1940s

Waldo Frank addressing a press conference;
date and location unknown

Waldo Frank, early 1940s.
Photograph by Lotte Jacobi.

Waldo Frank's home, Truro, Massachusetts

Jean Klempner Frank and sons
Jonathan (standing) and Timothy, Truro, 1955

Waldo Frank, about 1955

Waldo Frank and Fidel Castro, Cuba, 1960

Waldo Frank in his studio, Truro, early 1960s

building where I had lived before, on the rue de l'Université near its intersection with the rue des Saints Pères. It claimed *chauffage central*, which meant that around midmorning the radiator in my room would get luke warm for a few hours. I was not used to northern European heating; or rather the lack of it; therefore, I stayed in bed reading or writing until it was time to dress for luncheon. I had a lunch date every day: at a restaurant with some-one like Gallimard or Vildrac for host or at Valentine Tessier's home. A little less frequent were the dates for dinner. For the interim afternoons, there were picture exhibitions or appoint-ments at cafés; and at night there were concerts and plays or cozy hours with Bazalgette and other friends. I seldom returned before midnight. In my letter box, off the narrow foyer where my big key hung on a brass hook, there would sometimes be a scribbled note from James Joyce who lived in the same house asking me to give him a signal. Joyce would come downstairs, and we would retire to a nearby café that liked late hours.

The invariable drink was a bottle of white wine, a dry one from the Moselle or the Rhine; and we would talk until it was time to go to bed and live out the cold small hours.

At this time, Joyce's sight was poor but not as poor as it became in the next decade when the little vision that remained seemed to turn inward and the face before Joyce's face, even when it was that of a welcome friend, seemed an interruption to his constant inward view. Joyce was what the new jargon, then becoming cur-rent, called an introvert but because the introvert was absolute he was not schizoid; he was a whole world of its own creating as mankind had, from its mysterious past, its own language. Joyce, it seemed to me, resembled the bottle of white wine before him. He was gracefully slender; he was externally cold; like the wine, he had an inner glow blended into a dry and dominant savor. He was thin and spare-shouldered like a student, trim-bearded like a pedagogue; and his pale eyes looked inward with a compassion for his fellows that was both hot and distant.

Later, when I knew Joyce's family—his wife, his son, and his son's wife—I recognized the patriarchial grasp of the man on those for whom he felt affection. And this embraced his friends.

What was talked of at those midnight meetings? Of the people I had met that day, in detail: what they thought; what they ate. But mostly of Joyce. He spoke delightfully of his years in Trieste when he had earned his living as an instructor of the Berlitz School of languages. His earlier years in Dublin he was more reticent about, perhaps because he had already said what he had to say. He found little good in Irish writers except himself. American literature for him meant Ezra Pound, and modern music (he was a good conventional singer) meant George Antheil. I must have told him about Pound's officious offer to be the European editor of the *Seven Arts*. Joyce was interested to learn of the horizons beyond Pound. He was sympathetic to my aspirations and to my fiction—notably *City Block*. Joyce's basic attitude toward literature was irony. His sight was failing; his attention was fixed, more and more after *Ulysses,* on the microscopic worlds within language. One or two writers were his friends: Valéry Larbaud, above all. What interested Joyce was the men not the works which, after all, seemed to vanish (as he saw it) in juxtaposition with his own mighty creations.

As in the work of Gide (but how different in form and expression!), Joyce's theme was the disintegration of the self and of the society which produced it. His method included satire, parody of literary forms, and a fragrant song in his style. Thus far, there is a parallel with Gide. But Joyce in *Ulysses* soars beyond Gide's chronicles of self-disintegration. There is no Bloom in Gide's exploded day; above all there is no Molly Bloom of the last Chapter: no reintegration on her primitive level of sense and the womb.

The Joycean whole was a *completeness*. Nothing remains to be said. After the Night-town *Walpurgisnacht,* the rest is silence. But I was beginning to learn that he did not share completeness, did not want to share it. Indeed, sharing was alien to him. Joyce and I, although it was with affection, taked from opposite slopes of a great mountain, not seeing one another.

I do not recall the scene that winter of my first meeting Hispano-Americans (since the glimpse of the Mexican workers in Pueblo, described in *Our America*). Perhaps it was at the house of Jules Supervielle, the Uruguayan poet and proseman who wrote in French . . . heir of that other Uruguayan Isidor Ducasse, who as the Comte de Lautréamont wrote *Les Chants du Maldoro* which became a textbook of the surrealists. But it was certainly this winter that my friendship began with Alfonso Reyes, the great Mexican man of letters: a friendship ended only by Reyes' death in 1961. Secretary of the Mexican embassy in Paris, Reyes was returning to Mexico and asked me for a message to the Mexican and Hispano-American writers. It was published and began a dialogue that never ceased. When I wrote it, I knew nothing of Mexican culture, nothing of America Hispana. But in my rounds about Paris, I met many writers of America Hispana. I did not know their work; they were of separate race and religion; they spoke to me in French. They should, by rule of reason, have been strangers to me. Europe should have been vastly closer than their countries and culture. But I felt at once an affinity between us. I would stand in a room crowded with guests: French, English, German, Italian—and a few from Argentine, Peru, Colombia. What could we have in common? Yet they seemed to share a quality, a secret, that made them feel closer to me than the Europeans. What could it be besides the delusion of geography? They were "Americans?" What was America, indeed, but a misnomer?

I had one clue to the meaning of what I felt. The Italians, the English, the French, the Irish gave an impression of *completion;* whatever they were or were to be was there, active within them. The Americans were *incomplete* to themselves and to one another.

All this made me oddly cordial when I talked (mostly in French) to an Ecuadorian, a Brazilian, or a Chilean; and they felt it and recognized it and responded. Most of them had read *Our America.* They did not understand it more intelligently than the Europeans. But it meant something to them that they all shared, that the Europeans did not feel in their more objective acceptance.

One night as we picked up our slender glasses of cool wine, I said to Joyce:

"I'm going to get out."

"Of what?" Joyce smiled. "Can one get out of life?"

"On the contrary," said I, "I need to get into life. That's why I need to get out. I'm going to get out of Paris."

I had been warmed in Paris. As a youth, I had read these remote masters, never dreaming that I would touch them; even in my previous visits, never more than dreaming. I had the dream, and it had happened! Ramón Fernandez, brilliant critic, had said with a sneer and a sour smile: "Pour la *NRF* la littérature américaine, c'est Waldo Frank." It was false, of course, and the *NRF* was soon to prove it. But I understood my malaise. The gods of literary Paris were not my gods. Their feasts left me hungry; their clever talk deepened my silence. But the unreasonable sense I had, when I was with Hispano-Americans that under all the differences we had America in common, gave me no bill of particulars to work on. Obviously it was not enough to intone Walt Whitman, to echo Thoreau, and to recite Rubén Darío, whose view of the American cosmos (unlike Whitman's), was voiced in a prosody pure as Mallarmé's. There was a completeness enough in Paris, and how warmly I had been invited to come in and join it. Yet, they who welcomed me liked what I wrote because of its incompleteness.

Their fulfillment beckoned to my unfulfillment to absorb it. What I needed was that my unfulfillment should take in and transcend their completeness. All this in a mood which made me, every day, get ready for my next engagements as if I were an actor who heard his onstage cue but did not know his lines. I could have said, like Maeterlinck's Mélisande: "Je ne suis pas heureuse."

Abruptly I got out. I took the train to Marseilles, where I wandered for a week (letting no one know I was there) about the streets of the Vieux Port: the cafés bursting with the energies and lusts of sailors from the Near East; the solid streets of whores, who smashed my hat, stole my cane, rumpled my coat trying to draw me in to their sultry rooms stuffed with bad bourgeois furniture, sentineled in doorways, whose doors were always open to the street until a customer closed it. Not a poet I knew in Paris included in his work this ferment of Marseilles. I boarded a cheap boat for Algiers. The mistral was blowing, and the dirty little vessel tumbled and tossed. I was sick. But when, recovered, I wandered up the rabbit warrens of the Kasbah in Algiers—the streets cut with stone steps like parts of vertical ladders—I realized I had exchanged one finality for another. This world, too, was complete. They had in common, Marseilles and Algiers, that they were irrelevant to Paris; and Paris was a collective art, the loveliest of Europe, but irrelevant to the present!

In an open dirty lorry I crossed the Atlas mountains and nearly froze in an oasis of the Saharas. But the market place Arabs and Berbers, vibrant and noisy, warmed me far more than the brasiers of sandalwood. I turned west. In cities half ancient, half modern —Fez, Rabat, Marrekech—I experienced the Moors. The Arab *Sherifs* in Fez entertained me. They were all poets; they were all sure the Arabs, beginning with the Prophet, were the greatest poets in the world. They had disobeyed Mohammed (they told me), whence in punishment the decay of the Arab world, soon to be restored to glory.

The bus that moved me from city to city stopped at a bleak station high in the hills where I got out to smoke a cigarette. Standing, I noticed three Arab boys laughing at me. I was puzzled until I found that the burning tobacco of my cigarette had fallen on my coat, and I was on fire. The Arabs' purely aesthetic response, to enjoy the spectacle not to save the man from being burned, was, I learned, typical of the desert culture in which strong men ate first, after them the young women, the old women, and only finally the children.

At Tangiers I looked across the street of Gibraltar and saw Spain. I realized that I was on a quest. I recalled the almost forgotten leap of the heart when I saw Spain in the body of the soldiers at Badajoz. I had returned to Spain because it was involved in my feelings for the Hispano-Americans in Paris. There had been method to this zigzag direction: France, straddling the Mediterranean and the western sea; the Moors who in Spain had conquered the Arabs, threatening both the Arab and the Christian cultures; all this, a complex heading toward Spain. I loved Spain already. Now, as if Spain were a woman with whom I had fallen in love, I meant to know her and to know why I loved her. That would make me understand what I had felt about the Hispano-Americans in Paris and the soldiers in Badajoz, and my need to move on from Paris. . . .

7

Self-discovery in Spain

Wanderings afoot and alone through cities were already my firm habit. (The reader will remember the walk in Paris when I was eleven.) Since boyhood I had known and loved the sidewalks of New York, as far afield from where I lived as Chatham Square and Brooklyn Bridge.* To go alone on these strolls was of the essence for they were really journeys into self, externalized meditations which, I believed, gave me insight. For the past decade they had reached far beyond New York. Periodically, and no less frequently when I was married, I felt the need "to get away." I would take a room high up in a tower hotel of Brooklyn with a view of bridge and harbor and work through the night or walk through the night. Less often, I boarded a coast-wise passenger boat (they have all vanished) to Charleston or Savannah, Galveston or New Orleans. I would rent a lodginghouse room and, for days, speak to no one except perhaps the landlady or a casual sharer of a bench in the square. Much of this experience had gone into *Our America* and *The Unwelcome Man*. By the time I had "escaped" (this is what it was to me) from Paris and was heading for Spain by the circuitous but organically direct route of North Africa (whence had come the Arabs, the Jews, and the Moors to create, with Visigoth and Roman, the Spaniard) I knew I was preparing to write a book on Spain . . . a portrait; and my walks would be part of my method.

Since the first encounter with Spain, I had read the literature . . . for the first time read *Don Quixote* in the original Castilian which revealed to me the immense loss of a whole living dimension when I had read it in English. Now began the true meeting with Spain, its lands and above all its cities. I don't believe I fig-

*This New York and those sidewalks, of course, have vanished. Today, the sidewalks are filets of human nerves lacerated by the perpetual city shrieks. A stroll must have its own pace. The traffic lights destroy all the poetry of walking by breaking the inward rhythm of the walker.

ured much on my motives. I had never loved the twentieth-century Western civilization; Tolstoi's rejection I had made my own. And I knew I was in love with Spain. That must mean Spain offered some quality of living the Western world did not give me. I did not want to imitate the Spaniard. I knew Spain's bad record of civil wars, of political incompetence and inquisitorial oppression. Not for a moment did I romantically forget. But Spain had remained outside the Western culture of capitalism, political democracy, mechanolatry, and mechanistic science. Its Renaissance had been marred or cruelly crushed by the tyrannies of church and crown. Its peasants were poor, and this was no virtue; its politics fitted the gone world of Philip II, and *that* was no virtue. Britain exploited most of its mines, its industries—and drank its best sherry. The little social unity Spain had was clamped down on it by the ecclesiastics who took their cue from Rome. What had I felt, that stirred me, in those soldier boys on the frontier of Badajoz? Love registers a need, and the need is in the lover. Spain, in my first encounter, had made manifest an incompletion in myself. My malaise in Paris, my dissent at home in America, that I was to call "the grave of Europe," meant an American need, since I was American. It must have an American form: aesthetic, economic, political. It must be a potential . . . a *possible* fruition.

This, precisely, was what Paris could not offer. The western European had a completeness . . . articulate . . . that *left something out*; something I had felt live, in however obsolete a form, in the Spaniard; and something I needed in order to live and that America needed. The Hispano-Americans I had met also did not have it, and its lack, like mine, was their positive incompletion.

The little boat crossed the tight Gibraltar Strait from turbulent Tangiers, and I was walking in a street of Algeciras under the Rock that the British had appropriated as tool and symbol of their civilization of power. I felt at once: These townfolk of Spain had a vigor, a vibrant erect rigor, like a tumescence. These men were *man,* these ample-bodied women were *woman;* almost motionless although they were walking, as in a balance of forces. Did I love this because it was the true human condition? And was it lost in the man and woman of the West? Some synthesis within these Spaniards of all they were held them in stance, as if their quite ordinary creaturely motions of body and mind summed to a moveless and timeless cosmos within each one.

By current standards these poor folk of Spain had little: no refrigerators; no correct hygiene, so that too many of their babies died; no cars; no respectable local government; no welfare state—and almost no welfare. Yet they seemed to have the strength and the music of great pines, each deep-rooted and beyond the dimensions of the people riding in the New York subway.

More than any land of the West, more than even Italy, Spain is a world of cities: each distinct, each unique and uniquely Spanish. I knew the way to be open to them and to know them, in an act that needed solitude and silence. I made my way northward through the fluid Andalusian Plain that terminated in Murcia, Córdoba, Málaga, Granada. (Only in Sevilla my solitude was broken by two cordial Spaniards, Ramón Carande the historian and the poet Pedro Salinas, now gone.) Thence, over the high *meseta* of La Mancha, Don Quixote's country, I approached Toledo and eastward Valencia, Zaragoza, stoney Jaca . . . to Castile Old and New, Segovia, Ávila, Burgos, the Escorial, and Salamanca.

This is the ancient university town and Don Miguel de Unamuno was its rector. The day I got there, he was leaving (the most Spanish of the writers of the "Generation of 1898"), exiled by Dictator Primo de Ribera. Instead of Unamuno, whose *Sentimiento trágico de la vida* I admired (it discussed Kierkegaard years before the Dane became a vogue in Europe), I found another Castilian, square-skulled and rigorous, Federico de Onís, on a sabbatical year from Columbia University whose Spanish department he headed. We went to the ranch of Onís's family, which bred *toros bravos* for the bull ring. I saw the peasants, their mouths and throats muffled against the cold, speaking a Castilian pure and rotund as Cicero's Latin. We sat in the broad kitchen before the great open hearth, where a whole side of beef was spitted, drinking the heady *Rioja* wine. And I realized that this group of Spanish landsmen—Don Federico de Onís the intellectual from Columbia, the peasants who could not read, and Don Miguel de Unamuno, poet and mystic—were of one body.

There were small cities, also, and villages to be sensed immediately as one takes in a person. All, with the great towns, had their roots far down in Spain and flowered together into Spain. It seemed to me I could stand at the Plaza Mayor of each and feel the whole as one senses a man whole by looking him in the eye. If time was weak in this process of knowing, space did not count at all; as it is nonexistent in one's pure sense of a person.

Several years later, when *Virgin Spain* was published, the unfriendly reviewer in the *New York Times* headlined her piece:

"Speaking of Spain Here is Waldo Frank." She meant of course that the author was speaking of himself, using his subjective vision of Spain as a projection of his lyrical outpourings. She was right. The book was a *self*-expression of its author. What the good lady did not mention and could not explain was why the Spaniards, beginning with Unamuno and the Hispano-Americans, all of whom presumably knew Spain, recognized the book as an *objective* portrait of their land and their people.*

So at last, after most of the Peninsula, I settled down in Madrid. Araquistáin, who had welcomed me first in Spain, introduced me to two estimable ladies who had an extra room in their apartment, heated by a bulky iron stove. One of these was Victoria Kent, a lawyer, who became director of prisons in the Republic and later, during the Civil War, ambassador to France. As her name reveals, Doña Victoria had English blood; but she was wholly the Spaniard, an archetype of Spanish character and beauty: sober, humorless, with a repressed intensity that perhaps was English. One of her innovations was to grant leave to the convicts of good conduct to spend a few days at home, periodically, with their spouses; on their honor bound to return to prison when leave expired. Of course, such imaginative novelties vanished when Franco, aided by Fascist Italy and Germany and even more by the betrayal of the democracies the natural allies of the Republic, overwhelmed the land in war.

Mornings, I worked on my book at the unheated *Biblioteca Nacional* if it was not too cold. After lunch I walked or took a trolley to some outlying neighborhood; perhaps stopping at a chocolatería for a cup of the sweet brew which was almost too thick to be called a *drink*. Or I dropped in to a café where at a long table Ortega y Gasset or Araquistáin or Ramiro de Maéztu, conservative but culturally open, held their *tertulia*.

Madrid had none of the stark, dynamic clarity of the great Spanish cities. As the political capital of Spain, it was full of bureaucrats, lobbyists, and speculators and their servants the churchmen, the lawyers, the moneylenders, the menial hangers-on. The crowds of the popular districts were coagulations. I was reminded of the ancient Roman slums, the *Suburra* described by Juvenal. No health, I thought, could come of this artificial city whose roots, unlike the roots of the great towns, were not in the soil of Spain but in the lust and will for power. I saw

*Unamuno, without asking permission but not without the enthusiastic willingness of the author, translated the last chapter of the book and published it with a long essay on *Virgin Spain,* in *Sintesis* of Buenos Aires.

Ortega y Gasset frequently at his home or his tertulia. I admired greatly the prose-portraitist, the cultural critics; but I was skeptical of Ortega as a leader of Spain: his values were too conventionally European, direct from the German schools and the Sorbonne.

The exiled Unamuno had settled at Hendaye, on the French frontier, to live as close as possible to Spain; but he had less direct influence in the tertulias than Ortega, the man of *ideas*. Unamuno rejected the *abstractly human*. He said in effect not "nihil *humani* a me alienum puto," but "*nullum hominem* a me alienum puto" (I am a man, no other man do I deem a stranger). Away with abstractions such as *humanus, humanitas*. Let live *the man* of flesh and bone . . . *hombre de carne y hueso* . . . who is born, suffers, and dies—above all dies—who eats and drinks and plays and thinks and loves. The brother, the *real* brother. Absent from the tertulias, Unamuno seemed to me very close to the people of this "Rome" which had lost its empire yet held a mysterious possession, deep as imperial Spain had been wide, on which the sun never set.

The great poet Juan Ramón Jiménez was not at the tertulias because of a self-imposed exile. He lived in a cork-lined room (Madrid is a city of noise), guarded by his wife while he spun his exquisite nebulae revealing the kinship between man and cosmos. Like William Butler Yeats (both received the Nobel Prize), Juan Ramón Jiménez wore a mask that never left his face. He looked the *hidalgo* he was: slender head, close-trimmed beard, and the eyes of a hawk spotting his prey from his sky, swooping down, and lifting it skyward. The people hardly read him, but he was acknowledged by people and by poets as a prince of the blood. His apartness and his identity with the folk were implicitly accepted. His verse was obscure with the obscurity of sky that never ends, the obscurity of life and love and death. His poetry was clear only as the mathematical equation is clear to the *cognoscenti*. The other two outstanding poets of that lost epoch of Spain were Antonio Machado and young García Lorca—the latter murdered by Franco's fascists, the former destroyed by them indirectly when he was forced, an old man, to escape afoot to France from the fall of Barcelona. They did not attend the tertulias; I met them only later.

I, of course, belonged to no tertulia but was made welcome in several. In one reigned Ramón Gómez de la Serna, versatile and almost as prolific as Lope de Vega. He called his countless stories and monologues and homologues *greguerías*, clamors, hubbubs.

. . . Indeed they were samplers of the multitudinous noises of Madrid. Ramón was a short, stock, witty, and potent Sancho Panza to Juan Ramón's Don Quixote. Of course, there were many tertulias in the cafés of Madrid where I could never have sat down: gatherings of church and army, or royalists and nationalists.

Pío Baroja, the novelist, was as far from the tertulias as Juan Ramón Jiménez and as prolific as Ramón Gómez de la Serna. Baroja was a Basque of the north Basque country with a Basque *boina* always on his small spheroid head. By trade he was a baker, and he turned out stories fresh and unspectacular as his loaves of bread. He was an anarchist and at contemptuous ease in all tertulias alike, since he despised them all together. In the Civil War that was still a decade ahead, he had to flee from both sides, the organized left and the organized right; both would have been pleased to shoot him. I saw him for the last time in Paris with Ramón Sender the novelist. John Dos Passos in his essay "Young Spain," which appeared in the August 1917 issue of the *Seven Arts*, called Baroja one of the leading writers of the West. This superlative was perhaps not quite earned. His work lacks selective emphasis and the strong formal texture of great prose. The Baroja novels are loaves of bread. But the man . . . wary, pure and jealous of his purity, loving the stinks of life as an infant loves its excrement . . . enriches the picture of that Madrid in which bread and hope were still common.

The king belonged to it, too. I got a ticket to the Palace to witness the Easter ritual of the king of all the Spains washing the feet of the poor, his masters. The carefully selected paupers sat with bared feet and scrawny legs in their mahogany chairs; the monarch took a towel from the large silver bowl proffered by an attendant, wrung out the excess water, kneeled, and laved the feet, stepping from man to man. Alfonso looked as if his mind was elsewhere—perhaps on Mary Pickford, the movie pet of the world? perhaps on his new racing Fiat? He drove well, and he performed this rite well, this king of dwindling Spain, as servant of the humble. If his mind and heart were not in it, perhaps he had no mind, no heart. . . .

One day as I strolled down one of the new avenues which were beginning to cut, ruthless and regardless through the sordid turmoil of nineteenth-century Madrid, I got the sudden answer to my love of Spain. *The average Spaniard was an integrated person.*

In the Western peoples, from central Europe to the United States, the immense pressures and invasions of modern science —the machine and, even more than its economic, its psychological effects—have alienated man from his instinctual counterpoint with his earth, his group and his self. Man always seeks a whole to live in; and if his experience and his doctrine leave out some element of the normal whole, he will make a whole of the remaining fraction. This was the modern peril which I was to study in my books of the next decades. So great was the success of Newton's mechanistic laws and the prestige they won that the intuitions of the real brought to Western man by his religions and his arts were relegated to inferior place or altogether exiled from what he accepted as "reality." In the brief modern era (brief compared to the duration of other cultures), self lacked a whole dimension. Power spread, and man's will spread which engenders power and embodies it in the machine. And the more they spread the greater became man's disconnection from the cosmos within him. All this I was to feel and to study. Western man was a splinter of himself and took the shard for the whole. The false whole became the genocidal cancer which the world calls progress.

For Queen Isabel, her husband Ferdinand, and Philip II, Spain was the organ that must unify the globe in Christ. The instrument itself must be whole. And the will of God must be done simultaneously within the conscience of every man, in his relation with his Christian country, with his universal Church of Rome, and with the empire whose every subject was in touch with the crown. The Catholic king commanded; the Spaniard obeyed— too well. Heretic, Moor, and Jew must be excised from the land since they could not be integrated in it. The Church stood guard, policed by Jesuit and Inquisition.

All over Europe, science and the stirring of the peoples were establishing a new economy, a new world. Spain fought and then ignored these innovations. The Spaniard continued to live in a synthesis that knew none of the victories of science over space and matter, nothing of the social and political science that was preparing the liberation of the masses from servitude and dearth. The Spaniard in his daily life carried the cosmos within him and related his self to the group whose leadership of Church and Crown he accepted. But the *materials* of this integration were obsolete—and impotent against the new rising world of the machine. The Catholic kings' success in making the Spaniard whole sped their failure, their growing isolation.

Other races, other cultures knew the instinctual integration of man within soil and cosmos: Africa, Asia, Indo-America were full of such simple forms of knowledge. The distinction of the Spaniard was that he had *not* gone back to primal unity, such, for instance, as had flourished in the isles of the South Seas or in the Andes. He was the heir of Europe's intellect, ethic and aesthetic, to which he had made contributions on a possibly smaller scale but as well as the French, the Italians, or the English. These peoples had suffered, along with the benefits of science the basic lacerations of maintaining the mechanistic laws of physics to be the sole real science. The Spaniard, because of the greater success of Church and Crown, had been spared that deadly error. The Briton, the German, the Italian, the North American had been depleted and wracked by his false sense of his own being which cut him off from his true self. Malnutrition and its deformities were the sequel, and I had felt it in my own hungers and in the spectacle of such monsters as the city of New York. The Spaniard lacked technique and method to articulate his whole nature in terms of contemporary life; but at least he had not gone off at sterile and dangerous tangents. His own hard-headedness had temporarily saved him during the centuries of rationalism and mechanism, whose symbols were perhaps the seven-year-old children toiling in the Manchester mills and the tight, complete "universe" of La Place which had no need of "the hypothesis of God."

The "backwardness" of the Spaniard among his European brethren paradoxically prepared him to advance straight toward a new "Whole" that would be *whole*. He had never succumbed to the superstition that Newton's mechanist laws were the ultimate and that color and an individual's emotion are on a lower level of reality—less "real" than mass or gravitation. The West now was also ready—even its physics, Einstein over Newton—to supplant mechanolatry. But only after what injury to the substance of man! What immediate peril!

My idea was not that Spain be imitated or emulated ... of course not! It was simply that if the Americans saw the perpendicular vigor of the Spaniard, as I had seen it, they would sense what was needed and missing in their own way of life. How could the Americas become a New World (rather than "the grave of Europe") unless they produced new men?

This was what I meant when I inscribed my new book to:

> those brother Americans
> whose tongues are Spanish and Portuguese

whose homes are between the Rio Grande
and Tierra del Fuego
but whose America
like mine
stretches from the Arctic to the Horn.

I was ready now to go home and write it.

II

Rout of the 1920s

1

Don Quixote: Man of Letters

In the early June of 1922, a hired limousine drove up an elm-lined street of Darien, Connecticut to a white clapboard house and unloaded its passengers: a new father, a new mother, their son hardly a fortnight old with a profusion of paraphernalia from bassinet to bottles. On May first I had begun volume viii of my notebooks:

> There is no reason to worry or repine. Everything deep goes well. If you could but be satisfied with this, with the deep, I mean. For look: you have elected to live and to work deep. The price of that is its consummation. The price of that is what you elected to be. There are swift surface breakings. Would they seem such shattering waves to one living deep indeed?

> You are not free of the most menacing American failure, which is the final failure to fuse into a person. You are not yet a person. It is clear now you cannot become a whole surface person. The alternative is to become a whole deep person. To work. . . .

That May in New York had been a poignant one of joy and pain. Spring was breaking out from every crypt and crack of the city. In a hospital on Stuyvesant Square, my wife Margaret gave birth to her son; and in another hospital uptown, the son of my brother, seven year old Roger, was dying of cerebral meningitis. I swung from one hospital to the other—the place of life, the place of death—aware of the balance and unity between them. The episode revealed the whole human story as of a single creature covering the earth, reaching invisible antennae toward the sky, beyond sky, and toward earth beneath earth.

My notebook continued:

> The having a baby is particularly painful mechanics since *you* are an inconscient part of the machine. Your spirit that cares

to refocus all life to itself as center is bruised and offended and not a little marred by its failure to do so here, where life so clearly centers outside the pale accessoriship of father.

Nor must your spirit ever in its future dealings with the child force your centrality upon him. It is a sin unpardonable though all but universal.

Two years later, after the bittersweet lionizing in Paris, after North Africa and Spain and the conceiving of *Virgin Spain* which finally appeared in 1926, I took up my notebook again:

This day in France I have read the page which I wrote two years ago in Darien. I must strive very hard to make a contact of recognition with the man who, in undoubted sincerity, wrote those words about "the pale accessoriship of father."

My marriage had failed (I realized how unconscious-deliberately I had sabotaged it) because I was not ready, not *willing*, for its burdens of responsibility, absorbed as I was by the problems of my career as a writer. I faced long absences from my son, and my notebooks reveal how I suffered from the separation.

This cross of will, not giving itself and not losing itself wholly in the emotion of father, I was to carry with me through the decades. The normal conflicts of the creator confronted by complex personal relations, biological and social, were emblems of the contradictions within the role of artist and husband, father and citizen with a social conscience. All this was already explicit in the year of Darien, before the home broke up (September, 1923): mother and son going west to Reno for the divorce she wanted; I sailing again (October, 1923) for Paris.

Rahab had come out in March after great troubles. The publisher, Horace Liveright who had made a national success of *Our America*, came to my New York apartment on the upper West Side late one afternoon to announce that his regular printers refused to touch the book which they called "blasphemous and obscene." I looked at my roused friend: "stalwart, svelte, and scintillant," I was to call Liveright in the *New Yorker* "Profile," a little later. Would he withdraw publication which might cost him dear? No, he was going to get *Rahab* printed and published if he had to set it up himself letter by letter. It didn't come to that. But in those days the Society for the Suppression of Vice, headed by Anthony Comstock and his successor John S. Sumner, was going strong. Even such classics as those of *Rabelais* and *Boccaccio* were attacked; and when Liveright read the manuscripts of *City*

Block, it seemed to him sure to be molested. It was always the publisher who was apprehended, not the author, as if the law knew that the business of books was more important than their creating. Therefore, I decided to be the publisher of *City Block.* Liveright gave me credit for paper, printing, binding, and the cost of a leaflet to go to the leading bookshops of the nation. The result was a limited edition of 1,250 published at Darien, Connecticut at $5 before, $7 after publication. Very few copies remained for the higher price, and I made money.

I was comfortable in my room, with both kitchen and nursery remote. The portrait on my table of Anatole France, treasured since college, still had meaning. I had a publisher who declared himself proud to produce me, a man of business who was yet capable of humanist emotions. In my early thirties, the century in its early twenties, I regarded myself a man of letters—quite humble, for the domain of letters in the vast American continent was thin compared with the scope of masters such as Balzac who had all France, Hardy who had all England, Tolstoi who had the whole world as precinct. Quite often I put aside my manuscripts to give a lecture or a course in such institutions as the New School, then on West 23rd Street.

I wrote in my notebook:

It is not enough to forgive those who have sinned against us.
I must forgive myself for having sinned against myself. . . .
The supreme law is joy! how else obey it? I must be forever
relaxed, forever forgiving even of my past rigidities. The
supreme sin is to have been wilful, to have been rigid.
But even this you must forgive yourself. For indeed the
one sin that cannot be forgiven is the state of unforgiveness.
Know that the true goal is hard because wilfullness, effort,
fixed determination never can attain it. It is hard because not a
million aeons of endeavor can attain it. It is hard because
only ease, only innocence, only the instant can attain it. It is
hard because all the soul's sophistications of effort, of virtue, of
the virtue of striving.

So spoke Blake and Meister Eckhart and, of course, Jesus inviting to his kingdom of Heaven only those who are *like* little children. So, Lao Tze and the Zen Buddhists, but no Stoic or Epicurean or Confucian, no European or American man of letters. I was a long way from a vocabulary adequate for the thoughts that a generation later became *The Rediscovery of Man.* But it was already visible that I would blend conduct and aesthetic creating.

Since I lacked method for this, I was related to Don Quixote. For this is the trait of the knight of the sorrowful countenance who sallied forth in modern imperial Spain to cure its ills, in rusty armor, with a spavined nag and a brain full of obsolete romances.

In a notebook of this time, I list the books that have meant most to me. The Old and the New Testament, the plays of Aeschylus and the dialogues of Plato (which I called comedies). Lucretius, Dante, Shakespeare, Rabelais and Cervantes, Spinoza, Goethe, Stendhal, Balzac, Dostoevski, Whitman. "Let a man," I wrote, "know these and win within himself response to these, and he is a man indeed . . . nor need he then read any other book." I think the list is careless and conventional. The young poet with mystic and anarchistic leanings was putting down what he deemed the structure of a "literary man," a man of letters. Tolstoi and Blake should replace Goethe and Plato who never meant much to me except in the dialogues of Socrates' death. I never finished Lucretius. England's seventeenth-century writers I disliked, except for Swift and Smollett. Blake fed me inordinately; the Blake who said that politics is no good unless it is part of religion. This burned into my brain. Of course, Blake was not thinking of established churches nor of established political institutions. He was thinking of the Hebrew prophets—the most successful, surely, of the world's professional politicians.

By its omissions as well as its inclusions, my list reveals much. In a statement of that time (published in a book of caricatures of writers by Eva Hermann), I declare aggressively that I am not a professional man of letters. Writing, I say, is a mission. Yet I practiced it as a profession.

I was in my mid-thirties. I had edited a magazine for which such critics as Gorman Munson and Van Wyck Brooks were to give me years later the larger credit, saying that with it I had introduced the 1920s. I had written *Our America* (1919) which was later to be called "the Manifesto" of the 1920s. My lyrical novels were recognized in many places, home and abroad, as authochthonous poems. As I sat in my tranquil room, my self-image of man-of-letters seemed sound, save for my own assaults on it.

In 1924, I wrote in my journal: "Reason is nothing. It creates nothing, it *is* nothing. But it is the measure of everything. . . ." Finally, in October of the same year:

A new phase begins. I am 35. I move into my new little home on East 54th Street, tomorrow. Within three weeks my new life should be in order. Margaret (divorced) will have gone to

Europe with Tom. There will be silence and a peace to work in. The latter-day struggles have availed. I am calm and I am ready to go on.

With improvised equipment, I sought to unite my life as an artist with my just place and privileges in the social order. I pondered much on "justice." Why need I try to be just? Why was my striving to write words of truth and beauty not enough? Justice, I learned, should be neither an end nor a beginning. As an end it was too cold and thin for life; as a beginning, with nothing to act on but itself, it was sterile. The Pharisees were just. The root of justice was love. Why should God be just, unless he loved his creatures? Why should any man be just except to a brother he loved? The entire notion of justice as primary could be ruled out; therefore, injustice too; leaving the mere processes of nature for which the concepts of the just and the unjust were equally null and void. (Why should nature care about the seed that falls into earth and dies? Indeed it does not care. . . .) The Old Testament already had made explicit the nonentity of divine justice—and injustice—in a Job's world where Jehovah visits calamity and death on the innocent for the sake of a bet with Satan. Justice by such a God does not exist. Justice is exclusively human. Only as the fruit of *Human love* is there justice.

And love is always deed. I looked then at my deed. I sat at my comfortable table in my well-warmed room. I had breakfasted well, this and every morning. My body was sound; my mind had been fed by the best available experts of the society I lived in. This education had been paid for by my father, who could afford to pay, being well-paid himself for his services as a lawyer in the maintenance of the system and of the rights of property which implied injustice. This son of this father did not approve of this society with its built-in injustice. To me, whatever its merits in the production and distribution of goods, a social order whose main motive was profit and power was an evil social order, fated to be short-lived (it was only a few centuries old) and to collapse or explode. (It was far younger than the ancient and medieval systems when they vanished.)

The postwar world, in which I willed to be both man of letters (who can be bred only within a stable social order) and judge and smiter of that order, was the America of Warren Gamaliel Harding, champion of "normalcy" to which he hoped to turn America "back," and of Calvin Coolidge whose proud word was: "the business of America is business." Emerson and Thoreau would have agreed—and wept. There were no tears in the people. Liquor had been denied them by constitutional amendment so that they might soberly contemplate their glories and powers. They had won the war without a city bombed. They had made the world safe for their kind of democracy, without the responsibility of joining the League of Nations. H. L. Mencken and Sinclair Lewis sneered at them as yokels and "the booboisie," but these louts and their prim-lipped wives had inherited the earth. The climax of their contest—Main Street against the Nietzschians of Mencken—was acted out in such scenes as the Scopes trial. Tennessee had forbidden its public schools to teach Darwin's theory of evolution. William Jennings Bryan led the state's defenders of its youth against the outrageous heresy that they were descendants of monkeys. And the liberal lawyers, Clarence Darrow of Chicago and Arthur Garfield Hays of New York, worried the poor man like terriers with a wounded buffalo. Soon he was dead of a stroke brought on by overexertion in the heat and the rage of frustration. My sympathy was with Bryan. The rationalist liberals could never know that the Old Testament story was a myth whose truth lay beyond reach of their sneers. Of course, the youth of the land followed Mencken; in hordes they left their bucolic homes and temples and flocked to Greenwich Village where they bedded in Freudian freedom.

All the groups, it seemed to me, suffered from illusions. The liberals were deluded thinking they knew more about the mystery of life's beginnings than the poets who wrote Genesis. The democrats were deluded, sure the majority is always right; and deluded were the oligarchs, sure the majority is always wrong. The America firsters and race supremacists were deluded deeming themselves humanly superior to the dark-skinned; and the highbrows who purged themselves of America in the cafés of Montparnasse were deluded laughing at the old home in Grand Rapids and Little Falls, and convinced they had escaped it. The champions of capitalism were deluded thinking their system guaranteed freedom and the benefits of competition. The Marxists were deluded in their belief that the nationalization of industry meant necessarily its genuine socialization and in their blind faith that the proletariat *must* win the world to virtue. (The Hebrew prophets were more wise knowing that the people could sin and could fail.) And the neo-orthodox of all religions were deluded assuming that their great myths and ancient methods could again work in a world utterly changed from the one the myths spoke for.

I found I could belong to no organized political or theological party, since all of them were based on untrue psychological interpretations of man's nature: Rousseau and Marx—and, no less, John Dewey, whose pragmatic view of truth lacked what in my later language I was to call "revelation." The followers of Dewey limited knowledge to what they called Instrumentalism, which was also a delusion; since the Real exceeds what the senses give us and what logic develops from the senses; and since the mind can be instrumental to apparent human needs only by achieving a dimension beyond them.

In 1922, T. S. Eliot published *The Waste Land* and inscribed it to red-bearded Ezra Pound, *il miglior fabbro*. The poem at once *fit école*, as the French say. Disciples sprang up in every college green. The language of the poem is the vernacular of the American hour:

O O O O that Shakespeherian Rag—

laced with refrains from the Sanskrit and every rhythm of English prosody from Thomas Gray to Ella Wheeler Wilcox. A working girl toasts a slice of sausage on the gas ring of her furnished room; her home: under the glory of a war won and of machines breeding like bacilli. The beauty of the poem's words lies like an old ache in the heart, a pain made sweet by habit. Loneliness is in the words, and a freedom from the responsibility of hope, shared by all together. The effect was achieved with shards of erudition: refrains of ancient Hindu Scripture so much more elegant than the Hebrew and the Greek. But the password, "We do not need, we do not choose, to hope. Despair and the dead victories of yesterday is better."

In the same year, *Rahab* and *City Block* were published; and these books were full of the challenge of form, which is life, within the chaos. The avant-garde turned away from them in defense of their own dear death. But Eliot also taught the singers of renascent life, such as Hart Crane, that their apocalypse must have a language.

Eliot too was deluded. He thought the answer to the world's void was his veneer of mystical unity surfacing the wasteland. He thought the Anglican Church could be still made to work. Despite their rich differences, all the *mauvais bergers* shared a delusion: they were certain they had the correct answers as to men's nature and the Real. But they were not sure, *and knew it*. We touch here on the paradox of the 1920s. The decade was one of hope. Hope of Darwinian survival; hope of the "animal spirits" of Santayana.

Hope of immediate goals. But a fever of asseveration, an awareness of imminent abysses, and a doubt of substance and health
wrecked this self-consciousness. Floyd Dell's "moon calf" and
Scott Fitzgerald's poor little rich boy became the archetypes. In
the 1940s, with the appearance of the bomb, hope was excluded;
and Eliot's earlier hopelessness, sophistical and definitive, became
the easy fashion.

When I wrote *Our America*, I felt myself a captain with other
captains. I had no sense of myself as a solitary. In that book I
named my brothers: Sherwood Anderson, Van Wyck Brooks, Carl
Sandburg, Alfred Stieglitz, et al: a remnant of the "chosen people." (Lewis Mumford, a little younger than I, as the others were
older, joined the corps of captains.) Not in possession of a Way,
Anderson's characters are seekers of the Real, not imposters (as
was the Knight). Mumford turned his inquiry for the good life
from the utopias to the cities men live in and to their possibilities
of freedom. Brooks gave his devoted life to finding and shaping a
"useable past" through understanding of our writers and their
milieux. Stieglitz kept looking for "an American place" and for a
way of life rather than of art to define it. He opened his door and
kept it open, letting drift in, drift out, the searchers; answering
their questions with a vast volubility which amazed them and
seemed to have no revelance to what they had asked until they
got away and realized—the brave ones—that all his talk had been
a parable of essential meaning. Stieglitz refused to call his photographs "art"; his sky-studies he named "equivalents," but never
asked nor told "equivalents of what?" His highest praise for a
painter was to call him not artist but worker. Marin, he would
say, or Georgia O'Keeffe or Marsden Hartley is a *worker*. He tried
to change no one, content with discovery. Indeed, he was convinced no one changed. He had none of the will to reform that
identifies Don Quixote. Indeed, none of these captains went to
Don Quixote's extremes of total commitment to either revolution
or revelation, except Frank.

2

Hollywood and Chaplin

In the 1920s, the decade between *Our America* and the great depression, I travelled much. Lectures took me widely around the country; they paid well, but their chief fruit was to acquaint me with the towns, people, institutions I would otherwise not have seen. Also in those years I went several times to France, Spain, and England (avoiding Italy because of Mussolini). And I came to know the South, the Negro's as well as the white man's South. One afternoon at home in our Greenwich Village flat I had a visitor worth a score of journeys. . . .

I had already written about Charlie Chaplin in an essay, "Valedictory to a Theatrical Season," which appeared in the *Seven Arts* in 1917. I said: "Chaplin is an extremely brilliant clown, but he is also an unhealthy one." In 1924, I collected some of my papers in *Salvos, An Informal Book About Books and Plays,* appending to each one a postscript in which I recorded my own dissents from what I had originally written. To the "Valedictory" I added: "The injustice which this essay does to Mr. Chaplin by a total disregard for the pure aesthetic virtue of his art, I have righted in *Our America* (1919) and elsewhere. Mr. Chaplin's art is far from unhealthy. His art indeed is a symbol of health in a complexly morbid world."[16]

This afternoon the bell rang downstairs, and soon there was a knock on the door. "Come in," I said, and in walked Charlie Chaplin.

"I want to thank you in person," he said, "for what you've written about my work."

I saw a dapper little man, carefully groomed, with a slender rhythmic body and eyes of every-varying blue; a man of charm like a spring day, but an early one still charged with the toughness of winter. It was about 4 p.m. when Chaplin sauntered in; and we talked till dawn of the next day, with an occasional pause to which Margaret brought coffee and a sandwich. There was no moment of embarrassed adjustment. Chaplin was having a good time with living, and he was grateful. For a few hours I was part of his pattern.

He talked about his start in Hollywood. "I'd have made a good banker," he said. His name was unknown. When a film with him in it—perhaps only a short bit—was shown at some nickelodeon, a cardboard simulacrum found its way to the lobby with "Funny-legs is Here" printed on it. Chaplin had to learn that *he* was Funny-legs, that *he* brought the bumper crop of nickels. When the producers wanted to sign him up for a long term at a price that was dazzling compared to what he got in London music halls, he went dumb and reluctant. He did not like the movies; he was going on the legitimate stage; he was going back to London; Hamlet was his aim, etc. He noticed that the money men turned pale. He refused to sign for more than one next picture at a time. If Chaplin finally left Hollywood with seven million dollars in his and his wife's luggage, it was not for want of effort on the part of his associates over the years to pry the dollars loose.

In those early days, Chaplin's favorite bedtime book was a fat volume of selections from Schopenhauer. He seemed sympathetic with the crusty German's attitude toward women. This changed later, when Chaplin married Oona O'Neill. The man who became my friend was a lonely man only as any conscious, deliberate, and busy artist is lonely. His high intelligence, moreover, filled him with disgust for Hollywood where he—and only he—built up an organism within the organization of what called itself "the Industry."

When he left the house at dawn, I asked: "You want a taxi?"

"Not one," Chaplin laughed. "I want a string of taxis."

For a change, he was alone and not recognized in a city street! The parade of taxis dropping him at his hotel would remedy this. In my judgment this most widely loved of artists of our age was one of the deepest of the age. In Chaplin's judgment the highbrow champion who thought this, and said this, was worth thanking. So, thank you. Was worth knowing—So here I am!

Chaplin invited me to drop around at his home in Beverly Hills. In those days one could voyage pleasantly and variedly from one edge of the continent to the other. There were coastwise passenger ships: New York to Boston or Portland, Maine; New York to Charleston and Savannah; New York to New Orleans. . . . I took an old Morgan liner for Galveston. We were struck, north of Cape Hatteras, by a hurricane. Over the ship's radio came news of the distress, then the sinking, of the *Vestris*, smart British steamer plying to Trinidad, Brazil, and Argentina. On the bridge I watched the skipper guide his ship with an *obbligato* of furious profanity whose purpose, I supposed, was to prove that he, the captain, not the wind was in command. As the huge blow carried us five hundred miles off course, I learned the vast flowering of the sea. The waves became mountains; then the wind flattened them out, and the ship was a cork racing down a smooth-sided sluice. The captain proved he was master, and we limped into Key West for repairs; the force of the water had stove in the hull and made matchwood of the tables in the dining saloon. The ship's frenzy was suggested by what happened to my steamer trunk: I had placed it under the lower berth of my cabin, and it had been tossed snugly into the upper berth.

From Galveston and Houston I rode through the Texan desert to Los Angeles. Charlie's house was a bit of elegant England with trimmings and bric-à-brac from China and Japan, and sliding screen doors opening on semi-tropical trees. Not used to the late hours, I always awoke too early with not even the butler stirring yet to bring me breakfast in bed. When it came at last, the tray had savory dishes: lamb-kidneys, grilled tomatoes, etc. Still in bed, I worked on the proofs of *The Rediscovery of America*. Around ten, I would hear the purr of the waiting Rolls Royce. By eleven, more or less, Chaplin would show up, popping with energy; and we would drive down to the studio together. For a couple of weeks I lived the life of Hollywood and of Chaplin—always at a disadvantage in that I could not sleep late, as the others did, when I went late to bed. They were rehearsing, and I was struck by the artist's study of every minute point. Chaplin weighed his effects like a chemist. To repeat a gag a hundred times with subtlest variations of light, place, speed was nothing. A week might be spent on an act that took seventy seconds to record. Intelligence was in control, as indeed it was at the Beverly Hills mansion when Chaplin discussed world politics. The difference was, of course, that on the lot Chaplin knew what he was doing; whereas in the realm of sociology and philosophy he was an ignorant man with startling intuitions. When Charlie said "box-office" at the studio, he knew what he was saying. At home, often, it was his emotions that spoke. I recall one instance. A French world-trotter with a title of the *ancien régime* was showing us some photographs he had taken in China of Kuomintang soldiers actually carving with knives the faces of captured Communists. The pictures were unbearable. Charlie paced up and down, tortured. Suddenly he cried out: "Let 'em, the bastards! They deserve it! Everything they do to themselves!" He was trying to justify his anguish.

Welcome everywhere as Charlie's friend, I got the feel of the place. We usually lunched on the lot of the United Artists, the organization of the great pioneers: Douglas Fairbanks, Mary Pickford, Cecil DeMille, William S. Hart, and Chaplin. Joseph Schenck would be there, Goldwyn and other producers. The golden couple, Mary and Douglas, stood best for Hollywood. Fairbanks was a poor actor and a good acrobat; an externalized man without temperament but rich in gimmicks. His wife Mary Pickford, "America's sweetheart," was beautiful like a chromo and hard as nails. She was more strictly business than all the Schencks and Goldwyns. Fairbanks accepted me as one of Charlie's odd friends. He was cordial and open. Not Mary. To her I was a stranger, an outsider; and she left me alone, even if I sat next to her at table. Griffith, creator of *Birth of a Nation*, was a sadly intelligent man who seemed somehow to have sold his mind to the satan of success. I was struck by his unhappiness, as if his soul had been left out and were clamoring to rejoin him.

There was fire in Hollywood, but most of it was cold. There was talent, but most of it was mortgaged. There were exceptions: Al Jolson, for example, a true troubadour who shook your hand as if he were hugging Mammy. Above all, Hollywood was a place of extremely busy people. Entertainment had been attached by business. There were parties, but they were strictly business; there were love and sex affairs, but they were promissory notes carefully audited. The parties were all alike in that they were cool: assembly line models with slight surface novelties. One, I recall most easily, was given by Bebe Daniels, then an exuberant star living with a protective mother. Bebe was beautiful—and neuter; she was a superb artificial flower which, if you dared touch it, you found to be real—and destined to fade and wither. Dozens of little tables were scattered about on the copious lawn, each with two folding chairs so that for the bulk of the crowd the party became a tête-à-tête. By some whimsey of fortune, I found myself at a little table vis-à-vis with the pugilist Jack Dempsey. Mr. Dempsey did not seem to mind. He ate the delicious food like a devouring furnace; he looked at his partner as if I were part of the scenery. It never occurred to him to say a word, and the silence between us did not disturb him. But I felt it my duty to say something to the world's heavy-weight champion, and above all to make the Champ say something to me. So the discomfort was all mine. The short man looked up at the giant as one might look up the craggy side of a precipice under which one sat suspended.

I recall another party, although I've forgotten the world-famous star who gave it: Chaplin and Maurice Chevalier, new and crisp as his straw hat, for some reason this night decided to be friendly rivals. One after the other, they fired songs, imitations, quips at the cheering guests who, of course, profited by the spontaneous show.

Most of the stars and starlets I met in Hollywood I don't recall. But they were all workers except for the hordes who were candidates for work. From every hamlet in the land, they came to wait for work. "The Industry" was single-minded as a mill: its will to succeed making a hum like a machine. There was no idleness, no sensuous indolence; and a sexually cooler place could not be imagined, than this where beauty crowded. I learned that there were brothels in Los Angeles patronized by the handsome and the successful of the movies who would have needed only to crook a finger to have the lovelies flock to them. The beds of "the Industry's" workers were too chilled by scheme and pean. If you wanted female heat or even feminine warmth, go to a whorehouse.

This does not mean there was no passion in such affairs, for example, as that of William Randolph Hearst and Marion Davies. But if passion was there, the approach to it, and the control were the mother-wit of the woman. Marion and I became good friends. Her mind overcame provincial frontiers more readily than the minds of most of the men in Congress. She saw the springs of power (as had the mistresses of the French Bourbon kings) and was at home in it. Hearst had found Marion in the chorus of the Ziegfeld Follies. Balzac should have recorded their talks.

When she sat at the head of the long table with her fifty guests, she made me think of Mesdames de Maintenon and du Barry. The monarch of course was W. R., as friends and associates called Hearst: less a monarch of France, however, than a decadent Caesar with his bland girl's brow, his treacherous cold eyes, and his prognathous jaw. Like me and unlike most of the others, W. R. was an early riser. We would meet at the pool, and then would have breakfast together. W. R. would never make up his mind about the nature of Chaplin's friendship with Marion. To Hearst, she was like a mother; and he spent millions trying to make her into a star. But the charming lady, alas, could not act. Mothers, of course, take their sons into their confidence only up to a certain point . . . never beyond. And W. R. was like a boy, a spoiled, unscrupulous child who needed his mother terribly. He would prowl the upstairs halls waiting for Marion's door to open and to be invited in.

Like an emperor of decadent Rome, Hearst lived in a world already vanishing, a world of power carrying on by sheer inertia. He loved to build; he loved to tear down. Over the breakfast rolls, I told him how, as a mere lad, I had been a watcher in the New York elections when he was cheated out of the mayorality. Hearst's eyes almost warmed. And one day he offered me a job on his papers. I declined. I knew, if I took the job, I would soon be fired. Nevertheless, it was perhaps an error not to sample it. Goldwyn also offered me work; but not the man of letters, not the prophet, not the Don Quixote, could "see" Frank in Hollywood as a studio writer. It would mean making a lot of money and wasting a lot of time. I did not have the time. I was in a hurry.

It did not occur to me to give a name to what I felt burgeoning within me. I did not call it "a spring." The bloom had no energy left over to identify itself. But I knew I must not hurry. A burgeoning spring must not be hurried. "Time pressed. America pressed," I wrote in my notebook. My ego's ambition pressed. Yet I must not hurry. Until the profusion of my busy life lay all within the hold of my hand, I must not hurry my hand.

There was another woman in southern California at the time who adored power—a crasser kind of Marion Davies's—the evangelist Aimée MacPherson. Chaplin and I visited her "show" one night. It was a well-run machine for extracting dollars from the distracted; less spontaneous than Billy Sunday's (I had seen him perform in New York); less sophisticated than the flossier more recent show of Billy Graham. When the tears and the musical shouts and the dollars had all been loosened (the pregenital phase of sex), Aimée stepped up into the center of the stage and took over. From the distance where Chaplin and I sat, Aimée needed only a pinafore to be a fourteen-year-old virgin, fragrant and shining with innocence. One almost expected to see Mary's little lamb. After the show we went behind the scenes, and Aimée was thrilled almost to speechlessness by this condescending visit of the master of their mutual art of acting. But the close-up of Aimée at least for me was shattering. The face geared to the dull audience of a packed theater became a poster, a huge oversize poster as if the woman with her megaphone voice had been sired by a bill-board monster. Both Chaplin and I left the view faintly nauseous.

Los Angeles and environs, now one of the country's greatest

industrial centers, was already a focus for every conceivable movement—political, mystical, Communist, theosophical—filling the suites of skyscraper office buildings.

Chaplin had few warm, close friends in Hollywood: who has more than a few? By doom of genius, and of nursing his money, he was a solitary; and it was the communication of this loneliness that won him his great audience: the New York subway rider, the cosmopolitan of Paris, the Chinese peasant, the American white southerner, and the black man of Dahomey . . . all drinking in together the tears within the laughter. Chaplin's chief appeal was to men. Women are never alone; for their world, being technical and economical, is ephemeral and fades in form leaving man alone. Chaplin's great image is of the poor devil who needs mothering and does not get it, who needs a girl to save him from the cold wilderness of machines and is brushed off. Women would rather mother Douglas Fairbanks, who might leap into their lap as he leaps from window to balcony.

One visitor I had in Hollywood distressed me. It was John Howard Lawson, the dramatist whose plays, produced by the Theater Guild and the Group Theater, impressed me by their masculine vigor and rhythm. Lawson, I guessed (it is still a guess), had become a Communist. This was because he (and others) felt guilt making big money in the Industry, and felt hurry. Lawson needed to believe that the script of the "new world" was written. Marx had written it; Lenin and the Russians had written it. All they . . . the Hollywood playwrights . . . could do was to ring up the curtain. I admired *Processional* and *Success Story* and liked their author. But I feared the premature in Lawson's hurry. I was sure Lawson left me that day with something like compassion for the bourgeois revolutionary, the parlor pink, who could not read the writing on the wall. And I shook Lawson's hand feeling lonelier, feeling envy of the man who could be so happily sure of what was soon to happen.

It was time to go home, and there was a last informal evening at Marion Davies' with the servants all out and W. R. bringing the sumptuous food from the refrigerator and sampling it before it reached the tables. I told Hearst that I had been invited to the University of Mexico to give six lectures. W. R. told me "the simple truth" about the Mexicans: Conquer them. Wipe them out. Take the country over, which they're not fit to govern. (Hearst owned mines and vast lands in Mexico.) Hearst smiled at me knowing the libertarian nonsense going on in that young head. He invited me to forget Mexico and come with him to his fabulous château-ranch at San Simeon. "You'd better go," Chaplin urged. "You may not get the chance again, and there's nothing like it in the wide world."

I declined. I was tired and surfeited with new impressions. I was a stranger in Hollywood, not to mention what I would feel in Hearst's luxurious fastness. I loved Charlie Chaplin, but I lacked Charlie's ability to flourish in a hostile world. We were, the two, like electric charges. Insofar as we were alike, we repelled one another and came together only insofar as we were opposites. I did not belong in Hollywood, and I did not belong in Paris. I loved the word of Chaplin, but our media and languages were too remote from one another—yet close!—for us to work together. And what did I have in common with the world of Mary Pickford?

What would Mexico bring me? Would it shed light on *The Rediscovery of America*, whose proofs I had just corrected? I knew at least a truth about myself: my living and my work must grow together. They must be as single as the seed which is also one, although it holds complex elements. Meanwhile, the world was at spring, and every day was bright, whether the sun shone or the rain fell. . . .

3

Mexico and Don Quixote

How travel has shrunk, its joys and revelations along with its pains, since a June day of 1929 when I sailed out of New York harbor bound for Veracruz.[17] I smelt the open sea before we had passed the Narrows, and it called me more urgently . . . more of *me* . . . than the piled skyscrapers of lower Manhattan fading in the wet air like a dream dying. A quiet euphoria of the sea possessed me. Habana, where we docked for the whole day, was an overripe mango. As we neared Yucatan, the sky took the form of Mayan sculpture. I could not see the temples glimmering in the jungle, but they saw me. My eyes saw, as we anchored at Progreso, a little group of faithful Catholics welcoming back with pathetic shabby pomp two priests exiled from Mexico at an earlier stage of the Revolution. At Veracruz, my sweat simmered through the night within my *mosquitero;* and when, before dawn, I got up to make my train my flesh had a sharp chill.

How that journey has shrunk! The insipid airport, mass-produced. "Please fasten your seatbelts," says the vapid, antiseptic stewardess, pretty and null as Mary Pickford. (In your pocket the receipt of your bet with the gambling machine: "I'll bet you forty thousand to two you get there.") And the doors slam, you're crated. Your head stays in New York; then after empty hours your head, dizzy, is stretched to Mexico, with no sea, no wind, no history, no gossip and ghosts. . . .

When I arrived in Mexico, I knew very little (not that anyone knows much) about the past Mexican cultures: the Maya, the Toltec, the Olmec, the Zapotec, and the final Aztec in whom the rite of human sacrifice, sparingly practiced theretofore, became the mass-madness that horrified the Spaniards. I could not identify the taste for blood, the cult of death, infused by the Aztecs in all Mexicans. But the day's dramatic journey up from Veracruz to the bleak *meseta* gave me much about the people bred in such savage soil and submerged beneath such volcanic mountains. I knew of the Revolution of 1910, whose slogan had been *Tierra!* Land! Here it was, and here were the peons who did not own their land. It was lush, down here, close to the sea level; and the Mexicans in their primitive floorless huts revealed poverty as extreme as the worst I had encountered in the Near East and eastern Europe. This indigence was different in kind. The slums I had seen in Poland and in Egypt were a shut-in pestilence of festering boils upon the social body of man, as of some leprosy. Here there was simply deprivation by a certain measure. After all, who said man should sleep on a bed rather than a mat of straw? Eat leavened wheat bread rather than roasted beetles? The Mexicans whom I glimpsed as the train hurtled through backyards shaded by twelve-foot banana leaves and palms, slowing as the rails laddered upward, revealing the snow-capped volcano Orizaba as background for heat-saturated villages where children shared life with pigs and chickens—these Mexicans were not so much deprived by their lacks as differently focussed. Even the death of a child meant something other to them—perhaps a victory, since the infant was sure to go to heaven. Now they had learned other wants: land *and* bread *and* freedom of assembly.

A small group of men awaited me on the platform as I stepped down from the train into the cool night of the *meseta.* I was lightheaded, heart pumping the thin air of a mile and a half above sea level. The Mexican handclasps were warm; the smiles seemed to know that I was short of breath. With few words and no effusiveness they took me to a hotel, *posada* or *fonda,* purely Hispanic, innocent of American tourists, on a midtown street noisy as only a Latin-American city can be. The room they showed me had no windows, only a door giving on a balcony around a roofed interior court. I was accustomed to sleeping in rooms open to the outside air. This avoidance of windows on the streets, with only a door to the balcony shared by strangers, made me feel, while my heart pounded, that I had crossed—as I had!—from one civilization to another. Should I breathe with every guest? Or stifle in private? Either way how could I sleep? I locked the door. I slept—only to wake with a bound, gasping for more breath . . . and again and again.

Diego Rivera offered me a dinner of welcome at a famous and ancient restaurant. The great painter chose the menu which was to introduce me once and for all time to all the classic Mexican dishes. My hosts at the long table watched me take on specialty after specialty. Innocently I delighted in them all, from subtle to fiery, with foretones and aftertones like music. Next day, I was deathly sick, intestines writhing, bowels flooding. The press got wind of it and accused Diego, who was already a Communist, of poisoning the *Yanqui* visitor. I had come to tell the Mexicans my plans for a cultural union of the Americas through the minorities of each: I had not guessed that my problems would begin with dysentary and acute indigestion. Before my first lecture, the Yankee invader had learned that it was possible for a radical head to be overthrown by a conservative stomach.

In the decades ahead, I would come down many times to Mexico and visit every part of it; multiverse and potential cosmos. I never dared forget to keep my diet bland. For breakfast: papaya, piña, other fruits; dinner, the one real meal, at 3:00; for supper at about 9:00 a pot of chocolate, a biscuit, again papaya (which contains pepsin); and between feedings, nothing. I also learned the treacheries of unboiled water, of greens washed in unboiled water, and of such innocent fare as milk and ice cream.

I will be excused for not recalling in detail the *Gran Salon de Actos* of the University, where I gave my first lecture (in Spanish.) I was too excited to observe sharply where I was speaking. I saw flags and blazons on the walls and pendant from the ceiling; I saw rows of heavy mahogony high-backed chairs like thrones . . . all the appropriate pomp of a university founded in the sixteenth century. I never saw that stately hall again. For my talks were transferred to the Escuela de Segundo Enseñanza, the largest auditorium in the city.

My first subject was "The New World"; my thesis, that this world did not exist; and my first words; "I have come to Mexico to learn." I stood on the mahogony dais under the gilded candelabra now equipped with electric bulbs and impressed on two or three hundred intellectuals before me that I deemed my coming to Mexico a mode of action. I did not learn until later that an overflow of over a thousand students heard me by loudspeaker in the yard. I did not learn until the next day that something unusual had happened. The leading morning paper devoted its leading editorial in extra leaded type to the lecture. It gave my thesis of the uncreated "new world" and said in substance: "We accept the invitation, the challenge, the collaboration." The *Yanqui* was not the expected academic event; he was *news*.

The keynote men I met on that first Mexican journey of 1929 expressed in their own vigorous ways the sense of America as "the grave of Europe"—and its destiny to become a new world. There was Diego Rivera, huge and silent as a cat, who wrought his peasant men, women, and children from the sunlight and the luminous earth. There was José Clemente Orozco, agonist and bitter satirist, who drew his revolutionary soldiers and their dolorous mothers from the moon's beams and the moon shadows. There was José Vasconcelos, whose books avidly taught the students of all the Latin American universities that their mixed bloods must make them *la raza cósmica*.

As national minister of education, Vasconcelos led the painters of Mexico to the bare walls of the schools and said to them: Paint! There was Alfonso Reyes, my first friend in the Hispanic world whom I had met in Paris: the urbane, Horatian poet and the writer of what Gabriela Mistral called the finest prose of our generation. At twenty Reyes had seen his father General Bernardo Reyes, chief of staff under the fallen President Porfirio Díaz, stride across the deserted *Zócalo,* the square and stone steps before the Presidential Palace. If he was not stopped and had entered the Palace, he would have made a revolution for the continuance of Mexico's "law and order." A volley of fire stopped him, and the son saw his father crumple and die in his own blood. This scene of terror was the root of Reyes' Virgilian verse, a paradox which explains much about the Mexicans. There was Emilio Portes Gil, president of the Republic since the assassination of Alvaro Obregón by a fanatical Catholic rightist student. Portes Gil was a full-blooded Indian and a dynamic lawyer. He was ready to discuss my program; he recognized its possible place on the agenda of the nation; but as I talked with him one afternoon I saw, behind the grey image of the politician, behind the mask of the President, an image that leered: the peon skeptical, pessimistic, resigned—and capable of ferocity.

There were in Mexico two potent musicians: strict Carlos Chávez who subdued native folk song to Western tonal logic without loss of integrity (he gave a special concert in order that I might hear Mexico's music and the orchestral instrument he had perfected); and burly, tender Silvestre Revueltas, whose want of control of the torrential music within him was soon to destroy him.

Moises Sáenz, assistant minister of education, had come to me in New York with the invitation from the University and settled the generous terms for the six lectures. He helped me in every way to profit by my visit: planning interviews, expeditions to villages and to archeological treasures under the expert guidance of such authorities as Manuel Gamio and Professor Gonzalez Casanova. I went along with mobile missions set up by the ministry. Our team consisted of a nurse, a teacher, a physician, an agronomist, and often a painter. I recall one, when Rivera went along. I had slept on a hard school bench, and before dawn the ungiving wood of the cold bed outbalanced my need for sleep. There was a hill above this village (in the state of Guerrero), and I climbed it to get warm and catch the sunrise. I stood on the crest facing the massive dark of trees that flowed to the horizon, bursting there into flame from the unrisen sun: a flame of earth and clouded sky that seemed closer to passion and ecstacy than to physical color. When the view relaxed into full day, it was joyous as release in sexual embrace. I turned and saw, standing beside me, a man of about forty dressed in the habitual village white pyjamas.

He must have come silently up, while I experienced the flame together of sun and sky and earth, and he was watching the stranger's watching. Now the man nodded and smiled, and his silence said as surely as if he had spoken: "I am happy, stranger, that you see the beauty of my earth. I happily share it with you." It came to me that a man capable of this act of empathy with an outsider—an illiterate man, doubtless—was a man of *culture*.

It was Sáenz who first took me up to Taxco (this was before Spratling organized the silversmiths of the town). The road was the old one of cobbled stones down which the Spaniards drove their mules and donkeys laden with silver and gold. When we came to a stream, now, the old Ford forded it. At the base of the valley was Cuernavaca; here at the top in Taxco was the church the Spaniards built, all gold and silver walls, to thank God for his good fortune.

Below the church, a few steps, was a rustic bench with a tumultous view of the valley. I sat there alone, resting . . . thinking of my lectures, now half done, full of the enchantment of success. I did not understand the success; I simply drank it in, hardly tasting it, as a very thirsty man takes in a glass of water. I was not thinking of the relation of the Mexican with this turbulent nature visible in the valley before me. Sáenz, a little breathless, joined me on the bench.

"Frank," he said without preamble, "you are a fraud, a cheat, a second-rater. Your visit to Mexico will accomplish nothing and will bring nothing about." I, without a word, listened. What should I do? Agree? Slap the minister's face?

I knew I was a susceptible man. I knew if someone rushed at me crying "Thief!" my first response would be that of a thief. But what had I stolen? Only my second impulse would be self-defense. Sáenz spoke in a clipped voice, with his eyes not on me but on the vast valley; and I sensed that the attack was not individual but general and collective like a cavalry charge in battle. Sudden as he had begun, Sáenz stopped, got up and walked away.

—Perhaps it's true, and I'm a cheat and a second-rater. If so, and Sáenz has discovered it, his bitterness is to be pardoned. Yet, his courage in speaking should have bowed to the courtesy he owed a guest. Perhaps he had to speak because he had to attack my country through me? If the bitter sense of fraud includes the United States, how else attack? Was Mexico the assailant? What is Mexico? A chaos of voices, many ignorant even of the nation's name; a folk living in floorless hovels, half of whose newborn die of filth diseases and over half of whose adults cannot read the editorials engaging Mexico to work with me—and Bolívar and Juárez and Martí—to create a new world. Fraud! But the United States no less a fraud, equating progress with refrigerators, prophecy with profits.

Insofar as I could, I had been honest. I had warned my hearers that when I defended Mexico against invasion, economic and cultural, I and my little band were defending *our* America, the America of Whitman and Thoreau. We, I said, were as hated or ignored in our own land—more inwardly exposed to the menace of business than the peasants of Tampico in the Yankee "kingdoms" of oil.

Sáenz had business in Taxco and did not return to the Capital with me that night. But a couple of evenings later, I was sure to meet him again at a party given for me by Tina Modetti, a photographer who had caught memorable moments of Mexico's revolutionary life. Meanwhile, I saw no clearer what I would say, what I could do, about the personal form of the affront. There was still no anger in me. Tina's flat was jammed with the usual noisy human substance. Sáenz was not yet present. Then I saw his tall well-groomed body push into the crowded room, making his way smile to smile, handshake to handshake toward me. We were face to face. Sáenz cried: "Waldo!" joyously, took my hand, clapped his left one on my shoulder—all as if nothing had happened or what had happened were of another world. There was no anger in me, but there was sorrow.

The episode had no overt sequel. Soon after, Sáenz went abroad on official business; and I was left with my deepening sense that Mexico, despite its gentlemen and ladies and students at home in the culture of the West, was at war with itself, like Don Quixote when he "repented" the journeys that were his glory.

Of course, I had been insulted by my Mexican host. (I had also

·

been welcomed and loved like no other intellectual in Mexico's history.) I had been rudely reminded that my crusade for a "new world" in the Western hemisphere could be interpreted even by my sponsors as fraud and delusion. Before Don Quixote's venture for love and for the justice that comes of it could become real, it had to be laughed at—and by himself. Before my image of a new-born world could become substance—substance of science and society and economics and ethic and art—it had to be received as fraud. . . .

4

Success and Defeat in Argentina

To move from Mexico to Argentina was to return from a strange world to one seemingly familiar. On the way, I got a first taste of another world neither old nor new: Brazil. Our ship was the British *Voltaire*, sister of the *Vestris* whose going-down in the hurricane the year before I had witnessed by radio. When we sailed into the harbor of Rio de Janeiro, I realized that beauty can be ineffable: literally stunning and unspeakable. I left the ship; wandered all day through the dark and luminous city; took the train to Sao Paulo, Brazil's great industrial center; and rejoined the boat three days later at Santos, coffee-capital of the world where the women sorters, squatting on the pavement before their pile of berries, had the dark body-smell of coffee.

On the three weeks' journey from New York, I wrote the rough draft of the new lectures. The boat was not crowded, and the Captain gave me an extra cabin for a study. Nothing was crowded in those remote days: nothing first class at least. I got a sample of why the British empire still worked. There was a lady on board, a British lady, wife of a British admiral, who made a point of having a friendly contact with each first-class passenger on board: with some she played bridge, with others deck tennis or shuffleboard, with some drank tea or cocktails, with another paced the empty promenade deck before breakfast. The noble dame secreted unction; and when she left the ship at Rio to rejoin her husband, the British Navy behind her wiles and smiles had become, in the flattered minds of several score passengers, a symbol of good will, not of destruction.

The press of Buenos Aires got on board at Montevideo, in true American hurry. With them came Alphonso Reyes, then Mexico's ambassador to Argentina. He had flown in from Mexico on a government plane and learning of my arrival decided to make the last lap of his journey with his American friend. Also Samuel Glusberg was there, who had first broached the subject of my visit with Dr. Alfredo Colmo, justice of a high court and president of the Institute of Argentine-American Relations. Also Coriolano Alberini, dean of the Faculty of Letters of the University of Buenos Aires, under whose aegis I was to give my first lectures. Glusberg wrote subtle stories and mordant critiques under the pen name of Enrique Espinoza and led a literary campaign that promised to make Buenos Aires the literary capital of the southern continent. Son of immigrants from eastern Europe—tall, thin, owlish behind his thick glasses, Glusberg looked more the scholar than the dynamic promoter he was. At the time, he was still riding high. When the democratic method broke in Argentina with the counter-revolution against President Hipólito Irigoyen (1930), he was to be one of the victims: his books, his magazines, but not his commitment to my "new world." Finally, he settled in Chile where the democratic movement ebbed but did not shatter.

Reyes, Glusberg, and I stood, that night, together at the rail of the promenade deck looking into the grey mist of the Rio de la Plata, whose breadth of eighty miles revealed no discontinuity between our vessel slowly gliding forward, the water, and the sky. But there seemed no continuity—as I look back—between the precipitous perpendiculars of Mexico, land and people, and this vast watery pampa without horizon.

I soon discovered that "horizontal" also described the people: the ten or twelve million Argentinians, half within the huge metropolitan area, half within the pampas bounded north and west by the Andes, south by Patagonia with its violent winds and by the green fjords of Tierra del Fuego. I had sensed in Mexico plenty of the corruption of power that infects every revolution. But its honest intellectuals and a few politicians with statesmanship in them had taken the "new world" I visioned as a serious proposition, to be studied, to be implemented by method if ideally accepted; if not, to be attacked and disposed of. One might say the Mexicans had accepted my challenge "standing up." The Argentinians were to make it a spectacle, a performance. This does not mean they did not take me seriously. Nothing, they knew, was more serious than aesthetics, which, however, was an end in itself.

One of the young writers who climbed aboard the ship at Montevideo was Eduardo Mallea, literary editor of *La Nación*, who was to become the leading Argentine novelist of his generation. A few years after my first visit, Mallea wrote a book entitled *Historia de una pasión Argentina* whose fifth chapter under the heading of "America" begins:

In those days there arrived in Buenos Aires a writer from another American latitude. He came preceded already by much fame and many people drew close to his voice; but the meaning of his message was hardly understood and soon forgotten. It was not an easy message, indeed it was a very hard one. Nevertheless, his language was not hard; and his general conception of problems . . . was as mature as it was precise. The difficulty was not the external body of the message; but its assimilation; and if one was not disposed to live it in its totality, it was useless; and in this case there would remain of it no more than a few phrases in a desert. . . .

These words were to become prophetic.

In the first days, I was invited to the house of Victoria Ocampo. A famous house, a famous lady (I describe both in my cultural portrait: *America Hispana*). When I first met her, Victoria was a woman of about forty: a tall, large, black-haired woman of classic beauty; a powerful woman; a wealthy woman; and, in her private life, an unhappy woman. Her ancestors, conquistadores from Spain and Portugal, had acquired huge haciendas far and wide which were now priceless real estate in Buenos Aires when it was still a provincial city of slight importance compared to other capitals: Mexico, Rio de Janeiro, Lima, Bogotá. Victoria worked to make Buenos Aires a cultural center. She sponsored, often financed, visits by famous writers and musicians. For a while, she directed the National Opera. In her land-owning class, as in old Russia, the children learned French before their native language; when moved, Victoria would spontaneously and unconsciously lapse from Spanish into French. And her English was perfect. One of her gifts was reading French poetry. How good she was is shown by what happened some years later when she asked me to bring Jacques Copeau, creator of the Théâtre du Vieux Colombier, to her apartment in Paris. She wanted a few lessons from the master. She recited a scene from Racine's *Phèdre*, a poem by Baudelaire, a page of Mallarmé. Copeau listened, got up, and bowed. "Madame," he said, "I thank you, and I regret . . . but I have nothing to teach you."

This fabulous creature, with her three curses upon her head—the curse of beauty, of intelligence, and of wealth—had her weaknesses. She overvalued, perhaps, her friends Tagore, Virginia Woolf, T. E. Lawrence, the coteries of London and Paris. She undervalued surely some of the Americans; north and south, past and present: Brazil with such giant works as Euclides da Cunha's *Os sertões* and her own pampa's Martin Fierro meant little to her. For these failings, if you will, she was savagely attacked by both the nationalists and the cosmopolitans. Unjustly. That she appreciated *so much* did not make it fair to demand that she appreciate *more*.

La Prensa, the greatest Argentine paper, invited me, when I returned home, to become a regular contributor. *La Nación,* the paper of most intellectual prestige, founded a century before by President Bartolomé Mitre, published summaries of my lectures, sometimes two columns long. And these were repeated by the press of Santiago de Chile, Lima, as far north as Bogotá. The paper with the largest circulation, *Crítica* of Buenos Aires, obviously patterned after the journalism of Hearst, kept me on the front page as if I were a visiting movie star. The press of the United States was not concerned. But in Madrid, a well-known Spanish writer began an article:

> Through Buenos Aires have passed some of the most enlightened lecturers in the world. The great intellectuals of Europe spoke to the Argentines—if not as mature to younger persons, at least as outsiders. But recently the North American writer, Waldo Frank, has put a stop to this practice. He has spoken to the Argentines as from within: that is to say, he has placed himself in the attitude of the American who speaks on equal terms with other Americans, and who speaks to them moreover on the destiny, responsibility and spiritual mission of America in relation to the problems of the new culture which must appear.
>
> This happy thought of the great North American writer has received its deserved reward. Although the public of Buenos Aires manifests its good will lavishly, and its applause, on all the notables . . . who reach its shores—beyond all that has been known up to now, the applause for Waldo Frank has gone the limit. . . .*

In Mexico, I had been a prophet—according to my doubters a false prophet. In Buenos Aires I was a literary showman. The successful lecturer is always something of an actor who makes his own lines, models his own image as he rambles along. The newspaper reports of my talks, as they appeared in Chile, Colombia,

*J. M. Salaverria, in *A.B.C.* of Madrid.

Peru, did not convey my person; and the people wanted to see me. Before I completed my schedule in Argentina, I had received invitations to come and lecture for the presidents of the Universities of Colombia, Uruguay, Peru, and Havana.

In Buenos Aires, I acted a kind of intellectual theater. I was not aware of this at first. Mallea in his book sized me up more sharply than I could myself. As a lecturer, I was "a natural," without theory or forethought in the bastard art of public speaking. I had something to say, person to person, and said it. My reward was to experience popularity, as no writer does in our country: to know what it was to be "the rage" among both the men and elegant ladies. But I was to learn that I also had the masses with me. Sure of their hearts and ears, I could subdue my voice, with sudden sallies, flares of emphasis—without shouting, which would have lost me. It is indicative to note that the accounts of my meetings in Buenos Aires describe my *person*. I was acting out a monodrama.

The earth of Argentina and the waters reminded me of Egypt; both lands are fertile like a woman; in both, submission can rouse to sudden ecstasy. I noted—knowing it meant something—the resemblance between the look of the women's eyes toward the far pampa horizons and the stance of Egyptian sculpture.

In the first years of independence, Argentina produced distinguished disciples of the soon doomed liberal movement in Spain (the name "liberal" was originally Spanish): disciples of Jefferson and Madison and Thomas Paine. But in Buenos Aires there were also other directions, other doctrines. At the welcoming banquet given to me by the Argentine Society of Authors, the chairman was its president, the poet, Leopoldo Lugones. "Our people," he said, "are both Latin and Catholic." He praised American democracy and said Argentines would have none of it. He praised the American Constitution as a wondrous machine of government by balance of laws and rejected it; for, he said, "we are authoritarians and personalists." In my reply, I observed that I understood the discrepancies in theory and ideal and value between myself and my hosts who had invited me in full cognizance of the facts. So be it! My reception by ideological adversaries proved that my presence in Argentina had a deeper meaning: it was an exchange among artists. "But you," said Lugones, "are an anarchist; you, too, are against all law but the authority of strength and merit." Lugones's destiny made that banquet a bitter irony. When Fascism rose in Europe, Lugones, the antidemocrat who had fostered it, would have none of it and sent a bullet through his brain.

The majority of Argentines, the vast majority in the Provinces, were conscious liberals and democrats; and their leader was the President Hipólito Irigoyen. He asked me to come to the Casa Rosada where he had his offices. A secretary led me through a long empty room hung with portraits of colonial worthies; opened a heavy door, mahogany with silver fixtures, that led into another vacant room at the far end of which an old man sat alone at a small teak table. The secretary shut himself out, and the old man got up to greet his guest. I had been introduced to Irigoyen a few evenings before, during an *entr'acte* at the opera: a tall, stooped country gentleman of seventy or more with thick white hair, a ponderous handsome head, who spoke a Spanish courtly and archaic.

Now, silently, he clasped my hand in both his: the flecked hands of an old man, pressed and released it, graciously gesturing me to the chair beside him. The desk top was empty except for a tall pile of papers which almost obstructed the view of the president's face. He spoke of his privilege and his pleasure in welcoming the young tribune of the North to Argentina. Soon he was speaking of the world's great needs and of the potential help of the social sciences, the philosophies, the arts and letters. Nearly an hour passed. The distant door where I had entered clicked, and another secretary traversed the immense expanse of carpet and in-laid floor to place a paper on the tower of papers already a foot high. The secretary murmured a few words I could not understand; the president nodded with a flicker of irritation in his eyes —and returned to the dangers of transition from one social order to another. Then, yet another official in a smart morning coat, bearing no papers, navigated the long room and whispered to the president who again gave a nod both disturbed and acquiescent. The official grasped the tower of papers and riffled them as a bank teller riffles bills, a gambler a deck of cards. From the heart of the pile, he extracted a single sheet and showed it to the president who read it, moving his lips like a peasant reading; nodded again; took an old fashioned pen and signed it; glanced at it hurriedly once more; and gave it to the official who bowed low and vanished. I had a clear impression of a conflict between a staff of secretaries who wanted papers signed, *things done,* and an old man who preferred to speculate on the world's situation. (This was Irigoyen's second term. During the first, he had angered the liberals and the rich alike by refusing to enter the war on the side of the Allies.)

"I'm afraid," I said, "I should not disturb you any longer."

"Nothing is more important," said the president, "than this good talk. Tell me, what can I do to help you?" He would not let me go. "How can I help?" he insisted.

He knew I had concluded my talks in Buenos Aires and would soon be leaving for lectures in Argentina's provincial cities: radical Rosario, clerical Córdoba, Patagonian Bahía Blanca, Salta, Jujuy . . . could Señor Frank use a private railroad car, to add comfort to his journey? I declined: the private railway car in my country, I said, was a boast of the magnate or the tool of a political campaign. Well, then, an airplane? This, I accepted.

Irigoyen in his second term, after the six year interval required by the Constitution, had infuriated the large landowners by devising means (punitive taxes, for one) of fractioning off pieces of the great estates. These small holdings, *chacras*, were then apportioned to immigrant farmers, largely Italian. His devises enraged, but were not thorough enough to cripple, the rich, leaving them scared but with room to maneuver. As to the Army, is it not always on good terms with the big money?

The following year President Irigoyen was thrown out of office. He had resided for decades in a simple flat over a tobacco store. Now one morning generals of the Army knocked at his door and told him to leave his home and country. The pretext for this action by landlords and officers was that Irigoyen neglected the duties of his mission and permitted subordinates to rob the treasury. It was true: Irigoyen's liberalism lacked method, and among his underlings were thieves.

For the remainder of this first Argentine visit, I taxied around the vast and nearly empty land (a million square miles) in an old single-propeller German Junker manned by an Argentine Air Force captain and his mechanic. We had unscheduled adventures. Meeting a steady and unpredicted head wind, we ran out of fuel aloft and made a forced landing in a field, barely missing a tree that would not move and a hostile bull that came at us. The north of Argentina is mountain, and we were among mountains on another day when a dense mist came down to blind us. We had to come down too; for night was gathering; we did not know where we were; but we did know that the mountains reached above us. Each time we dipped we were in peril. All the Argentine visit thus far had been in a brilliant world with human faces shining: a euphoria of color. Now the bright shining world was leaden grey, with the road of the propeller. A grim promise of death waiting for us in the grey shrouded mountains. But I could not believe this death. I sat beside the pilot, my tense clasped hands lifting the plane by empathy to safety. The life problem was to find the valley with the rails which we would follow. We must fly low to find it because of the mist; face death to find life. I knew I was near death, and did not pray because I was too alive to fear death. Suddenly we dipped and swooped sharp to the right, and for an instant I feared that the pilot had gone mad. There were the rails, shining and winding safe within the lethal heights! The captain had only to follow them to Salta.

The climax of these flights was the last. My work was done in Argentina, and the captain was instructed to drop me in Santiago, Chile. The routes over the Andes were not yet determined in 1929. At Aconcagua, the Andes are second in height only to the Himalayas. The mildest and lowest valleys, the safest from the mighty winds sweeping like suddenly jetting glaciers, had not yet been routed. Now the plane leaped up into the thinning air and our ship became a midge against the ice flows. I had neglected to fix my oxygen tube; now as I surveyed the inchoate turbulence I forgot. An ecstasy overtook me. We rose . . . rose almost at the height of Aconcagua. I saw a condor, a black speck, and recalled the great-winged bird I had recently read of in the press that crashed into an airplane's propeller bringing his own death as he dealt it.

The thin air, acting like ether, exalted my consciousness; the irrelevant, the trivial, vanished. Peoples, places, and time went before an absolute Real beyond space and time. All was understood. The plane's single motor softened, we began to descend, and I saw the sapphire of the Pacific.

The reader must understand: what I felt in this leap of the Andes was not concept, not verbal. The spoken translation comes now. But under what conditions had I seen and experienced the Real? I had been deprived of the oxygen requisite for living. The earth had faded; its splendor a barren tumult of ice and crag. If the single motor had failed, we would have died. Even if we had landed alive, we would have died in a few moments in that desolation. What did this signify? This had been perhaps a mystical revelation. It is not enough for man. *Revelation must become incarnate in man's way of living.*

I would have told anyone that by far the most important result of my Argentine visit was the magazine I thought I had persuaded Victoria Ocampo to found. Toward this beginning, I had brought her and Samuel Glusberg together (they had never met). Their varieties of cultures would enrich one another and the New World organ I envisaged: Victoria's contribution, her closeness to the classics and to the latest arts and letters of Paris and London; Glusberg's contribution, a sound recognition of social subjects and the prophetic vision of the Americas. Victoria founded *Sur,* and a very respectable display of culture it turned out to be. But Glusberg, the dynamic immigrant Jew with a Prophet's America in his heart, and Victoria Ocampo, princess of good taste, separated almost as soon as they met. My cultural union remained a dream. My concept of the magazine as an organism meant nothing to Victoria for whom most of the American and Hispano-American authors, loved by Glusberg more for promise and intent than for complete achievement, also had no meaning. The elegant *Sur* published many a good piece, but it was remote from what I wanted and the hemisphere needed.

A dear friend of Victoria's was Maria-Rosa Oliver, another of Argentine's remarkable women. She had been crippled in childhood by infantile paralysis, which appeared to launch her into endless expeditions. Sympathetic to the Communists to whose will to disarm she gave more credence than to that of the United States, she covered the globe in her peace efforts. She visited the United States where she was for a year consultant on Latin America for Vice-President Wallace. She visited China and wrote a book about it. She attended Congresses far and wide. She wanted the magazine I wanted. Victoria could not work with her. The ideational split of Victoria, Glusberg, and Maria Rosa was a symbol. The "parts" of America were not yet ready to grow together.

From Chile, where I was welcomed by the Peruvian poet José Santos Chocano, in exile from his country, I went on to Peru. The intellectuals of Peru had asked the dictator, President Augusto Leguía, for permission to invite me. It had been granted, and I was made an honorary doctor of Peru's University of San Marcos, oldest university of the Americas.

Leguía was a very small old man in a black suit with black tight gloves forever on his hands. He tried to explain to me the three cultural strata of Peru: the chaos of races on the coast, the mestizo of the mid-plateau, and the (culturally) pure Indian of the Andean Cordillera. He tried to convince me that this divided Peru could not be governed by democratic methods. Many Peruvians, particularly among the youth, disagreed, of course. If they were dangerously subversive, Leguía exiled them. If they were young students, he "bought" them: gave them a purse and let them pursue their studies in Europe.

Among these was José Carlos Mariátegui who spent three years in London, Paris, Rome. But he did not remain "bought." (There would have been a post for him, academic or diplomatic.) José came home a Marxist—with Peruvian and Franklin modifications and with the will to relieve the unbearably exploited Indians.

I had already encountered the Peruvian student. At Arequipa in south Peru, I had been met at the station by about forty youths who marched me up into the town, fragrant as an orange blossom within the cool embrace of snow-capped mountains, and by exterior stairs to the flat roof of a building where they asked me to speak to them. (There had been many of these "forced" meetings, perhaps this was the best of them all.) Over them loomed the volcanoes—Misti, Chachani, Pichu-Pichu—while I told them of my dream of an integrated world where the whole man would function and transform the institutions. These youths were in touch with Mariátegui through his magazine *Amauta*, where such vigorous artists as José Sabogal and Julia Codesido celebrated the Indian and where Mariátegui published his remarkable "Seven Essays in Interpretation of the Peruvian Reality."

Mariátegui, when I met him, was already a sick man confined to a wheel chair by a tuberculosis of the bone. He was a short young man of slight build with a ponderous head and a lock of black hair on his brow like a nineteenth-century romantic poet. But he was no romantic. I spent long hours with him and loved him and knew we must work together. But Mariátegui must come east as San Martín and Bolívar had marched west: a long and expensive journey. I, at once, wrote to Glusberg asking him to manage the economics of the "march." Mariátegui must get well in Buenos Aires. Then he would return to the Pacific, his native land, his battle field.

Meanwhile I comforted myself, in Argentina a true liberal was in the saddle: Hipólito Irigoyen.

The following summer my family was occupying the charming house of Severo Mallet-Prevôt in the White Mountains. I was happily at work on *America Hispana*. I worked joyfully. The journey had been of good omen. Then the news came of Irigoyen's fall— and of Mariátegui's death.

I wept. . . .

5

Crash

On my first visit to Buenos Aires, I was lodged in the villa of an absent British business man in Vincente López, a suburb about half an hour by train from the center. It reminded me of a cottage in Surrey or a chalet in Switzerland. With it came the maids, the chauffeur, and the limousine; I seldom used the trains.

On a morning in October (1929), I came down as usual for breakfast; and as I drank my orange juice, I glanced as usual at the headlines of *La Nación*, which with the sedate *La Prensa*, bulky as the *New York Times*, lay beside my napkin. *La Prensa*, like the London *Times*, gave its first pages to advertisements and public notices; and it was the headline of *La Nación* that announced for me the crash on Wall Street. I was not disturbed; no foreboding spoiled my excellent bacon and eggs. I knew that the politician-pundits, such as Hoover and Coolidge, prophesied the endless rise of the market; and in general I doubted politicians. But neither the rise nor the fall of prices interested me. It had been silly to predict that stocks would go up forever; it would be equally absurd to read in their slump the signal of disaster. I was lecturing on revolution of a deeper pitch (of the arts, of the person): the revolution of a profit system into an economy of use. The Wall Street jitters meant nothing to me.

Chaim Weizmann, the Zionist leader, had asked me to lunch at the Commodore in New York. The other guests were Schmarya Levin who, prophecying there would be prophets again in Israel when it was free, was himself a Hebrew prophet and Ludwig Lewisohn, the literary critic who became a fanatical Jewish nationalist and could not forgive me for falling in love with Spain. The whole spectrum of Jewish colors was at that luncheon table, in that Babylonish hotel.

After the lunch, Weizmann hailed a taxi and asked me to accompany him downtown. As we dodged the traffic of Broadway which seemed to pour on us and vanish, he invited me to Palestine. Before the cab reached Wall Street, plans had been made. There were no strings to the journey. But Weizmann, I knew, was sure that I would be inspired to write about my visit. I agreed about this probability. We were both wrong. I was indeed inspired by what I saw—but not to write.

(Of course, I am setting this down in the perspective of nearly forty years, which unites experience and events into a pattern of awareness. Within it, the visits to Palestine and the east European ghettoes [1927]; the writing of 50,000 words of the *Markand* novel; the *Markand* myth; and the tearing up of every word; the visit to Russia and the immediate publication of *Dawn in Russia;* the 1929 "Crash" and its relevance to my relations with the Communists and my awareness of poverty, specifically in the American industrial cities after the "Crash," all came together.)

As I sat with these conscious Jews at that luncheon table— Weizmann, the scientist and world statesman; Schmarya Levin, the prophet; Ludwig Lewisohn, the neurotic zealot—I was poignantly aware of my ignorance of the culture that had formed and weaned my forefathers. In a mystical experience, years before, I had heard the voices in Alexandria, city of Philo and the Apocalyptists. But I knew no Hebrew, no Yiddish, no Talmud, no history of Zionism, no hermeneutics. This meant study for which I had no time, although I promised myself to make time in some future never to be captured. At least I began to read what was available in English, from Bible to Martin Buber. Began the debate with myself about the methods of survival so wondrously practised by a dynamic little people. And I had the foresight not to enter Palestine directly; instead, to visit orthodox communities in eastern Europe in order to gain some sense of the human beings who were reviving Palestine—some of them after thousand mile treks from Galicia or Lithuania. As a threshold to Palestine, I saw Warsaw (my guide there was the novelist Scholem Asch), Lemberg (Lvov), Vilna, and many a village ruled by a holy Zaddik whose joyous doctrine came from eighteenth-century Baal Shem Tov,[18] and clear down to the oil fields of the Romanian frontier where men in filthy rags scooped up in tin cans the oil mixed with mire which they would then try to sell as fuel to those slightly less impoverished than themselves.

For the first time, I saw poverty as a way of life.

It meant the gnawing void of hunger, the constant exposure to disease and to death without the chance of defense. It meant filth and rat-ruled cellars. But it meant also, here in eastern Europe, transcendance from dearth into spirit. In German, I could communicate with these people whose Yiddish consisted largely of German words. But far stronger was the handclasp; more healing, the tears of empathy between us as they worshiped God in their scrubbed *schule*. I felt the separation from these Jews and did not want to be separate; I felt shame in my nescience, among these scientists of ethics. And I saw beauty. These Polish and Galician Jews were, for the most part, ignorant of what had happened in the world since the eighteenth century. In time, they were laggards; and under the squalor and the fetor of their filth-cursed homes, they touched eternity and were of it.

Now suddenly, as revelation always is being outside time, I understood the meaning of the 616 Mosaic Commandments. By attaching to common daily conduct the dietary human relations and to the celebration of historical events with games and song the command, hence the presence of God, the Jewish people became saturated with Jehovah. In waking and in sleeping God was with them. Not for a moment did I believe that the specific 616 Commandments should or could be revived or retained. They had come forth from an agrarian, intuitive culture. For our civilization of science their *equivalents* must be created: commandments (of course, under another name) to rediscover the whole society, the whole man.

This was the deepest meaning of Zionism.

And this was the motive driving the myth-mad *David Markand* away from home, across the country, and home again. . . .

My second wife Alma had met me that early spring in Paris. I had spent a month in Heidelberg writing articles, a few at fabulous prices for *McCalls*. We had gone by train to Marseilles (I recalled "the escape" from Paris five years before), where we had taken the boat to Alexandria. There, on the rue de Menasce, Jean de Menasce had received us in his home and showed us the sculpture and landscape of Egypt. Menasce, scion of a Jewish family of bankers, an Oxford graduate, an exquisite of culture, was a recent convert to the Catholic Church. He was also a passionate Zionist, drawing from the Scriptures the event to come: the Jews' conversion, the Jews' messiahship, conquering first Palestine, then the world.

Scholem Asch went with us from Egypt to Jerusalem. There we found Adolph Oko[19] waiting to travel the length and breadth of Palestine with us . . . "Dan to Beersheba."

Oko was to become my closest friend, certainly the wisest. He resembled a little medieval monk, and he possessed a range of experience and emotion beyond friars, unless it be a Roger Bacon. He was a soft-spoken man, giving judgments true as steel, making observations exquisite as the touch of a young woman. His mobile mouth could be warm with tenderness or icy in contact with the false and mediocre. Born in Russia, educated at the University of Berlin, he came to America and accepted the post of librarian at Cincinnati's Hebrew Union College. His conduct there reveals him. Quietly, he collected millions of dollars from the Jews of America and made his Library into the greatest Jewish collection in the world—safe from the talons of Hitler. And although the Library was, of course, an organ of the college (which trained for the Rabbinate), he let no student take or touch a book without express permission. The students, he made his point quite clear, were expendible, not the precious manuscripts, incunabula, and scrolls. Oko's great literary loves were Spinoza, on whom he was an authority, and Heine. He knew the moderns, too; and if they wrote well like Eliot or Santayana, he respected them despite discrepancies of doctrine or aesthetic.

Until Oko's death in 1944, his closeness to me meant a lucid strength—a strong light—in my intricate problems of pursuing my aims as artist and cultural critic without falling into the peril of aloofness from a world in revolution. When Oko died, I mourned him; and there was instinctual anger in my lament. "I needed you," I seemed to be saying, "you had no right to leave me in the fight without you."

My friend's last years were made a nightmare by the rise of Hitler within the supineness of Germany. The doctors spoke of low blood pressure as the cause of his death. But Adolph Oko died of a broken heart.

Our our first day in Jerusalem, my wife and I looked down from the high balcony of our boardinghouse room upon the valley of Gehenna and David's Mount Zion and the whole stone-strong city, and upon the embowelled sites of Jericho, the Dead Sea, and the river of Jordan.

Alma exclaimed:

"This beauty is to the beauty of other lands as the beauty of the Bible is to other literature."

It was a true saying, and I soon hunted out the physical cause. In other lands I knew . . . the American Southwest, Mexico, Brazil, Europe, North Africa . . . the variations of earth . . . garden to water, jungle to desert, mountain to prairie . . . were cast in a scale too vast to lie within one glance. They came to the eye seriatim, not instanter. The immediate, perpendicular wholeness of Israel's landscapes was like the immediate wholeness of its history: the flight of an insect, the thunderous word of God, were together.

After Palestine and Egypt, we went to La Rochelle (admiring the medieval chains which still shut the harbor every night) and by a little boat to Saint George, of l'Ile d'Oléron, to a rented house on the single village street. I labored at *Markand,* filling notebooks with discussion, and destroyed what I wrote. I was too close to my myth; his image kept interfering with the saga of my hero: a *mature* man's emergence in the contemporary chaos. In May, I went to Yaddo. I read most of Marx there, noting the contradictions: the pages where Marx wrote in an organic teleological sense of man, and the pages where he implicitly accepted the mechanist vision of human nature borrowed by Engels from the Darwinians. Marx was a prophet with a charisma apt to move multitudes, but a meager psychologist, a poor logician.

When the six Yaddo weeks were gone, restless, I drove up to Quebec with my wife and did not like it. Here the flavors and fragrances of France had grown rancid and black in the struggle of the French and their church against the British. We returned to Cape Cod, and I hired a shack overlooking the valley of the Pamet in Truro and could write no word of my *Markand.*

Finally at the hot close of July, I retreated alone to our apartment in New York between Columbus Avenue and the Park (almost under the equestrain statue of Bolívar) to do nothing except simmer in the city's torrid breath, waiting on the travail of my novel.

The hot August was an ordeal. There were beckoning articles and stories to write, friends to be visited, a family to rejoin. There were enticements and temptations. I saw no one, did nothing. For example: I had walked on Riverside Drive at dusk, above the river, and caught the eye of a young woman. I could imagine in her breasts and thighs her need to be taken. She too was living a vigil which might melt into delight. As she was about to pass, her face turned toward me; I held my eyes forward. I could feel her fury—physical as a flame against me as I let her go.

Mornings, the sheets under and over my body were drenched with sweat. Until one early September dawn I awoke cold; the heat was gone; I reached for a blanket; and I began to write. In a month, Book One of about 50,000 words, new and final, was on paper.

In 1932 I went to Russia, stopping on the way in Finland to win a sense of a durable people and in Stockholm to talk with Alexandra Milhailovna Kollontay, ambassadress of the Soviet Union. She presented a paradox to me. Strong, *individual,* guided by the courage to be herself, she fought for a *collective* way of life. When it came, as it threatened to come, would it produce more Kollontays, more Lenins? Or would the genes that bred such solitary heights have been levelled by the new rigid social order?

I had written virtually nothing about my month in Palestine; not only because of my self-discovered ignorance of Jewish culture, but because I observed the Arabs and the British, and feared what I saw. I did not trust them. I was right about the preparing treacheries against the Jews; I was wrong not to have seen, when the attacks came, the Jews' miraculous prevailing over foes that outnumbered them forty to one. If I had written on what I saw in Palestine, I might have expressed my fears—and harmed the *Halutzim;* if I had suppressed my doubts and fears, I would have been a dishonest reporter. I kept silent. But after my visit to the Soviet Union, I had no such incentive to be silent. The result was *Dawn in Russia.* The book anticipated my fears of Stalinism, which became explicit fears in *Chart for Rough Water* (1940). But despite ideological differences, my report on Russia was warm and hopeful. I realized that what I saw was *old* Russia turning toward the new rather than *the new.* The book was treated as news in the *New York Times* but sold only moderately. In *America Hispana* the authorized edition published in Madrid was swamped by pirated editions.

The book closed:

> We must defend the Soviet Union with our spirit; if need be, we must defend it with our bodies.

> But this does not mean that we must intellectually submit to Russia or imitate its ways and dogmas. That would be to betray the spirit which makes Russia worthy. . . . We must be loyal to the social aims of Russia; loyal to the soldiers of the revolutionary ranks, and ready to take their side in every feasible way. But above all we must be loyal—like the men of Russia—to our own needs and intuitions. *We must forge our part of the world future in the form of our own genius.*

During this time of the deepening depression down from 1930, the man-of-letters, the cultural journalist, was busy. My friend Harold Rugg, professor of education at Teachers' College, Columbia, called them the years of the Great Armistice; and it was Rugg, long before President Kennedy, who first spoke of "New Frontiers." I contributed regularly to the *New Republic* and the *New Yorker*. I gave courses at the New School in its new home on 12th Street —well-attended lectures on the aesthetic revolution. I expounded Dada (I had known Tristan Tzara in Paris) explaining why the surrealist movement was a legitimate heir in Europe and a sickly bastard in the United States. I was among the very first in the country to discuss Kafka. My greatest discovery for my own growth was that poverty had come to America. Of course, there had always been the poor in the cities and in the sharecropper farms, but not the poor hardened and fixed and frozen. The old frontiers were still open, but they were closing. Poverty as a way of life was clamping down horizons.

I saw the American hard times; went deliberately out to see and to feel them . . . in Chicago, Pittsburgh, Detroit . . . giving talks to pay my way: talks on the revolution in the arts, on inter-American relations, on Brazil's solution of the color problem (discussing color even in Southern cities), on our need of cultural vitamins, which could not be bought in bottles or in books.

Chicago's winter any year can be savage. In the black slums, in the empty stomachs of the depression, it became ferocious. The air seemed to freeze to iron in the streets of stone. The rooms, unheated or defiled by the stinking oil stove, tore at the flesh of the unemployed. When you are cold and hungry, the blood stops flowing. I knew each moment, if I could no longer bear it, I could retreat to the house of the friend with whom I was staying, which had a furnace, or to a hotel. What if I, and my friend too, were as poor as this Chicago? What if there were no furnace?

Having given a lecture in Pittsburgh (before some genteel body such as the Foreign Policy Association), I visited the neighboring steel towns. The streets, except for a few lone workers with a slender paper bag containing a can of beans, a loaf of bread, were empty. At a factory gate I saw the idle men, not even dreaming of the sun, only of the chance to earn a dollar over a pool of molten iron. The organizer of a block committee (probably a Communist) climbs on the shut iron gate and tells the men what to do about the rent. Don't pay it! Buy milk for the kids. If you can't buy the milk, take the milk. The streets of a town defend its men and women. Not these streets. Men in this industrial system had *built in* their own enemies. And now, in the cold, in the dearth, the enemy streets attacked.

One of my sallies into America was to the coal fields of Kentucky. The coal industry was ailing everywhere. But the miners of Harlan and Pineville had joined a Union more radical than the United Mine Workers led by John L. Lewis; and the operators, glad of a pretext, locked them out in their hill hovels, where they might stay and starve. Theodore Dreiser headed a committee of investigation which came back to New York with tales of terror. It was not possible, reported Dreiser, to bring in food:

> The Kentucky coal fields, where within ten years a pioneer agrarian race has been changed into a fearfully exploited proletariat, represent a danger to every one of us. Here men receive as little as 40 cents a day, and this not in cash but in the inflated form of private currency known locally as Scrip. Here miners and their families are not allowed access to the U.S. mails nor frequently even to receive visitors within their homes without permission from the superintendant. Here are year-old children forced to feed on beans and fatback bacon. And their parents must regard milk not as a food but as a medicine. . . .[20]

An independent group in New York decided to find out if this was true, and if so to act. Among us were Mary Heaton Vorse, Edmund Wilson, Quincy Howe, John Henry Hammond, Jr., Polly Boyden, Malcolm Cowley, Charles and Adelaide Walker. The train rolled them south in their comfortable pullman, as they made themselves into a committee with me as chairman.

We got off at Knoxville, Tennessee; hired two trucks; loaded them with food; wired the Mayor of Pineville, the seat of Bell County, Kentucky, that we were on our way and our intentions. At the entrance to Pineville, we were stopped by armed deputies who overturned one of the trucks and began pillaging the food. The miners had been barred from their own county seat, and the committee decided to go out to the hills to find them. But again we were stopped. Armed deputies escorted us to the police station, where we were booked for "disorderly conduct," and from there to a hotel where rooms awaited us in our virtual house arrest.

It was already dark when we were taken from our rooms, marched across town under guard, and arraigned in the crowded but silent basement court. One of the deputies dropped his gun with a clatter on the floor, marking the silence hostile. The county attorney rose and moved that the charge of disorderly conduct be quashed; the judge quashed it; and the unwelcome visitors were escorted back to our hotel and told to pack our bags.

I went up to my room, and about half a dozen citizens crowded in behind me. Someone shut the door. Their leader, who was very drunk, swinging his gun, began provoking me with insults. I packed my bag, piece by piece, while he abused me, careful to say nothing. The insulting words poured out as toothbrush, shaving kit, pyjamas, went one by one into the small suitcase. And as he spoke, he waved his revolver up and down, wildly. I was careful to say nothing, as if my life depended on it—as possibly it did. I shut the bag, opened the door. . . .

(I can still see that deputy of the law: a short, dark man with sallow skin and eyes of an oily gleam.)

The lobby was crowded and humming with excitement. We committee members, two by two for the most part, were led through the constantly banging or swinging doors into the sudden sweet cool of the mild night and into cars—a long line of cars with their lights on and motors idling. I was placed in a sedan with a man who was not of the committee: Allen Taub, a New York radical lawyer who had been retained by members of the new union and spent a week bravely and vainly seeking justice for his clients.

Taub and I occupied the rear seat, separated by a heavy man in a dark coat; another townsman sat beside the driver. It seemed to me that these men had no faces; they were all body; and it would be as useless to try to touch them with words as to speak with stones: but they were more like wood than stone, wood uprooted, no longer growing, and cut into boards.

There were voices and then a scraping sound running the whole length of the line of cars as they thrust into gear; and the cars moved slowly through the town, more swiftly out.

Death, I felt, was at close range; although I figured it more likely we would be beaten up than murdered. But my consciousness was grey and ready for death, half dead already. Fear was grey, and dull pain; death, if it was here, was grey.

The line of cars suddenly made a scimitar-shaped curve and halted. Some one shouted, "All Out!" but our driver said, "Stay where you are!" Lights vanished, and I could suddenly see the rise of the earth (we were at Cumberland Gap, where three states meet) into a spangled sky. The road broadened into a parking space for tourists stopping to see the view. But for me, the cosmos was two simple substances: earth rising and the stars.

Men approached, opened the door, and told Taub and me to get out. We stepped into darkness. I heard a shriek behind me, where Taub was; and at once I, too, was struck in the head from the rear by some metal weapon, perhaps a jack or the butt of a pistol. Some one flashed a light on Taub, and I could see Taub's brow bleeding and knew my own blood flowing, warming my brow, my scalp, and the base of my neck. There was no pain.

Someone yelled: "They've had a fight!" Another: "Who hit you?" A third: "They've been fighting together!"

I did not feel my wounds, but the lie cut me like a knife. These men were ashamed of *themselves*, did not believe in *themselves*. Their talk was that they were "defending" their homes from the foreign invader: the *Communists*, the New Yorkers. If they believed it, would they need to concoct the grotesque fraud—which went at once over the wires—that Taub and Frank had attacked each other!

I had suffered a scalp wound, a slight concussion of the brain, and a shock at the mendacity and treachery of man.[21]

6

A View of the Communists

The reader will recall my early awareness of poverty. I had found it as a boy venturing throughout my city, not only in Chatham Square but around the corner from where I lived. It was not a fixed, institutionalized state like that which, years later, I was to discover in eastern Europe and the Near East. Poverty in New York was undermined by Jefferson's democratic credo *that it could cease!* True poverty has no horizons.

Nonetheless, I poured over *How the Other Half Lives* by Jacob Riis with its gruesome photographs of city slums; studied the statistics in Robert Hunter's *Poverty*. And I was ready, before I went to college, to go along with Tolstoi on the literal Christian ways to bring poverty to its end. I was impressed even more by the anarchist Prince Kropotkin who taught that a city could feed itself adequately with intensive scientific farming on its house-tops! I read Nietzsche, Max Stirner, and Walt Whitman—none of whom was concerned with that dismal science, economics.* A favorite motto of mine was Proudhon's "La propriété, c'est le vol." (I did not know that Proudhon became a neo-Fascist, and why.) Marx, in those early days, I knew almost not at all. But I knew about him. I remember that at Yale in an economics course the professor (was it Irving Fisher?) referred just once to Marx in passing, as if he were unimportant, if not indeed a crack-pot.

When the revolutionists took Russia and set up Kerensky as premier, I turned for my accolade not to economics but to poetry, publishing "Holy Russia" in the *Seven Arts*. I recall, one day after the Bolsheviks seized power, strolling through New York's Union Square with a friend who, if my memory is correct, was a nephew of Emma Goldman and asking him who Lenin was. He replied:

*In his old age, according to Horace Traubel, Whitman leaned toward Socialism.

"Oh, he's a theorist, some sort of scholar. Writes books, knows nothing about real revolution. Lenin won't last."

Only when Lenin and Trotsky had "lasted" nearly a decade did I feel it my duty to study the texts of Marx. As I have already said, I found him wanting in a proper logic. His dialectical materialism seemed to me a quibble of definitions. If you ascribed to matter the qualities of human growth and the conscious destiny of abolishing poverty, injustice, and the class society that engendered them, were you not endowing matter with Hegel's "Absolute Spirit" or accepting Spinoza's "Substance" as God: *Natura sive Deus*? And if you conceived the proletariats of the world as bound by the laws governing Nature to replace the present world by an ethical one in which each man gave according to his means and received according to his needs, were you not restoring the Messianic role of the "Chosen People"—the workers instead of the Jews? With this grave difference; that the "Chosen People" of the Bible could sin and fail as their prophets and history showed, whereas the proletariat, according to Marx, *must* conquer, being an instrument of a law of nature. Marx, I found, went back to the meager psychology of Rousseau with its "natural good of men." Man was subtler, deeper, than that: was good and evil together. But the Messianic role of the world's proletariat had a charismic value, needing only leaders to assume it.

This was the romantic period of Communism, and I was soon swayed by it.[22] I accepted the workers' "saving grace" that fated them to change the world. Yet, I never lost my critical stance toward the over-simple Marxist psychology. Man was more than the product of his material conditions; evil was more humanly inherent than the corruption of a class society. And if you reduce man's dimensions by the dogmatic rejection of the cosmic within his self, your society will be unprepared to cope with reality and will be overwhelmed by the unadmitted in man's nature.

This is where and why religion and politics come together. I found much naiveté in Communism, whose ideals, I enjoyed saying, were "too bourgeois for me." It claimed to have the truth of the social processes working toward an absolute solution. It had a party whose decisions took the place of revelation. It saw nothing incongruous in establishing a police state to *enforce* freedom and an academy to expound and shape the truths of science according to an a priori doctrine. I was in a dilemma. I could not join a party that had doctrines and methods I considered not only wrong but dangerous. Yet so long as I was convinced, in those early

1930s, that the Communists were the sole organized instrument for the transformation of the capitalist into a socialist society, I could not oppose them. And I had been exposed to enough Marxist persuasion to feel guilt if I confined my support of a cause I believed in to writing articles and speeches at my comfortable desk. In brief, I must somehow *act*. Conviction without deed is bad ethics. This the Hebrew prophets taught as well as the Marxists.

I devised a plan. I could not join the Party; but I accepted its professed fundamental aim, the creating of free persons; even if its doctrines of the contingent nature of man and necessity of monolithic industry, and its practice, barred free persons and suppressed them. I invented the term *integral Communism* and first used it in 1931 in my *America Hispana*. I collaborated in a limited form with the Party: defending Russia's right to its own way, speaking at open meetings where that way was explained, participating in protests and in strikes; such as, the textile workers' in New Bedford, the coal miners' in Kentucky. My cunning plan was to be a "spy of God"—gain the confidence of the "comrades" by sharing their perils and their pleasures and thus gradually to win them to a deepening of their doctrine. I knew that they exploited my prestige, that they laughed at me when I insisted on "giving beyond Marx." I was a mystic; for them, almost as bad as being a moron. Nevertheless, I figured my ideas, if they were true, would move them.

Whether the folly and naiveté of this stratagem or its insolence impress you most, dear reader, you must admit that Don Quixote was again riding high. They listened to me as I expounded in my lectures, essays, books, the thesis that only the whole and integral man can create the fertile revolution—and did not hear me. So far as I know, no one took up the term *integral Communism*. No one looked, so far as I know, into the proposition that democracy must include not only all men but the whole man.

This private definition allowed me, on one or two occasions when I addressed an open meeting, to say: "We Communists", without too great deception. Or so I figured. Actually. I spread confusion about myself and failed, therefore, of the communication I desired—a failure for which I paid all the ensuing years of my life.

Could I have improved my method of communication with the American public? Doubtless, the possibility was there. But I must not regret my failure with too much masochism. I was trying to engraft some of the ideas of anarcho-syndicalism upon the still flexible body of socialism. Nationalism of industry is *not* necessarily socialization. Vision was needed that is found only in the poets: a Blake, a Whitman, a Nietzsche. But their works and values were neglected no less than my own. The time was not propitious. Only now, as I write in the 1960s, with the serious errors of orthodox Communism and orthodox socialism visible at last, is there again the opening promise of a creative social order.

My book *Dawn in Russia* revealed both my empathy and my intellectual differences with the Party. The Party discipline and order were of the sort youth loves: and drew the humblest members, for youth will pay any price to "belong", any price to possess a little reflected power. The attraction of youth is: "youth is youth is youth. . . ," ad infinitum. Among the Party members were idlers, psychopaths, schemers for getting something for nothing, half-wits, libertines, and compulsives. But the *majority* were lovers of life, haters of hate, boys and girls longing to be brave in self-bestowal. I was always stirred by their innocence, their lyricism of body and mind. But in any organization the men at the top have the qualities that push to the top: shrewdness, cunning, greed, and indifference to truth.

Came the shattering Trotsky trials, in which leader after leader of the Old Bolsheviks confessed his betrayals, pointing to Trotsky as their master in crime. The peoples of the West were floored. It was to the American mind as if Jefferson and Madison had confessed conspiring to return America to England. I wrote a "proposal" which was published in the *New Republic*. The Soviets, I argued, claim to be the fatherland of all the world's proletariats. Our concern is deep; and international, our right to hear the truth. The Soviets must heed. I proposed an international tribunal; tentatively suggested for it Romain Rolland, Bertrand Russell, Charles Evans Hughes (then a Supreme Court Justice). Let them hear the evidence on both sides and give a verdict.

Perhaps the suggestion of an international tribunal was not viable. In making it, I had a secondary motive. I was presumably a friend of Russia, of the Party, and of its American leaders. I needed to learn how free I was to express my mind . . . to speak out . . . even to make mistakes. Also, I was receiving for my books published in Russia small sum in dollars (about $1,200 a year), as part of my royalties which were in unexchangeable rubles. Were these real royalties or a retainer of my good will—in fact, a bribe? The year before, I had written to Michael Koltsov, editor of *Pravda* (he was to vanish in the Purge), asking if I had enough rubles in the Soviet bank to take my son Thomas for a visit to

Russia. He had answered: "You have enough rubles to come to Russia with your son. You have enough rubles to put him into school and to rent a villa in the Crimea. You have enough rubles to place a mistress in your villa. And if you need more rubles, we can always order a few articles for *Pravda*."

I did not like this letter. Now I might learn. . . . Word came in the next issue of the *Daily Worker*. In a signed editorial, Earl Browder, the leader, attacked me as a fool, a weakling, a hopeless bourgeois. This was in May, 1937. The days of my attempted relationship with Communists in any shape or form were over.

At about the same time, I published another proposal in the *New Republic:* an open letter to Léon Blum, premier of France. I urged him to send all possible aid to democratic Spain, which was threatened by the generals, chief of whom was Franco. The letter warned that if the Fascists were allowed to win in Spain a world war might follow. The letter, translated, I was told, became a poster on many a blank wall in Spain. Blum did nothing about it. And the War came. . . .

The flower of any revolution is its youth, even the Hitler youth had beauty. Youth, as Stirner said, is always right: "Jugend hat immer Recht." The turnover of Party members was rapid and voluminous. This meant, of course, that the eager candidates for salvation, once they were in, learned they had made a mistake and decamped, possibly for reasons as wrong as those moving them to become members. My sense of guilt and debtorship, in having profited by an unjust social system, was certainly present in my feeling for the Communist youth; but youth itself . . . just youth . . . counted also. One saw no such youths at gatherings of Republicans, Democrats, followers of Norman Thomas. Nor did the older Communist leaders have stars in their eyes like their own followers. . . .

The secretary, Earl Browder, came from one of the corn-belt states, Nebraska or Kansas. He was a dry, pleasant, reliable, transplanted Yankee, the sort that teaches in the Methodist Sunday school and helps out with the church finances. He was not brilliant, not tough; and he knew that Marx was right and Lenin, the greatest man who had ever lived, and that to speak to Trotsky was to parley with the devil. The Party president whom the secretary preceded in power was William Z. Foster who had brilliantly run the steel strike in Pennsylvania. His background also was Yankee, but he smelled more of the mill than of Methodism. He was narrow; intense; devoted, as a machine might be called devoted, to its single task. And he was tough. Somewhere along the line of his life the masters of the world had humiliated Foster, and he would make them pay for it. Browder had read books; Foster made no pretence to culture. I could not be at ease with him as I was with Browder; I was, for Foster, a member of the enemy class—even if I was smart enough to try to get out of it while there was time. About Browder, there was something boyish. Foster was cold as a jack hammer.

His running mate on the presidential ticket was a Negro named Ford[23] whose chief political asset was his color. Can deep black be flamboyant? The Party's fervor for the Negro knew no bounds, and Ford's six feet of nigrous hue endorsed it. Some of the young white girls proved their freedom from "race chauvinism" by going to bed with the black comrades. I recall one such rebel from an old family of the South, white and slender as a lily, who succumbed. But the gesture availed her nothing; she could feel nothing but distance and separation.

Robert Minor was a cartoonist of genius who gave up his art to become a Party functionary. He was a man with a mission, convinced that his faith in Marx was objective and precise as mathematics. I recall an argument with him on the beach of Truro on Cape Cod. We were talking about the "certain" Marxist future; and I cried: "But the imponderables, Bob! The imponderables—." His smile were somewhat a sneer: "There are no imponderables," he said.

The Party attracted also men of charm. Granville Hicks might have been a strict and pure Yankee deacon. His insight into books (for years he was the Party's main literary critic) was small, but his narrow vision for all works of the imagination gave security to the reader who needed to conceive himself as "chosen to have all the truth." Through Hicks, Presbyterianism; through Minor, Catholicism; through Browder, Methodism got modulated into the revolutionary symphony. By the same process of analogy Mike Gold, lovable columnist of the *Daily Worker*, might stand for the enraptured Chassidim. Mike was sentimental, effusive, sure-eyed in tilting against such bourgeois aesthetes as Thornton Wilder. He had written a book about his childhood on New York's lower East Side, *Jews without Money*, which has authentic value. When Mike came to Paris as one of the delegates to the Congrès pour la Défence de la Culture, André Gide was particularly drawn to him. Here was the real, rich proletarian odor! The man who published the proletarian books and pamphlets, read almost exclusively by bourgeois malcontents, was Alexander Trachtenberg who had the air of an itinerant Armenian rug merchant. You felt, observing him, that he would lie like any man of his trade as he spread carpet and rug on the pavement of the café terrace. Yet he was sure, selling you the Communist scriptures, that he was selling you salvation.

Because he had a better mind than most, Joseph Freeman's case was more grave. By intuition and intellection, he felt the hurdles in the Communist command. But he was too close to the political apparatus to criticise, to reject, to choose. Thus, he was forever defending what he disapproved, explaining away what remained perilously *there*. Small fish swam comfortably in the aquarium of Communist orthodoxy. Freeman's larger and more generous mind got hurt by collisions.

There was something specious in the Communist combine of Rodin's *The Thinker* trying to be Irving Berlin's Singing Waiter. A tournament of vulgarities. Good and generous minds, like Freeman's who got entangled in it got twisted.

These were all, and many others, vivid men and women: officers of an enterprise for action whose *methods contradicted its aims*. And as Marx himself said: "The means is part of the end." But he had also said: "ich bin kein Marxist"—the conflict made me unhappy because it left me homeless. I had no place to go . . . no place ready-made. The fate of my "integral communism" was a portent; I had not lost hope, but its symbol had become my friend, the crippled Randolph Bourne.

Symbol of what betrayed the hope was such a man as "Jake" Stachel, executive committeeman of the American Communist Party. I shared a hotel room several times with Jake during the presidential campaign of 1936 which I covered as correspondent for the *Daily Worker*. He was a considerate, sensitive roommate. But he was also a short, dark, cigar-smoking politician of the "manager" type to be found in the smoke-filled caucus room of any American city. Jake was smooth and slick. He could swiftly size up a situation and make it serve his purpose. Why on earth was he a Communist and not a sachem of Tammany Hall? He had got his computers mixed. There was so much of the archaic in socialist tactic and Communist strategy.

The Stachels had no use for the Bournes nor the Bournes for the Stachels. The Stachels would prevail; Bourne would die—always to be reborn. The Fosters and Browders were intermediate between them. They wanted their ideals to live, but also they wanted action. If deed issues from a false concept of man's nature, it will produce falsehood. This has been the fate of revolutions: consider our own of the eighteenth and nineteenth centuries.

When Lázaro Cárdenas was president of Mexico, he granted asylum and haven to Leon Trotsky. Diego Rivera lent his villa outside the capital; the president provided a permanent guard of soldiers to protect him and his wife from possible attacks by the Stalinists. I went to see him. My position must have seemed unfavorable to Trotsky. I had had as yet no open break with the Communists in or outside Russia. Of the innocence or guilt of the accused, I had carefully said nothing . . . indeed, knew nothing. I had also never aligned myself with Trotsky whom I respected as a man of genius. All this must have seemed to a zealot like Trotsky almost tantamount to Stalinism. My ideological criticisms of Marxism applied to Trotsky as well as to Stalin. The horror of the great Purge in Russia had not yet begun; or, at least, I was unaware of it. I did not like Stalin's police state; but I assumed that with Trotsky in power there would be a similar apparatus to implement the dictatorship of the proletariat, in which both believed. I admired Trotsky, the cultured European intellectual, more than I did Stalin, the blunt proletarian of whom I knew very little. I respected Trotsky's literary and historical writings: not deep but respectable. Yet, I suspected that Stalin was closer to the Russian people and that his program of socialist nationalism by force appealed more to them than Trotsky's thesis (inherited from Lenin) that a European revolution was more important than the Russian—even for the Russians!

When I entered the room, lined with books from floor to ceiling and colorfully furnished with much *tezontli* hue (more luminous than terra cotta), a small bearded man in *pantoufles* and a loose gown that looked like a bathrobe came forward from his desk; and his first words after the handclasp were:

"I don't know that I should shake your hand. You have been lenient with the Stalinists, to say the least. You have tacitly and implicitly aided a clique of murderers and traitors. You have certainly given no recognition of the very clear lines in this contest between true socialism, true world Communism, and the grossest sort of betrayal."

As he spoke, his face was not unfriendly; indeed, he was reservedly smiling. And he kept moving as he talked, finally beckoning me into a chair facing his own beside the table crowded with manuscripts and magazines; his words flowing, giving me no chance to defend myself against the accusation of the guilt of those I helped since I did not reject them. He gave me no chance to say anything. His smile had seemed to invade his face; now it left, but the eyes, although no longer smiling, were pleasant. He was giving me a précis of the history of Russia since the beginning of the Civil War. He knew his subject, rather more he loved it. He analyzed the power-clusters in Russia: how they came into being, how they had displaced the life-giving nuclei of the lower echelon Soviets, stifling the Soviets, self-aggrandizing, until the Soviets were choked—not dead, but helpless against the bureaucrats. Their master Stalin, he said, represented this gross phenomenon, the "rude" Stalin of Lenin's description.

A detailed account of what Trotsky said, even if I could give it, would falsify the nature of his monologue. He spoke with passion; he spoke also with compassion. And there was no personal anger in his words on Stalin, whom he seemed to regard as a natural phenomenon like a plague. Also, like the disease of Stalin, the Revolution was a *fact*. Socialist Russia was not dead, and there was no fear in Trotsky of its dying.

The flood of words was the scene of a tragedy by Euripides. Trotsky spoke in French, with a bad heavy accent more Germanic than Slav; but his vocabulary was ample. He was a tragic actor, as in Euripides, recounting the story of disaster and betrayal. He was obsessed with it; more exactly, he was entirely absorbed by his theme: this betrayal of the Revolution. But there was no hint that the Revolution would not in due time proceed. And as he spoke and spoke on his grandiose subject, he became warmer, kindlier, more aware of my presence as of a human being's. He showed me photographs of his son who, he feared, might be in Stalin's hands (it was months since the last word from him). His wife came in and I was introduced; they seemed a homely elderly pair, very Jewish, very bourgeois. Yet I knew, looking at this man, not whether he had plotted Stalin's death but that he would plot anything, and carry it out, that the Revolution, as he saw it, required. What was any single life in value?

As he stood up, silent at last, I looked at my watch. Trotsky had spoken, virtually without taking breath, for over two hours and a half. I had said nothing. He made an appointment for my return when, presumably, he would be asking me, not telling me. As I drove back to my hotel, it seemed to me that I had been with a mad man: mad in intensity, in singleness, in absolute conviction. Such a man could not "ask." He was playing a role on a world theater. This was his certainty, and he was right. Right and mad went together. Mad simply expressed how the outsider saw the right.

About this time there were two large meetings held in New York on a single night: one in Carnegie Hall, the other in a hall whose name I do not remember. I had the uncomfortable distinction of being attacked in both: by the Stalinists and by the Trotskyists. A group of liberals and radicals, headed by John Dewey, proposed to "try" Trotsky in Mexico. The entire proceedings of the first Moscow trials had been published by the Soviet government. The plan was to go through the evidence, show the absurdity of the confessions, tear them to ribbons. Dewey invited me to be one of the tribunal;* after long hesitation I declined. In a letter to Dewey, I tried to explain that I did not feel competent to weigh this evidence. The trial would be as slanted and steered as the one in Moscow. John Dewey did not like my stand and told me so in a letter that made me sad; for despite our differences I loved John Dewey. But the Mexican "trial" bore me out. The judges were all convinced beforehand that Trotsky et al. were innocent and brought in a verdict which meant nothing.

An average witness of the liberal-radical scene in those days, who had not read my books (and that was average enough!), could hardly be blamed for assuming that I was a Communist of the Party. My own brand of *integral Communism* was not noticed. It was true that even my brief articles showed deep fissures of difference from Communism and Marx; but in the temper of the times, the difference did not seem to matter. Americans have never been strong in concepts. The comrades themselves appeared to take me for granted.

For example:

1. A Writers Congress, of left complexion, was held in New York at the New School and established itself as the League of American Writers. It elected me its first chairman, by acclamation. This meant, of course, that I was the choice of the steering committee, which was almost entirely Communist. No other candidate was named.

2. Paris staged a Congrès pour la Défence de la Culture. I was invited to attend by cables signed Maxim Gorki, Romain Rolland, André Gide, André Malraux, Louis Aragon; and headed the American delegation. It was a spectacular affair held in a sweltering

*Among its members, beside Dewey, were Suzanne LaFollette; Ben Stolberg; Otto Ruehl, a personal friend of Trotsky, and Carleton Beals (who withdrew properly for the same reasons that made me decline).

July in the Palais de la Mutualité, one of the largest auditoriums of Paris. The public, at nominal cost, sat in the rear of the *parquet* or the balcony to hear the great writers. In the front were the delegations, facing the podium table. The Russians alone were over a hundred strong, including Alexis Tolstoi, Ehrenburg, Koltsov of *Pravda,* Pasternak the poet. Among the British were Aldous Huxley, John Strachey, and E. M. Forster. Heinrich Mann, Ernst Toller, Anna Leghers, and Bertholt Brecht headed the Germans (Thomas Mann was too cagey to appear). The show was generously financed by the Soviets. We were instructed to give Aragon (of the French party) a full list of our expenses including travel, and our statements were immediately paid. There was nothing wrong in this. Without Russia the congress would not have taken place, and Russia's role was not hidden. But wait. . . . The Soviets issued a sumptuous volume (in Russian) giving the principal papers and discussions, photographs and sketches of the chief participants. My paper before the League of American Writers had been: "The Writer: Minister of Freedom;" in Paris, I spoke on "The Writer's Part in Communism"; and I discovered that in the book several of my paragraphs critical of ordinary Marxism had been omitted—without notice!

3. The American magazine field remained vacant. The *Masses* and the *Liberator* were gone. Max Eastman, whose physical beauty and verbal glamor concealed his weaknesses, had betrayed their cause when the editors were tried for "obstructing the draft" by declaring that he was in essential agreement with President Wilson! So the call went forth for a *New Masses.* Charles Garland, an idealistic youth from Boston, established the Garland Fund with his inheritance and devoted it all to the destruction of the capitalist system. He offered $17,000 to the magazine if it raised $8,500. Those who attended the first meeting or sent messages included Joseph Freeman, Mike Gold, Granville Hicks, John Dos Passos (who wrote in, "I am absolutely with you"), Susan Glaspell, Eugene O'Neill, Carl Sandburg, Sherwood Anderson, Elmer Rice, Lewis Mumford, Stuart Chase, H. L. Mencken, Bernard Shaw, E. A. Robinson, Rex Stout who donated the office furniture; and Freda Kirchwey. Those who attended (twenty-three) were summarily made associate editors, and I was voted chief editor with Edwin Seaver as my editorial assistant.

Before the first issue, I had resigned, and Seaver too, to be replaced by Joe Freeman and Mike Gold. What had happened? Had I learned I was a Communist "front?" Not at all. When the Left writers wrote they wanted "space for the type of discussion of spiritual values for the younger generation of which Waldo Frank has been the exponent," were they hypocrites? Not all all. I had been moved in the heat of the meeting to accept, partly by vanity (venial sin), partly by pride (mortal sin); and I was not ready; I would never be ready, because I had no time. I felt that my unwritten books came first and that an active editorship would hinder them—the more creative the magazine, the less time for my unwritten books.

4. Lázaro Cárdenas called a Congress of "American Revolutionary Writers and Artists." It met in Mexico's huge, hideous Palacio de Bellas Artes, final monument to the insincerities of the regime of Porfirio Díaz. I was invited to give one of the opening addresses and also the valedictory. My paper, similar to the one I had read in Paris, included a passage critical of the conventional Communist *agitprop* attitude toward art—like the ones the Soviet edition had deleted. And as I delivered it, I felt the mass before me of young delegates, mostly writers and painters of the Americas, turn cold. When the general public seated behind them applauded, *they* remained silent. I felt significance in their coolness, and it frightened me. Was a whole generation coming, who would be insensitive and calloused?

In May of 1937 came my proposal, in the *New Republic,* of an international Trotsky trial and Browder's immediate angry rejection of all I stood for. Since then I have had no relations with the Communists. Which I regret. But I realize how quixotic was my plan to influence a monolithic movement set up on the premise of war and with a psychology for war. President Cárdenas thoroughly understood this. There was nothing in him of the milky liberalism of Argentina's Irigoyen and nothing like the fanaticism of Lombardo Toledano, the strongly pro-Russian labor leader with whom Cárdenas worked. Cárdenas sped the establishment of the *ejidos,* the communal farms; and, after long self-searching, he nationalized the entire industry of oil. It seemed to him the only way to cope with the little Yankee oil "states" within the Mexican state. In addition to its economic values, it was a step toward freedom. Cárdenas told me that when he was overcome with doubts he had been helped to his oil decision by my book *The Rediscovery of America.* It gave him, he said, courage and insight to reach his verdict. I was moved by this. Every writer, I suspect, wants to play a role of action.

Cárdenas worked out a strange method of being president. He was almost never in the capital, constantly on the march as if his journeys were campaigns. He made it a goal, before his six-year term was over, to know every community in the country. He invited me to come along with him on several of his journeys, as far north as Chihuahua, as far south as Tehuantepec and Oaxaca. We went by plane, by train, by car along dusty roads. Often, in the mountains, the way was too steep for cars. Then we went by horseback (Cárdenas had some splendid mounts); and, I recall to reach one village in the Sierra de Juárez we had to leave our horses and proceed by muleback. These visits would never be announced in advance by more than a day or two: just time enough for the surprised hosts to get a feast ready and a long list of complaints and statistics. Here the señor presidente was welcomed by the town fathers. Here a little later he was seated at a table, perhaps outdoors, flanked by two secretaries who put down names, details of grievances, promises. If the town was large enough to have a plaza, Cárdenas would stroll through it chatting with the neighbors.

Despite Mexico's bad record of political assassinations, he took no precautions on these journeys into the heart of his land. When the end of his term neared, friends began to urge him to evade the constitutional law of no re-election. Cárdenas' work, they said, was too vital to delay or to cut short or to place in new hands. Communication among the people was too delicate, too young, too open to the hostility of oil and State Department, to risk a change of regime in midstream. Cárdenas turned down the proposal with a flat no. What his country needed more than any specific leader or reform, he said, was the habit of obedience to the constitution. He went farther. The true heir of President Cárdenas was General Francisco Múgica, a socialist of irreproachable ability, from whom Cárdenas had learned much. He could have thrown his influence to Múgica's nomination in the Party where it meant election. He refused, fearing the United States would find pretexts to intervene, choosing to propitiate the deadly northern danger. (The successor turned out to be Manuel Avila Camacho, a dull middle-of-the-road man who brought the doldrums to Mexico and had one virtue: he reassured the nervous State Department.)

This book is a portrait of the author. It should convince; and perhaps the reader does not see how I could be drawn so close to a regimented group—the Communists—whose ideology was alien to my basic anarchist temperament. First of all, I disliked Marxism's foes; I despised a civilization whose central motor was "the market" and whose leaders were men willing to serve "money."

Also, I realized the existence of a crisis which called for organization if the good in our culture—the great good—was to be saved. I never joined a political body; I rejected the authoritarianism of all or any; but in those years of stress (they have continued), I realized the necessity of order.

Most of all Communism, although I could not accept it, tempted me, I believe and—when I saw the Communist youth—moved me—because it seemed to offer a *community;* and to belong to a community was what I needed.

My way of life, by the time I had passed forty, had brushed by several communities which failed to hold me. The community of the Orthodox Jews that had deeply stirred me in Poland, in Palestine, was not for me. The community of Reform Jews, dwindling down at last to the Society for Ethical Culture, was not for me (it seemed to have satisfied my father) because it ignored the plan of ritual and myth to express the truths of deep religion, which a rationalist ethic cannot touch. I had had a fruitful time at Yale but found there no community to share. Nor could I make a whole of the entire country or city to dwell in it—dwell in New York or Paris or Spain except as a visitor. I was interested in the psychological techniques of India, versions of which came to us through Gurdjieff, Orage, and Ouspensky. A handful of us met one afternoon a week at the house of Herbert Croly, who had been baptised in the Positivist Church—quite a gamut! But these were all methods, however disguised, for getting free of community, free from social human life as *not good*—the contrary of the Hebrew community in the Bible which learned from the Creator that Creation is *good.* The great Eastern techniques all led to the symbolic forest and its escape from family, city, and state.

In the thirties, I wanted to be ravished by a community; and it was tragic for me that the Communists would not do, until I had made amendments which exiled me from *their* community as surely as theological differences exiled me from the communities of Jew and Christian. This was the search which traced the death and birth of *David Markand,* and for which I was ready to risk my life.

One summer morning of the thirties, I had looked out the window of the little cottage we rented in Truro on Cape Cod and saw a young man on a bike draw up at the front door. He was a short, soft-bodied man with fine features stamped sharp within the surrounding contours of his face, already heavy jowled. It was Edmund Wilson, and he had done me the honor of pedaling the twelve miles from Provincetown to see me. I have no memory of what we discussed but what he wrote at that time can serve to summarize what we both were feeling.

"Let's Take Communism Away from the Communists," wrote Edmund Wilson.

What he meant, of course, was that there was much in Marxist Communism which our Judaeo-Graeco-Christian nationalist culture of the West could integrate into our way of life: avoiding the alien ways of Eastern peoples who had never had a Wyclif or a Milton nor experienced the social-democratic dimension within the cosmic . . . the cosmic within the social . . . of the Hebrew Prophets.

It was a genial *aperçu*, this slogan of Edmund Wilson, far transcending cleverness. But, as we learned, it was disqualified by the irony of facts: by an East trying to achieve equality through a police state which, according to the theory, would permit itself to dwindle and die out, and by a West trying to achieve freedom in a system whose essence was the ignoble scramble for individual profit and gang power.

Wilson's happy phrase was repeated for a while and then forgotten. No more than my *integral Communism*, did it make a clearing for itself in that decade's jungle of loose thinking.

7

Freud and the Shekhina

I first heard the name of Freud in 1913, when he was already famous—or infamous—among the alert of Europe, and had already visited America and been honored by Clark University in Worcester, Massachusetts. It was at a small gathering in the New York Central Park West apartment Margaret Naumburg shared with her parents. I had recently been introduced to her by Claire Raphael (the reader will recall her and the trio evenings at *her* Central Park West apartment). The two young women had plans to capture and revolutionize New York's Board of Education and had opened *The Children's School* which later took the name of *Walden* in homage to Thoreau.

Margaret was a beautiful woman, dark, with great luminous eyes and a dynamic compassion that was not ready to settle for less than a totally new world. She had just returned from Rome where she studied primary education with Maria Montessori and from London where she took courses with Graham Wallas at the School of Economics. She spoke of Freud as if there stirred in her a prescience of the psychological revolution Freud would bring to the world in the next five decades. She lent me a book, *The Psychology of Insanity* by a man named Bernard Hart, another by Ernest Jones, and a third which was part of the "gospel" itself: *The Psychopathology of Everyday Life,* translated by Dr. A. A. Brill. His muddy English could not slow the recognition that this was a great writer. In fact, Freud had already written his masterpiece *Traumdeutung*, "the Meaning of Dreams," a self-interpretation which should rank, through its influence wide and deep, with the great Confessions: Augustine and Rousseau, Amiel and Henry Adams. . . . Freud had granted Brill permission to translate him into English, casually and carelessly, because he was convinced that no one would want to read him anyway.

My first exposure to the cosmogony of Freud elated me because I had had glimmers of intimation in my own life. I had guessed, for example, a connection between what I felt for the southern girl in Lausanne and what I felt for my mother; and that the chaste, inhibitory mask over my love for my mother corresponded with the repressed passion for the girl making it equally "pure." The pieces of the myth of Oedipus fell into place for me like an easy picture puzzle. A few years later I was writing *The Unwelcome Man*. According to a recent essay by Gorham Munson, this is the first psychoanalytic novel in our literature. I do not know how correct that is, and from the standpoint of literature it is unimportant. The novel, and its successor *The Dark Mother*, were experiments that did not succeed as *novels*, wanting a form adequate to their substance. I mention these *oeuvres de jeunesse* because they reveal an affinity to this story. In the same essay, Munson gives the chief credit for starting the 1920s to these early novels, to the *Seven Arts*, and to *Our America* (1919). More significant to me, however, was my disagreement with Freud's metaphysics —or want of one.[24]

I must have sent Freud a copy of my book, for I got a card from him that I treasure. He thanked me for "Ihr ausgezeichnetes Buch," *Our America*.

Freud, in those days before we entered the First World War, was a guide to our immaturities and a balm to our guilt of having abandoned the house of our fathers. The heart of this ferment (it could hardly be said to have a mind) was Greenwich Village. The Liberal Club and Polly's restaurant on MacDougal Street provided a stage. George Cram Cook, Susan Glaspell, Floyd Dell, and Eugene O'Neill wrote plays overtly or implicitly Freudian. The sliding doors dividing the entire first floor of the old house could be opened, and there was an auditorium ready made for argumental meetings. At Polly's the neophytes of the new revelation wrangled, over their dime's worth of beans served in wooden bowls; and such hierophants as Brill, Paul Federn, Smith Ely Jeliffe, in more formal meetings, led the devout down into the intricate dark of what Freud was to call id, which "must become ego."

Brill had named his daughter Gioia, Italian for Freud(e) (joy), and this was typical of the invasiveness of Freud's new presence. He opened a way to life, and the others had a good time living it. I insisted that the self had a dimension Freud ignored, "the direct conduit to Cosmos"; Freud ignored it, indeed, but he was later forced by indirection to acknowledge its existence. Consciously, his philosophy, like Darwin's, was a biologism. The cosmic was nonetheless there, but I was too hurried to remark it. What we wanted, once he had showed us the way, was release from the obsolescent ethic of the middle class. Freud made the mistake of confounding ethics with a particular form of it. What Freud called libido was an indefinably pervasive as Bergson's *élan vital.* It unified life, and this unity was implicit in such conceptions as the "polymorphous perverse" love of the child for his mother or the incestuous appetite of the daughter for her father. My knowledge of Freud was too shallow not to be derouted by his aggressive searchings for the laws of life.

The fervor for Freud among the young people who gathered at the Liberal Club can, of course, not be explained as mere sexual licence; although this played its part. Sex was justified as the life-force and this draws together—as we shall see—Freud's libido and the kabala's Shekhina in all its mystery. The most impassioned posts of that day were priests seeking temples in the "sticks and stones" of modern cities, to use Lewis Mumford's words. We all read D. H. Lawrence, the prophet angered because he had no church; and Joyce who tried to build a church of his own from the rubble of Europe's civilization, achieving only a stupendous solipsism; and Proust whose remembrance of things past was clouds of many colors between the earth and the sun. The world of Freudian wish was a fantasma befitting the disintegrated world of Western culture. Novelists, dramatists, physicists, and poets confronted it. Franz Kafka struck the tonal note. The best audiences went to the revealers of nonidentity, of nescience. The apocalyptists, as I was to call those who saw with inward eye the lineaments of a new culture and strove to place them, had fewer followers. I was among them.

Meanwhile, it was a thrilling adventure for me to talk with such a man as Paul Federn, one of the Austrian group closest to Freud. He was a blackbearded pale-faced man gaunt with Svengali eyes. Since I understood German, I could receive from him the excitment not of so slight a thing as a new continent but of a new morning . . . like a Spaniard who has sailed westward with Columbus and tells his experience to another who remained behind.

Freud of course by his own definition was an antireligious man. The definition was wrong; his vision was right. For him the human world, even unto the will to die, was a structured organism suffused with an energy as dynamic as the "Absolute" of Hegel, the "Substance" of Spinoza. The kabalists also knew it, and it joined them together with Jehovah. They called it Shekhina. It vastly transcended the specific sex of Freud; and Freud knew this, at last. There were contradictions in Freud no less than those I found in Marx. *Totem and tabu* "explained" everything except the emergence of a society as differentiation of the cosmic within man's mind and the mind's transcending of space and time. (This the id revealed in the death wish, in telepathy and prevision; and Freud in his old age admitted it.) Freud's study of Leonardo da Vinci made no distinction between the biological and the symbolic mothers; and his small volume *Moses and Monotheism* was a downright bad book, like the scribblings of a naughty boy on the walls of a privy. Why does Freud need to shock? To rob the Jews of their mythic hero by "debunking" Moses? Was Freud still immersed in, and rebelling against, the barrens of Victorian puritanism? Boys and girls bounced from bed to bed. To be a virgin was a disgrace in Greenwich Village. But I suspect a far subtler displacement. Freud overstresses the specificities of sex because he is fighting the religion in himself.

Not understanding the depths of Freud, I feared him . . . because of what seemed to me his metaphysical limitations—and his social, too. A revolutionary like all the starters of my generation (how we ended up was a different matter), I resented the nature of a therapy that implied adjustment to the detestable capitalist world. I rejected Freud's limited naturalism and the arrogance with which he turned out such shallow phrases as "God is the father image." We knew, despite the poor translations, that Freud was a great writer; but what we wanted was release from our own bourgeois culture; and this we sought in Nietzsche rather than Freud. Dr. Brill saw my fear of Freud; and his eyes twinkled with amusement when he said: "Why don't you visit Vienna?" Brill was a penetrant and tender man. His trouble as a divulger of the new Austrian "gospel" was that he did not know how to write English.

Marx was a sometimes surly man with a huge beard, whose linen was frayed and often soiled. His myth has moved mountains of men. His dialectic is the progress toward the Messiah and not more "scientific" than the theoretical theocracies of Alexandria. Day after day, year after year, Marx worked at his chilly British Museum table, "proving" that the classes and class strife would disappear, for man was "good." Seven times in the first chapter of Genesis God beholds his creation and finds it "good." History as the approaching Messiah conceived by Marx is a poem, and now is being written by the multitudes of Asia and eastern Europe.

Freud at work converges with Marx, seeking a unitary principle in the libido which is wounded by life and heals as it becomes whole consciousness. Freud at work, like Marx, is really Freud at worship; for his confident faith is in the efficacy of the Ego to transfigure the Id and make man whole. The kabala moves toward the same end with its primitive instruments of symbol and allegory. Freud's *method,* unlike his enthusiastic faith, is the strict observation and analysis of science—the microscope turned inward—this is its sole superiority over Western religion. But Freud's end is the *end* of true religion. Man, it says, is potentially good. The kabala, with the presence of the Shekhina, teaches that the creation of worlds takes place within God who then contracts and withdraws leaving a part of himself "outside" to be re-integrated. This is close to the procedure of Socrates, separating by analysis in order to reunite as synthesis. And it is the method of the psychoanalytic hour—or should be. For, of course, error crept in at once. There were analysts who mistook adjustment to a sick society as "cure"; there were others who mistook dream for apocalypse and taught that what the dream revealed must be the "Truth" and be followed.

I was discovering in the 1930s that the "materialism" of both men was a colossal fraud. Marx's masses moving ineluctibly toward Utopia and the classless society were as organic as a breathing body and as steeped in mystery. And the foundation of Freud was that man not only could be healed but was worth healing—even by a long and onerous process. Freud's libido is premised on an indefensible optimism—the ultimate triumph of Ego over the ferocities of Id—which is both blind and clairvoyant. Man *must,* according to this doctrine, reach the good. The Hebrew prophets knew no such fantasy. The Hebrews could do wrong and be punished by disaster. The Marxist, and likewise the follower of Freud, is moved by an immutable "law" which is not discernible by scientific method.

Of course, a doctrine with such deep roots and voluminous foliations as Freud's inspired extreme responses: the age rejected it as the plague or swallowed it whole as revelation. But major allies of Freud began to appear: the American Trigant Borrow, and above all the Swiss C. G. Jung who might be called the first master of psychic paleontology, tracing the geologic strata of the mind back to a "collective unconscious" that corresponded to the findings of Hindu and kabala mystics. Plunged into this sea, I had to swim hard in order not to drown; and there were times when I appeared to be drowning.

In the *Targum,* the Aramaic version of the Scriptures, and in the medieval mystical literature of the Jews known as the kabala there occurs this word that is crucial—and never precisely defined. It is Shekhina. When Jehovah appears to Moses on Mount Sinai, it is Shekhina that is present and that speaks. In another passage, Moses becomes the husband of Shekhina. It is "the Great radiance," in which Jehovah maintains his silence, carrying the universe. It is the "inner glory"; it is "no form but a voice," appearing in place of body. Gershom Scholem, the subject's great authority, observes that Jewish mysticism differs from all others in the total lack of a feminine element.[25] Shekhina is the exception. Every true marriage binds Jehovah and Shekhina in symbolic union. There is no passage, of course, in Jewish letters where the divine body is revealed. But Shekhina bares cosmos in erotic terms. One can transpose, without loss of pitch, the Shekhina into Freud's libido. This is a default of the literal truth perhaps—but Russia and China are here to prove that it raises armies.

I remembered my reading at college: the Jewish, Christian, and Islamic schoolmen. I realized sharply how much shallower were the eighteenth-century empiricists. I knew nothing of the kabala. Therefore I was not ready to understand what Freud meant by libido and by his relating all energy to sex. Freud, indeed, did not understand until late in his long career. He was a neurologist and a therapist because he needed human material for his laboratory. But he was a physician because of his compassion for suffering man and woman. His search was close in aim to the kabala. Man was to achieve power over himself by the achievement of *knowledge*. And this knowledge was like the engineer's, making faith and intuition secondary. This instrumental knowledge would shape man in health, in love, in illness . . . in the will both to live and to die. These words sound equally like Freud and like the kabala.

My own sex life was full of trouble. I could not carry on the mental posture common to the West, particularly the Latin lands, toward the sex act as *la bagatelle,* making it a game like tennis. I had encountered it, of course, in Paris and elsewhere, and I had more than once tried it. Literally it made me sick. There was a deeper pagan concept of sex as mystery and ritual. I accepted it. The Hindu cult of Tantrism, which ennobles the act as the archetypal union of two into the One, attracted me. My sex partner had to play a conscious drama of fusion and of union with my *idea.* Of course, this caused trouble. It was a burden for the woman to find her body exalted as an allegory and ignored as a fact. If they are honest with themselves, women do not like it. My second wife, for instance, who was a blue eyed, golden haired Yankee from New Hampshire found that her "accepting" me meant (to me) Anglo-America's acceptance of the dark Mediterranean "outsider." We did not know each other, not physically, not emotionally. My image of her was a barrier between us. And while for a term the myth flourished, love, which *is* knowing, agonized.

In the twenties and thirties the invitation to sexual experiment and experience prevailed wherever youths and girls emerged from their cocoons and buzzed about like newborn flies. Like every presentable young man, I was constantly being tempted to play the game of *la bagatelle* and constantly failing. And when I did not fail, I suffered more. I recall a typical encounter with a lusty woman who adored the play of sex as a ravenous child loved food. We dined over two bottles of wine; we went to my apartment, and the embrace began. It was highly creditable to the male ego. The woman responded and responded. I was a good instrument. Sated, the woman got up, dressed and left. I lay in a violent tremor that lasted twenty-four hours; and when the woman next day again offered me her superb body, I was nauseous.

I recall another typical episode with a very modern daughter of the "earth." It was October, and I was alone in my Cape Cod house. The ocean beach was empty, and I went in naked. A woman came out of the surf, and I saw that she was also nude. There was no embarrasment between us. We dressed silently and drove to her home. There, still without words, we undressed again. I achieved the detachment she desired and became what is known as a good lover. From that day I could not bear this woman. Alone with her I succumbed to the devotions of sheer sex she wanted. I was enslaved. Since I could not avoid her otherwise, I ran away from the Cape.

There were ignoble passages. . . . In the third floor hall room of my lodging house on Washington Place lived a girl whom I occasionally crossed on the way to and from the floor's common bathroom. She was a homely little mouse with small scared eyes. I had noticed her smile and was aware of what it meant. One evening I passed her in the hall, but turned and went with her. She locked her door; and I saw her meager home, barely wide enough for the cot, the bureau, and the chair. I helped her un-dress, for she was trembling; and I embraced her to combat her chill; and this desire to impart my warmth was the nearest I got to union between us. As if I were in a hurry with an engagement elsewhere, I entered her dry little body and ejaculated almost at once. Then I threw on my clothes, not even kissing her goodbye., and left her.

Returned to my large room, I pulled a small notebook from my pocket. It contained the list of names of women I had gone to bed with. I realized then that I did not know the girl's name.

This episode also is misleading. I refused many an invitation to the feast of sex after I had won it, overcome by a sense of disharmony with the woman. Often I was like a virgin whose desire takes the form of freezing fear because it is too great to bear. I found as I passed thirty that I was trading on my gifts. I don't think I was an unusually attractive man; and there were several types of women who looked through me as I were not there, so little did what *was* there interest them. But there were others who were romantically thrilled by the poet, the rebel. Women of this ilk climbed the five flights to my attic in Paris or came to my room in New York. I found I was exploiting my talents to ready women for bed. I would read a poem or a chapter of my own to thrill them. My intellectual and aesthetic powers became secondary sexual characteristics. In the hush and heat of the room, I could not resist this dishonesty. I resolved not to permit it, again and again.

But it is also falsifying to stress these abuses as if they were alone. The dominant will and trend of my sexual life was probably to *allegorize*—as in the case of my wife who had to represent Anglo-America welcoming the little Jew. Nothing could have burdened a woman more, and satisfied her less. For woman is the realist of the human story; man being the discoverer of mystery, the dreamer of mystery within mystery, against whom woman musters facts that ignore mystery altogether. Which leaves it nonetheless true that woman is the arch-conveyor of mystery to man.

I suspect that this idealizing was as destructive as my deliberate sabotage of the marriage vow with my first wife. We had wanted to live openly together because we loved each other. She was an educator of whom "respectability" was expected; therefore, we had to be married. But it was understood between us that we were not really married. And I kept the matter clear by my infidelities, of which I always told her. The birth of my first son changed my heart; I wanted now to be truly married to my wife. But it was too late; she had suffered too much; she insisted, now that I was more than willing to be a husband, on the sundering at Reno.

A paradoxical fact: despite my normal "successes" with women, I could not believe that any woman loved me. Was this because my mother represented woman's love for me and I did not believe her love? And if not, why not? The modern psychologist would hunt for some flaw in my mother's love for me; and, of course, since she was human he would find it. (My mother longed for the applause she would have had as a professional *Lieder-saengerin,* if her parents had permitted.) I think a likelier interpretation of the paradox would focus on the overbearing contradictory demands of my ego to possess my mother and yet be free of her, which meant that my love for her could not freely flow, nor hers for me. It is common for the child to feel he is neglected by the mother when in truth child and mother both are defending themselves from being—and longing to be—devoured.

The most witching hour of home, when I was still a child yet old enough to share the evening meal with the family, was just before dinner. The delightful aromas of the feast to come in a half hour rose from the kitchen; and they were merged, of course, with mother the provider. While we waited, she would place herself at the piano and sing songs of the romantics, Schubert and Brahms and Hugo Wolf, each one a dish that blended with the aromas rising from the kitchen. From the street came the night and shut out the street, and made itself a fastness of deep security. (The children of the Great Depression lacked this deep security forever.)

When the time arrived for our separation, Margaret proposed an alternative: that we go to Vienna and see Freud. This help I feared, as I rejected Freud's seeming lack of conscious metaphysic. The analytic process can be a dangerous simplification of life, which may block the organic syntheses of living before they can mature. The analytic process (if it is alone) may distort and sterilize experience unless it is matriced in the intuition of wholeness. Quite crudely I feared Freud. I think I was wrong. Freud would not have substituted in my mind analysis for living, despite his biologism. He was deeper than he knew. Yet perhaps also I was right. Freud was the older and stronger man. And there was an arrogance in Freud; there was a rancor, a petulant wilful child's, best seen in his worst book, *Moses and Monotheism,* where Freud seeks, on very weak ground, to destroy the Hebrew's role in revealing the One God. Perhaps I was a coward. Yet my refusal to go to Freud, also perhaps, was wisely self-defensive. I learned only later, as we have seen, that there was in Freud's concept of the libido room for the acceptance of the unity of cosmos *within* each man, symbolized in the kabala by the Shekhina and by the open questions Freud allowed for such phenomena as telepathy, clairvoyance, and prevision: all proving that space and time are real only as appearance is real. For extrasensory perception and prevision of future events annihilate space and time as we think we know them.

If Western man survives, a new religion (probably under another name then religion) will carry on the task proposed by such books as *Rediscovery of Man*: the task of relating man socially, esthetically, and *effectively* with the cosmos that is in him. This transformation of the ego, infinities of physics and biology can not touch. This *is* religion. The ultimate science. Freud's part in it—a method for revealing and classifying the dynamic elements of the individual—will then be seen as central.

The base of communism is a *faith* in the ultimate reason and reasonableness of man, causing him to move mountains—and in the direction of human love and justice. This is a wish outside the intrinsic nature of nature (which knows no justice and no love but the draw of gravitation). The Messiah-wish of the Jews or the nirvana-wish of the Hindus lies outside physical nature. Therefore communism is a religion. And religious, also, is the faith of Freud in the capacity of the Id to rise into Ego and of the Ego to rise into cosmic consciousness.

III

"Death" of Waldo Frank

1

Violence and Queen Victoria

Cicero, Roman rationalist, in his *Tusculan Disputations* wrote, "Almost all things are arranged in sevens," and believed with Pythagoras that the universe was built of numbers (our nuclear physicist might agree). Newton, archmechanist, who gave the physical cosmos of Descartes its language—mathematics—spent more hours in deciphering the Prophetic Codes of the Book of Daniel than in discerning the laws of motion. But then, all intelligent men are more or less superstitious; and there is reason for it. The intelligent mind, which is good insofar as it knows its place, is aware that its structures expressed in the three dimensions and in time are *impossibles*. How can space end or time begin? What is before and what beyond them? Rational man, as he looks at his own measures, finds them suffused with the immeasurable, unbearable to our mind. The infinite is unthinkable in terms of the mind. Try to spot it, and you will find you have swerved back into the finite. But no less is the finite unthinkable, which constantly "leaks" into the infinite which issues into nothing and rejoins it: the nothing of the future, the nothing of the past. Finite like infinite erase each other.

The structure of the wildest dream is solid contrasted with the foundationless derangements of the real according to time and the dimensions used by mathematics. From Plato to Hume or Kant the philosophers agree at least in this: the finite that leads to the infinite or adds up to it is nonsense; likewise the infinite that backs down to the finite is nonsense. There is no language of the mind that can modulate from finite space to infinite, and there is no language of the mind that can touch the beginning or the end of time. If a method exists for expressing space and time, it is beyond our logic, but not by way of the positivists who simply omit from the real what they cannot grasp. For our existence is saturated by what we cannot understand. The reader will now know why the intelligent are prone to being soft toward superstition. The rational is superb for plotting and practicing the motion of the planets, the atom, and the stars; for these activities are still entirely within the matrix of appearance, as are the motions within our body entirely within the matrix of appearance never touching the real *noumenon*.

A line can never express a life. Life is not linear. Wherefore, the conventional biography is a fraud, and I have attempted to avoid the imposture.[26] The latest and last decades of my existence cannot be limned in a Euclidean graph. From one year to the next my actions and emotions follow no simple statement from the yesteday to the tomorrows. My friend Stieglitz used to say, "no one ever changes." On the level of essence this is true: all I ever became was implicit in my earliest hour of "revelation." All my search for methodology to reach the truth was already present in the child making a continent of his body in the bath. Another beloved friend, Reinhold Niebuhr, when I once asked him why he did not write his life, answered, "no man writing his auto-biography can help lying." But the lie as one bespeaks one's life can reveal the truth. The lie can depict the man as faithfully as the sincerest statement.

Now I return to my unfinished remarks on superstition. The man who respects the superstition of astrology reveals that he knows the connectedness of all things, the continuum of all matter and life. The Roman who defers a journey because he stumbled over the threshold of his home reveals that he is aware of the false step in his stumble. I have been superstitious, without solemnity, indeed with more than a grain of salt, since I was a child walking on the stone pavement of the street, avoiding the cracks as if they were indeed an abyss I had to leap across as I leapt across the lime kiln. I would come to a town where I was to deliver a lecture and add up the digits of my hotel room. If they came to a multiple of seven, I knew that my lecture would be good. If no such figure emerged, I'd forget about it in a moment. It never occurred to me to change rooms. If I had, the game was over.

In a sense, as author of this autobiography my task is finished. In regard to the facts, there is not much more for me to say. In regard to the dimensions which contain a living life, everything is yet to say. I was this paradoxical man of letters crusading as fondly as Don Quixote. I was also a man of family with wife and children, generating the common glandular excitements and inspirations. I was a man of letters where there was no audience for letters. Citizen of a republic which equated the laws and justice only by elimination. The wonder of life which was constantly with me, on the other hand, was not an ethic. I found and loved beauty decades before I asked what it meant. (I did not know that when I could define love and beauty and did define them my commission signed with God would be done.) None of this could be touched by a line. The linear testament has no place here whatever. But on the other hand, the child lying in his bath, which his body displaces, and observing his male organ is related immediately with the man at his desk writing and with the man on the platform explaining to his hearers the democracy prevailing in Brazil or the desperate lost fear in Franz Kafka.

Is there perhaps a relation, acute and earnest, between man as an organism that in our dimensions seems to cover the earth and that long lost boy in his bath, or equally naked as he goes about the country giving lectures?

Yes, I have been trying to say all my life, a good mind is one that knows its place. Mind's place, its function, is to stand amazed before concepts of structure. There are other conduits to knowledge which, as I lived and wrote, became books and ways of revelation.

One fact is clear to me after more than a half century of seeking: man is not running this show. Every cue, every stance reveals this if only we would look and see that the eruption of forms—be it a toadstool, a virus, a flower, a human emerging from a fetus to human being—do not reckon what they are nor even guess where they are from and what they are. This is an epiphany of not knowing, not knowing which becomes the human advance into a knowing that we know nothing. Not a cell, not a myriad of cells forming an organism knows . . . first anything then nothing. We become aware of our unawareness within which we stumble and labor . . . first anything then nothing, we become aware of our unawareness; and that is something.

Life as it seized each of us has been exciting to consider. We are *fired* into living like an explosion. The implosion of a nuclear bomb is a more faithful expression of what happens as each child is suddenly exposed to the limitations of daylight. From the true seeing dark it has been borne away into the constant burst of being he will namelessly accept as living. The vast mushroom of cloud rises; the air withers into orgasm, into ecstasy; and all that is no ecstasy is destruction: thus a child opens into life. He devours: first his mother's breast, soon plant and beast. He is no less the devourer, eating his way into weaker lives that cannot resist him. Yet the converse is true no less: life rapes the newborn.

Everything the child experiences and learns is this organism of living. Out of this hugeness, peculiar, purblind little men and women whittle down their rational conclusions, citing Euclid or the positivists; but it is evident to the wielders of logic that logic simply leads to its own annihilation.

Youth of today will never know what the world was before the bomb. The decades since the close of the Second World War could be divided meaningfully between the bomb and the experiences which preceded the bomb and still function as if the bomb were not yet present. My existence had varied categories which seemed almost to have created themselves, to have made their own way. There was, for instance, the relation with America Hispana. I had had what I thought was a love affair with this great inchoate world, and it had turned out to be a marriage. I did not slight its importance to me; I merely marvelled at the stubborness of the organic process. No matter what I say, America Hispana insists that I am an expert, an "authority"; and nothing I can say breaks that image. A man's life—and this I am sure is true of everyone —is a palimpsest: many themes of lives and ways are written on it. My love of America Hispana and of Spain, my self-discovery in Don Quixote, my loyalty to liberalism and its response or want of response to me are all lives together.

In these times[27] Venezuela threw out its dictators, whom the Venezuelan oil fields had made among the richest men of the world, and elected, by the first honest election of the republic, Rómulo Gallegos as president. Gallegos was one of the outstanding novelists of his hemisphere. I was invited to his inauguration, which turned out to be a cultural rather than a political affair. To celebrate it, there was an exhibition of paintings by American artists, and each night a tournament of Venezuelan and other Latin-American folk songs and dances in the great illuminated bullring. Gallegos entertained his fellow writers at a luncheon. A few days later I was dining at the house of Rómulo Betancourt, and we were discussing how many were the books on Bolívar and how inadequate all of them were. Betancourt, who later was elected president, turned to me, smiled, and said, "Frank, why don't you write a book on Bolívar?" I laughed and added to myself that I could not afford it. A few days later I learned that Betancourt had spoken of the matter to Gallegos and the book was commissioned. This required of course extended visits or visits to the Bolivárian countries: Venezuela, Colombia and Panama, Ecuador, Peru, Bolivia. A few months later the family, consisting of my wife, our son Jonathan, and our spaniel Pablo, and I were on our way southward. The day our ship reached Le Guayre, the port of Caracas, the soldier boys threw out Gallegos, who had lectured them each evening on the blessings of democracy. The counter revolution began. I walked through the streets to the Ministry of Education to learn if my contract was to be honored. The new minister of education, descendent of the Counts Mijares, received me warmly. He told me he had attacked me in his books as a bad influence on the Catholic youth and said they wished to make only one change in my contract: to raise my monthly stipend which they found inadequate. This I declined, saying I would stick to the terms of the original agreement. Walking back to the hotel, I heard the sporadic shooting suddenly increase; and, with all the others exposed on the block, I rushed for shelter. I landed in an advertising agent's office. He recognized me, for I heard him at the telephone mentioning I was there. A few minutes later a jeep stopped at the house and a detail of soldiers entered and respectfully inquired for my name. I told them, and they asked me to come along with them. I wondered what was to take place. They drove me back to the hotel and saluted and left. A couple of days later the family, except for Pablo, was having dinner at the hotel, which was being served in an open patio divided by a wall of tropical plants. In the other part around the pool, the new boss of Venezuela, Colonel Pérez Jiménez, was holding a cocktail party for his victorious soldiers. We could hear the laughter and catch an occasional glimpse of the women. A man whom I remembered as a reporter for one of Venezuela's best newspapers came up to my table (he had interviewed me before) and said he had an invitation from the colonel to come to meet him. I had to think quickly. I realized that if I met him I would have to shake his hand and there would be photographs of me shaking hands with a fascist in every newspaper of America Hispana. There was nothing for me to do but decline. The reporter turned pale. I wondered whether in some way the Colonel would express what must have angered him deeply, but nothing came of it except that when we went around town there was always a jeep and a squad of soldiers to defend us. My wife, the boy, and Pablo returned to New York and I continued my researches, going from one Bolivárian country after another.

By the time I completed the last of my journeys of research for the Bolívar book, the essential ways of my life were drawn.

The reader should by now, if ever, know what I am, what specimen of nature. He might indeed know better than the author with his outward and inward perspective. Yet much is missing. Friends who have seen the first two parts of the book have complained that they are not "personal" enough, that the "me" was not sufficiently given. I think this reads their mistake that they without knowing were looking not for "me" but for some conventional interpretation of "me"; and of course they have felt deprived. As the reader should be aware, I differ from my contemporaries in my sense of the ingredients my self consists of. For me the self contains three dimensions, or more directly three elements: One, the ego, in which I would include much of what Freud means by ego, id, and super ego, as well as what Jung means by the collective unconscious; two, a social dimension by which is meant not banal social exterior of a man's dimension but the inwardness of the self which contains the social; the third dimension within the self, equally there with the ego and the group, is the Cosmic, by which I denote what Spinoza experienced equally as God or the unity and singleness of substance. Since it is, and has been all my life, this which I see when I see a human being, of course, this is what I am looking for; and therefore, do not see a conventional portrait of a person. Whence the confusion in such an age as ours when old images of man have broken and new ones substituted, none adequate, all shards and shallow fragments.

Of course, in writing this self-history I have matriced it in my own self-image. The image did not change through the decades after the euphoria of the twenties to the revolutionary years of nuclear and capturable fission which characteristically fits in with our profit civilization. They all, like the electric charges in the atom, swim together in a mighty *néant*.

The 1930s and 1940s were decades in which America began to learn how little it had learned in the 1920s. Renaissance and reformation, the romantic age of science and the liberal era of Queen Victoria had heaped up values. These decades had squandered them. I was a man of letters and a disciple of Prometheus, which meant I must not be afraid of fire. I must help the people use the flames of life which they burned for their own well-being. But also I was a poet; and poets are masters of precision, hating the "approximate" as Rilke put it. It was, one might say, "a large order."

Victoria had become a symbol throughout the Western world for the latency of violence. "Big wars" were over, I had heard at our dining table, when the century was new. From India to the Falkland Islands, British power herded the "natives" into corrals and slew them under the blessing of British peace.

Seven-year-old children in the mills of Birmingham were weaving Pax Britannica with their tender bleeding fingers. Square rigged windjammers on all the seven seas were teaching the young British sailor the most remarkable blend of gentillesse and bestial toughness since Rome rotted. There were other, more inward latencies of violence. In Vienna, a good physician revealed in a bloody story of the Greeks the common psychological foundations of mother incest and patricide. What Jung called the collective unconscious—and Nietzsche and Adler the will to "power"—was equally pregnant with vast violence. But the more explosive seed was the atom of the physicists. It consisted of electric particles more remote from one another within the atom than two coral islands in the Pacific Sea, one close to America, one close to Asia. And the men of the new alchemy could with precision implode this charge without missing one of the billion billion, trillion trillion, quadrillion quadrillion live organisms in it. The violence whose emblem was Queen Victoria was latent in the unswept gutters her coach rode through and in the sidereal fire of the constellations and the galaxies where space crumples back, we are told, and time too. Hydrogen, such astronomers as Boyle calmly assure us, is forever replenishing the cosmos. Where does it come from? From *nowhere.*

The violent world was at times less latent than muted. When Britain needed to put down the rebellion in Kashmir or to sell her Brummagem shirts to the masters of fine hand looms, a stick of news in the London *Times* told the story. This was the "Genteel Tradition," so called by Professor Santayana.[28] I knew the title of course, but I had never read his essay. The name was enough. My intolerance was rigid. I'd stand for no compromise: let the violence speak, let the "Genteel Tradition" be blown up, with Melville and Walt Whitman to conduct the explosive obsequies.

It cannot quite be accident that I recall the day of Queen Victoria's death. My cousin Helen was at the house that evening, and Helen was by long odds the most beautiful woman I had so far seen. Her loveliness was illicit. Genteel Victoria and glamorous Helen did not go together. Seeing Helen meant to covet her. It was sinful. I could never touch my cousin with my desire, and listening to the ladies praise the superlatively proper queen while I desired Helen was a kind of incest. I shall not forget the occasion (I was about twelve, Helen about sixteen) when Helen was ill in bed and I, visiting her brother Arthur who was my dearest friend, saw her in bed properly sheathed by the covers but for me searing as a flame.

2

Thespis Approached

All this was decades past and the good queen's bones long since mouldering in her grave, when I re-encountered the "Genteel Tradition" in a form I could accept: the American actress of highest prestige at that time, Katharine Cornell. Her most famous role, perhaps, was Elizabeth Barrett Browning, in which she performed the breath-taking acrobatics of kicking over the traces of the "Genteel Tradition" and enhancing them at the same time.

I had never met Miss Cornell, but I had written a play. I called it *Malva* and it told the tale (remember this was the 1930s) of a half-breed girl from a Caribbean isle, cultured, chaste, and rebellious, who breaks all laws of the day (how obsolete already in the 1960s). I sent the play to Katharine Cornell with a note saying I had written with her and only her in mind. Within a week I got a letter from Miss Cornell's husband and manager, Guthrie McClintic, with an option on the play of $1,000 and an invitation to their home on Beekman Place. Miss Cornell at that time was playing a confection, *The Red Hat,* by the Armenian Michael Arlen. When the run waned, they would be ready for my package of fire which dared to show on stage the white man with a colored girl, dancing together and in love with one another. Aaron Copeland was invited to compose the music, which was important. Robert Edmund Jones also read the play with enthusiasm and was commissioned for the scenery and the costumes. The stake was set, needing only the awaited waning of the Arlen opus.

Meanwhile there were good times at the Cornell-McClintic house. A frequent visitor was Al Woods, one of the producers of *The Red Hat,* a theatre man of the old school with a *Havana Puro* forever in his mouth and, if my memory is not playing me tricks, a black derby on his head. Al would sit silent while Guthrie, Bobby Jones, or Kit went through a scene. What Al thought was obvious: the play was "crazy;" it would never "get across;" they'd all land in the soup—not to mention that we'd "lose our shirts." I soon felt the reverberations of what Al was saying in private to both Katharine and Guthrie, "These damn highbrows!" Here they had the best theatre property in the country, and they were ready to lose it because *Malva* carried a wonderful message.

Dear, poor Kit Cornell when her husband began to waver before the built-up objections of Al Woods who knew the theatre "like no one." I was able to map the workings of the "Genteel Tradition" and what it concealed. Kit's enthusiasm grew pale and withered away. Perhaps the play was too daring to make money . . . it would cost a lot to stage . . . if it wasn't a wow, it would be a bust and I could do nothing. I'd written a play and obviously that was the most I could be expected to do: not stage it, not judge its potentials of success. Katharine Cornell was a remarkably fine artist. Stark Young, drama critic of the *New Republic*, said "she was one of those very rare actresses who knew how to walk across the stage." (Bernhardt was another). Her face was a mask for all the allowable emotions shown by the "Genteel Tradition."

You'd think the energy represented by Cornell, McClintic, the author of the play, Copeland, and Bobby Jones—all more or less liberal and progressive—would have been proof against the fears and bad grammar of Mr. Woods. No, he was more certain than we. Meanwhile *The Red Hat* continued to prosper. It had already earned a fortune, and Katharine Cornell was no pauper needing a bank full of money. She might without pain have given up the money-maker, but how refuse money? How slight the ritual of making as much as one could? It seemed that the god of money was favoring *The Red Hat* by postponing its finish till the last gold nugget had been squeezed out of it. I do not mean to say that there I was consciously witnessing a drama of the liberal tradition typically surrendering to the perpetual Al Woods, but the significances were there, and I felt them. The play was strangled. A half dozen of the talents of the time believed in it—up to the point of fighting for it.

The group of youths and young women, who in the 1930s founded The Group Theatre,[29] despised the "Genteel Tradition." Not for them the mobile and immobile mask of Katharine Cornell, making a theater of echoes and attitudes frozen from Ibsen and Molière. Among the leaders were the directors, Harold Clurman, Lee Strasberg, and Cheryl Crawford, and such outstanding actors as Luther and Stella Adler (children of the great Yiddish actor Jacob Adler), Elia Kazan, Morris Carnovsky, and Phoebe Brandt. The Group had a model and an acting method: Stanislavsky of the

Moscow Art Theater. It had several ideologies to debate (Clurman was a devoted reader of *The Rediscovery of America* which after serialization in the *New Republic* was published in 1929). Marxism was more available to the younger, less intellectually independent; and soon there were bonds between Group members, always from individual to individual and the Communist Party.

My play *New Year's Eve* was rehearsed by the Group, but not produced. These were the needy 1930s; and Otto Kahn, a banker with a generous record, an American Maecenas, was feeling the pinch himself and for a time ceased supporting radical and aesthetically revolutionary plays with his profits from Kahn, Loeb. Kahn and I became good friends in the 1930s. He consulted me about the artists and writers who had appealed to him for money. "Banking," he used to say, "is an absurdly overpaid profession." He was a true gentleman; but you had only to see the gleam of his cool blue eyes, to watch his blunt, powerful, acquisitive hands to know that he knew exactly what he was doing. "I give the capitalist system another fifty years," he said in the early thirties. He was no lover of the "Genteel Tradition."

The Group showed its fertility by producing not only its financiers but its playwrights. The first of indigenous impact were John Howard Lawson, Paul E. Green, and the deeply gifted Clifford Odets. Odets wrote dialogue that was expressive music. The action of such plays as *Awake and Sing* and *Paradise Lost* was a lyricism that lifted the American Theatre into significance, social and esthetic. O'Neill's theatre, which we have already observed, bogs down in a mire of dialogue;* but it is dynamic. O'Neill and Odets fused into one would have made for greatness.

Lawson's *Processional* is an authentic permanent contribution to our theatre: its song and dance, its shouts and tears and laughter point a fecund way for the American theatre to have gone. Unfortunately Lawson's *Success Story* is a regression into the well-made Boulevard Theatre of Paris which such men as Henri Bernstein brought to sterile perfection—a malnutrition of the marrow with hypertrophe of the surface. Odets died before he could begin again at a more complex plane the clear song of his earlier lyrical stage. But such a play as *A Country Wife* shows that Odets was seeking.

There are, of course, great differences between the *Seven Arts* and The Group Theatre, and between the causes of their deaths. More meaningful are the analogies. In both there is a common

*With exceptions such as the masterpiece *Desire Under the Elms*.

vision of the Cosmic within the life of the Group, as expressed in *The Rediscovery of America* and more loosely in the impromptu talks of the Group leaders about the Group's meaning. I was occasionally present and did some of the talking—in New York and Stockbridge. To me it was great and exciting that my ideas for American potential should have so swiftly found a fertile field. The Group broke, disintegrated, and died because of inner weaknesses, helplessness against centrifugal social and ego pressures bearing on the actors.

Causes for the downfall can easily be traced. If the Group hired a cheap loft somewhere "off" Broadway, they might sustain their independence; but no one was sufficiently clairvoyant to see the "off." But what would it amount to if, on the other hand, they went to Broadway and interested regular theater money in their project? What would happen to the real project of the Group? Invitations began coming in from Broadway also. It was not long before such able artists as "Gadget" Kazan and the Adlers found that they already had a certain superiority which could immediately bring them roles. What could Clurman and his Group offer them to balance a real job which a nod could bring them? It was a sad spectacle to watch these gifted boys and girls.

The confusion of political radicalism did not simplify or strengthen the poor aesthetic of *agitprop;* flattening the function of the artist to the thesis propaganda did not help. Perhaps the situation was one which required the incursion of saintliness and martyrdom into politics, as with the followers of Gandhi in India, of Martin Luther King in our South and elsewhere. But to become martyrs was not the nature of the Clurmans and the Adlers. To survive in the world of theater u.s.a. in 1930–1940 required an outright unwordliness beyond the Group, and also an intellectual clarity which was wanting. Was it not for the unclarities of these earnest and admirable young men and women that such plays as *Awake and Sing* and *Waiting for Lefty* got their afflatus?

No one was ready. Above all, love was not ready, whence anger and frustration—and violence, which is always ready.

This could be seen in the acting art of such men as John Garfield and in the directing of such men as Clurman, Bobby Lewis, and most notably of all, perhaps, in Kazan. His actors did not move. They rushed and sped. They flew and spun and fired so explosively that when actors of conventional intensity such as Franchot Tone were set before them they seemed flat and out of place.

Bobby Lewis Strasborg, producer, and intellectual guides Clurman and I were ready.[30] But the complex social body, so much more than the simple addition of these, was not ready. I had had contact with the creation and miscarriage of theaters. The reader will recall how I walked out of the initial meeting of the Washington Square Players which became the Theatre Guild because I found no aesthetic substance, no organic intensity in these men and women; blaming myself, perhaps unjustly, for my failure to collaborate with whatever was *there*, however poor. In Copeau's Théâtre du Vieux Colombier, and Jouvet's, and Dullin's, and Valentine Tessin's, and Suzanne Bing's, I had found a true theater in the making, but of course not possibly my own since France and its theater tradition were parts of their birth. Through the works of Synge and Yeats and other hardly lesser men, I had a sense of the Irish National Theater. Yeats had said that when a man created a thing of genius, he knew it was some objective focus that let in the miracle. They were concrete for Yeats: he even had names for them: "Gates and Gate Keepers." In less esoteric language they were the living flesh of Ireland, its folk, its Church, its green and narrow land and the struggles for that land by nationalist and unionist locked in an embrace of war suddenly become creative. The birth of a theater is a mystery force. Nothing can explain it. Most of the world's peoples never have it; and even if they do (China, Athens, England, France, or Spain) it may live for years within a millennium without it. When the theater is there and has it one may describe and explain. Why did little Ireland produce a major dramatic poet, Synge, and a whole solar system of dramatic poets, while America, after the beginnings of O'Neill and Odets and Saroyan, produced merely some fragments of more sterile beginnings? Was the social pressure on the Abbey Theater fertile, the pressure of middle-class New York audiences sterile? Did Ireland's intellectuals make a harmony with its peasants, while America's intelligentsia and laboring men were never tossed into isolation together by the vast land's centrifugal pressures?

But this is not supposed to be a study of the miscarriages in American culture, a quest for the reasons why the American analogies for Synge and Yeats, Lady Gregory and O'Casey eschewed the Theater. Specifically, here, an inquiry is in order as to why I became so easily discouraged in my love for the theater. For I was hardly persistent. After Katharine Cornell's cooling, I tried to do nothing, about *Malva*. After the Group's rehearsals, I tried nothing with *New Year's Eve*. Later, the Group Theatre—soon to be dispersed for good—commissioned me to write a play.

I wrote it *(Woman Alone)*; Lola Montiz and they did not want it. Lawrence Langner of the Theater Guild warmly praised it but was afraid the Broadway customers would not buy it. I put it away. My whole experience with the theater was a first scene, hardly a first act. It would have heartened me, knowing the peripetias of the theater. I seemed to be not interested. A few conferences with possible producers bored me. I forgot where the manuscripts were and let dust cover the plays. I went back to my work, back to my cultural portraits, back to my notes on psychological technics. Why? . . .*

A variety of reasons, shallow and deep. I knew, of course, the dominant social dimension in the art of Theater, one of the crucial elements of which is the public that comes to see the play —and that unconsciously produces the play. The final blend of qualities—ethnic, social, intellectual—must be a balance delicate and yet dynamic if the final blend is to be great theater—which explains the infrequency of great theater in the world. I, who knew the people and the intellectuals, had no confidence that their values were sufficient for the making of great drama. The characters of Synge's plays were simple in their depth and viable for the poet to work with. In the United States the simple was gone; the depth was not yet matured; and the result was fractions if not shards of the whole the play must be. Before 1920 I had already written, in the *Seven Arts*, an article about the *advantages* of the German Irving Place Theater on Broadway: it had a company, a repertory, a tradition, a stable public; none of which was in the scope of the native American theater except in very simple forms, such as vaudeville and musical comedy.

America's most gifted playwright, Eugene O'Neill exemplified my reasons for discouragement. His plays teemed with seminal theatrical ideas. In one play, *Desire Under the Elms*, a stark and sufficient body rose from its idea to create the language of an objective action; but, for the most part, the O'Neill drama was never written: the language remained unrealistic. Although the Theater was there, O'Neill plays were the opposite of Shakespeare where the language becomes the drama, takes over an idea and plot, and becomes the free work of art. O'Neill's successors had no language to inherit: characters and remains fragment; action, unintegrated, becomes a series of neurotic moments, as in the plays of Tennessee Williams. I don't say that I figured it all out,

*Excluding the *oeuvres de jeunesse* written shortly after college, the plays were: *New Year's Eve, Malva, Flamingo Isle, Woman Alone*.

224 | "Death" of Waldo Frank

as here; but instinctively I knew that *theater* was not the means whereby my own art could make its body. True, my novels and my cultural portraits were dramatic; but they were not, they could not in this present civilization become theater.

All this rational explanation might well have vanished if the Group could have survived and if such men as Clurman, Strasborg, and Odets had kept on carrying the torch of their illumed will to make a theater. But for this to be would not America have needed a more humanly culture, more favorable like that of Ireland or the Old Don-Cote's on the left bank of the Seine?

3

Irresistibly, Politics

I'd been in England with a new friend Sir Richard Rees, a baronet with an uneasy conscience who set aside from his income a minimum of shillings to live on and gave the pounds to the radical labor movement (noncommunist) and the *Adelphi*, a magazine which he edited together with John Middleton Murry. This was the one British answer to the *Criterion* of the esthetes under T. S. Eliot; and it was, in regard to influence, not effective at all. Richard's flat was in Chelsea, in view of Battersea Bridge; and one could almost hear the angry paradoxes of Thomas Carlyle who had lived a stone's throw away. Through Richard more than any other man I got to know the working man of England. Traveling by bus we went north into Lancashire and northeast into Yorkshire. We stayed with the workers, many of whom lived on the dole. No house was too humble to receive us, and in all when morning came there was a knock on the door and the woman of the house brought us our cup of tea.

In most of my trips to Europe after the twenties I had gone straight to France or Spain because I had friends there and had business there. Now there was this little *Adelphi* group, Murry's quicksilver brilliance (heir of Lawrence) comfortably balanced by the profound stability of Rees, of Max Plowman and others; but more important for me there was this hospitality of the true Briton and his gracious wife. I loved the English home. I wondered at its ease with the baronet. A young poet whom I met at Richard's, and whose name, Dylan Thomas, meant nothing to me, taught me the unity and the continuity of British culture. Joyce, the Irishman, of course belonged to it; and, looking back on my earlier hours with Joyce, I understood him better. There was an almost schizoid rift producing the cosmopolitan Shaws and the George Moores, the dogmatic Marxist John Strachey (he would vanish in the feeble Labor Party), and the brilliant Harold Lasky who, with less coruscant mind and more animal cunning, might have become the Lord Beaconsfield of a new British Empire turned Commonwealth. Murry, almost every year, wrote a book which contradicted the ones before. Until he lapsed into the Anglican Church—which killed him. I'd been introduced to Lasky by Sir Stafford Cripps, and one day Lasky invited me to lunch. I knew at once that this was a courtesy for Stafford. Lasky did not like me nor did I like Lasky. He was a cold man for whom all my work on dimension and revelation was nonsense; a cold man artificially heated, or if you will, a hot man chilled by his devotion to a socialist church which with a sort of intellectual perverseness denied the present mystery of life in order to extoll its past mysteries, such as, "survival of the fittest by natural selection" which is as great a mystery as the wings of the butterfly.

In the mid-summer, depressed, I returned home. I did not have a home. My marriage had broken. Europe, frightened to death of Hitler, even of Mussolini, and of war, was sinking toward war. Ignorant America, sliding toward war, seemed incapable of speech, of self-confrontation. It seemed to me irrefutable that *war was*, and we were in it. I wrote a long article in the *New Republic*, resigning as a contributing editor because that excellent journal of opinion could not see the war and our part in it, our part in fascism (Lewis Mumford faced the same problem, wrote his essay and also resigned).[31]

I do not recall very well the elements of my depression except that I felt irrationally homeless. After all I had friends, true ones, men and women. I had my work. By this I meant primarily my symphonic novels. These were the decades of *Markand* (1927–1934), of *The Bridegroom Cometh* (1935–1938), and of *Island in The Atlantic* (1940–1946). But my resignation from *The New Republic* did not mean entry into an ivory tower. *Chart for Rough Water* (1940) was an essay in politics which I was soon to come back to: an essay in the integral relation between politics, ethics, and religion. I'd been saying for some time: the Hebrew prophets were Western history's most successful statesmen. Blake and Whitman knew what they were saying when they related religion with political action. In the decay of the marrow of our churches may be traced the corruption of our statecraft. Already in *The Rediscovery of America* I had insisted that religion and political action must live and work together at far deeper levels than what our constitutional fathers meant by "separation of church and state." There was here no contradiction, only counterpoint and redefinition.

Coming home that mid-summer in the heat of New York like wet blankets stifling every pore, I came into overt violence. "Everybody" was away. I was alone in New York. I'd stopped by in Paris at my publishers to pick up due royalties and changed the francs rapidly into dollars. I had several hundred dollars in my pocket. I took the subway to Harlem whose streets bloomed like a virus. One could feel it, hear it, smell it rather than see it in the black population. A tall youth came close to me. His head a square box with tight yellow skin like parchment. "Yaller girl," he whispered, "want to meet some yaller girls?" And when I seemed to be interested, he speeded his pace through the throng to an alley with a door which he opened. We hurried upstairs, and I felt the loneliness of the silent distant streets just as three more young Negroes rushed towards me on the stairs brandishing open razors. I gave them my money withholding a dime for car fare. They also took the gold watch given me on my twenty-first birthday by my father. The razors seemed clean, cleaner than I. I was not worthy of such cleanliness. They did not touch me.

I had met violence in other forms before I sailed from France. With a day to spare I went to Le Havre for a swim before I boarded my ship. It was a clear day of hard wind. I took a little yellow trolley out of town and when it stopped walked on until I came to a rocky coast of the Channel. No one, and no building, was in sight. I saw the waves and the tide spuming over the rocks which seemed to bind the water. Water and rock were of one substance, and they were inviting me to swim. It did not occur to me that rock is not fluid. Not a liquid element to swim in. I took off my clothes, folded them into a little bundle in the shade of some huge ferns, and walked into the catapulting water. Soon I was swimming, my bare body an arrow of swift freedom. A side-ways landing wave lifted and tossed me. I felt the smooth almost imperceptible kiss of the submerged stone; but not until I had retreated, walking at last on the stony shore, did I realize that the whole side of my belly just above the appendicitis scar was bleeding. I ran to my clothes and staunched the spurting blood with them. I put on shorts, trousers, and shirt, still profusely bleeding, and raced in the direction where I had left the trolley. The motorman saw my stained clothes and instructed me where to get off. My luck held: it was a clean wound, the doctor said laying in a stitch, and antiseptized by the good salt water. It was a safe inch or two from any crucial artery. The wound itself was a mere bland lip of fat and flesh, and it healed before I reached New York, nine days later.

I distantly sensed that I had invited destruction two times: in the perilous Channel swim and in the imbecile seduction by the poisonous Harlem "spades," who did not sink their razors into my throat after they had rifled me only because I seemed to want them to do it.

4

Operation: Labor

It was in the early 1940s that I received a letter from a man I did not know, who, his letterhead told me, worked in Washington and was connected with the C.I.O. The man's name was Smith— Anthony Wayne Smith; he had just read *The Rediscovery of America* and wanted to talk to me about it. Pretty soon he came down from the Capitol; and I can still see him as I saw him that first time, with a head like a walnut and the fine chiselled features of a Yankee. He was, I believe, related to the general of the Revolutionary War after whom he was named. He spoke in a low scarcely audible voice; his lips were thin, straight, and hard bitten; and I saw that he meant business.

What he meant by *business* was not too easy to fix at once. For instance, he questioned my book's use of the term God as possibly misleading, and yet it was plain that he meant what I meant when I spoke of religion . . . what Whitman too had meant. But this was no lyric bard waving superlatives. What interested Smith, I found, was *methods* for the modernization and rehabilitation of the essential experience of religion. Smith, a lawyer by training and a reader of Freud and Fromm, was a critic of the inadequacies and incompletions of Marx. He had liked my book because it was so full of questions leading to method; and he assumed, since I had written the book, that method interested me also. To be precise, it finally came out that he wanted to work with me in the transforming of the American labor movement which, he said dryly, had no values, no strategy, only the most superficial tactics.

Tony and I became good friends. He and his wife Anya usually spent a month's vacation in Provincetown not far from my Truro home on Cape Cod; and it was he who urged me, before it was too late, to call a small meeting at my studio to save the Cape by absorbing the best of it into a National Park (this was several years of course before the Kennedy seashore was more than a dream).

Over the years our discussions grew until we saw that we were making what might be called the features of a culture which alone, if it lived, could replace the current capitalist culture that had become rotten ere it was half ripe.

We made plans that might be called Continental, with Chicago as our probable center. Thence would radiate a weekly newspaper, lectures, a literary magazine, and theatre, something of a university and something of a social clinic. We gave ourselves a name: The New Century Fellowship. And we saw ourselves out of the red in perhaps a dozen years. But of course a baby could not start self-supporting, so we needed money. Meanwhile we made ourselves a "temporary organizing committee" with Ernesto Galarza, Tony's closest friend, as our secretary. Galarza was a Mexican with much experience in the exploitation of the "wetbacks" who swam the Rio Grande each year to harvest the fruits of California and Texas.

On the committee were exemplary men of broad gifts. Harold Clurman and Lewis Mumford I have named before. Frederick Redefer was an educator close to Harold Rugg who also joined us (Rugg almost single handed was fighting the hegemony of John Dewey in American education). Arthur Root lately invited me to give talks that were more like seminars than lectures. But many other men, especially of the powerful labor echelons, showed an interest even if they were not Committee members: such men as Walter Reuther; Emil Rieve, leader of the textile workers; George Baldanza, his aide; Frank Rosenbloom of the Amalgamated Ladies Garment Workers; Louis Hollander, New York representative of the C.I.O.

Extraordinary about these professional labor leaders was that they were like other bright and pushing men in business and the professions who had also come up from the ranks. The ranks of labor had the same smell and feel, when added up, as the small numbers of the little millionaires. Reuther, with whom I had breakfast (his beginning of the day's work), was smooth of bearing, swift of thought, controlled and cautious as if his background had been not an assembly line but Yale, and wielded the same power as the Ivy League sons of bankers. Dear old Emil Rieve was the expansive, protecting mother of his men and women. Frank Rosenbloom was the neurotic, sultry, intellectually able Jew who lived out his victory by sitting at a desk, bare but for the telephones and big as the side of a barn.

It was a broadening, perhaps a deepening too, of my equipment as an American novelist to parley with such men. My principal point with them all was that an economic program which is no more than an economic program must fail as an economic program. I pointed out some of the failures. The American labor movement needed another dimension in order to absorb labor and exploit its dynamic energy. They all listened politely and said they agreed. Would they back the movement? To the full. Would they help finance it? Not to the first penny. They had, all, such strains upon their purses. Most of them before they closed the interview mentioned the Communists; the urgent need to root them out. And to fight Communism before it became a danger to the U.S.A. They were ready to go to Italy and France to fight it. That would cost money and most of them seemed to assume that this was enough. A campaign *against* the Communists and a campaign for the place of the *whole man* in life seemed to them different terms for the same operation. It was simpler to take on the "Commies" —and so much cheaper. A few were a little more aware. Walter Reuther for example, but Reuther knowingly reminded me that although he was a socialist, a word admitting it to his men would blow him sky high. They were "no socialists," his men. Most of them believed in the American system of "free enterprise," although it did not exist.

The New Century Fellowship Committee collaborated in a sixteen-page "beginning statement" that reads pretty well today (1965), nearly twenty years after it was written. Except that much of the enthusiasm has been rubbed off and a new delusion hatched: that the liberals' and radicals' purposes and such hokum as Johnson's "Great Society" coincide.

When we asked for contributions, the response was one hundred percent not a dollar.

Such activities did not mean that I had shifted or was prepared to shift my focus of action from novelist to promethean labor man. It did mean that any fusion, beyond that of rhetoric, of labor with the so-called intellectuals seemed out of the question. In Latin America these deep infiltrations existed—going so far in some instances as osmosis. The universities were autonomous. The writers and the artists worked with the workers and the peasants. A classic example of this was José Carlos Mariátegui. The social fabrics of the land in America Hispana were filmsy so that there was much incipient fascism as well as romantic communism. But at least the spirit, if not the structure, for organic

Operation: Labor | 233

growth was there. And this is still one human superiority of America Hispana over the capitalist culture of the United States.

I had not ceased to be a creative writer. My publications in the 1950s make that clear. *Birth of A World: Bolívar In Terms Of His Peoples* came out in 1951; *Not Heaven,* in which the friends of my work found some of my very best stories—and the world's—appeared in 1953; *The Rediscovery of Man,* in 1958. Despite the book's length and difficulties, *Editorial Acquilar* got out a Spanish edition in 1961. Nevertheless, in regard to my individual career as a man of letters, there were bad signs. With the cold war and Senator McCarthy my invitations to lecture had shrunk, particularly from institutions with money. Audiences no longer paid to hear the other side. Indeed the rich ones did not want to hear it. My lecture agent, W. Colston Leigh, told me that my western tours were among the most brilliant he had ever managed. But my patrons seemingly had had enough. Also the number of my articles in well-paying weeklies and monthlies began to shrink. For this also, there were palpable reasons. I was in too serious a mood to go on indefinitely with such special styling as the *New Yorker* pieces. I had resigned from the *New Republic;* the *Nation* paid poorly. *Commentary* had fallen into the hands of mine enemies, shallow and brittle men who called themselves the successors of my dear departed A. S. Oko—and then forgot about him. Most cogent reason for the seeming withdrawal was my absorption in such major enterprises as *The Rediscovery of Man* and *Not Heaven.* Also, I no longer had the gusto that good literary journalism requires. For a while there were exceptions. There were, for instance, the monthly or more frequent pieces I wrote for a large group of Spanish and Portuguese language papers. A delightful assignment under the auspices of that good man Joaquin Maurin. I could write what I wished on any subject little or large, until my defense of Castro's Cuba lost me that commission. The trend was wide-spread. A tide was ebbing, and I alone on the sands. To celebrate this new solitude, I wrote two brief novels which have not yet seen the light; and one of which, at least, may be among my best.

5

The Magazine

I had not exhausted the all-significant question of method, as I interpreted the interest of Tony Smith. The bid from labor took many forms. This was the year before the war began, when it was still the style to call it hopefully a "phony war." To my furnished one room apartment in the seventies between Central Park West and Broadway came one day by appointment my two good friends Reinhold Niebuhr and Lewis Mumford to have a serious talk about founding a new magazine. We were agreed that the extant magazines little or large, however meritorious, were not adequate to America's need for a consciousness of what and where we were in our dark age. We needed a word-organism to bespeak what was silent in America. We would call it the *Western World* or something similar. We would publish stories, poems, essays—anything that illumined our state and the stage of mankind—both equally ominous and auspicious. We hoped to begin already possessed of sufficient funds to launch us. For Reinhold thought he knew some potential angels in California, and both Lewis and I believed the hour for getting funds propitious. The world had sunk so low that, in grim irony, it did not challenge profits of arming against Hitler for the purpose of abolishing the threat of Hitler, did not question the end of the depression and the business boom brought about by a race of armaments with Hitler. America was getting rich arming Europe, and from these resources we hoped to draw our pact for a magazine dedicated to peace and to the health of the West.

I can still see us in that mid-Victorian room with its tired furniture and its little old landlady serving us English tea. Her name I believe was Mrs. Bagby; if not, it should have been. Reinhold Neibuhr was there, with his head of an eagle and his eloquent warm words assuring himself that he was a rational student of the world's irrationalities. And Lewis Mumford, our America's most lucid and embracing mind with its confident discovery that mankind was rational, if only we could find the reason. We were sure that America was ours. So José Martí of Cuba had meant it, "Nuestra América" already in 1891 . . . so thirty years later I had meant it (not having heard of Martí at the time) when I called my book *Our America*.

We were amazed at the enormous wealth of matter, of subject and problem, our organ would exploit: virgin soil of the Western world. What Romain Rolland had written in 1916 to hearten us again, now was an accolade and a literal fact. "Tout est à dire. Tout est à faire: A l'oeuvre."

Finally we were talked out, at least for the present.

One of us quietly said, "Who is going to edit this magazine?"

It may have been I who spoke: "We three will be the editors, we three will share the work and the time."

"It won't do," one of us said, "unless the three are nominal editors, what we must have is a focal responsible editor who with a managing editor under him *makes* the magazine, issue after issue."

"A full time editor?"

"Absolutely . . . a full time editor."

"And then some. This is more than a full time job."

"Lewis and Reinhold—" I began.

"I'll be glad to give all the time I can spare, said Lewis, "but I cannot be *the* editor. I haven't the time. I have my lectures. I have my articles. Under and above all I have my books. I must put them first, my still unwritten books."

"No," Reinhold Niebuhr shook his head. "I cannot possibly undertake it. I have my classes at the seminary; I have my sermons; I have my lectures which keep me hopping from one end of the land to the other." He got up (he is a tall man). "You must do it, Waldo."

"Yes," said Lewis Mumford, "you're the most qualified, Waldo. You've already edited a major magazine. You have the closest connections—U.S.A., Latin America, and Europe, except England. I'll help all I can. I'll assign fixed times for being in the office. For editorial conference, for seeing writers, but you Waldo, definitely."

Reinhold Niebuhr approved and said so.

My next thought, unlike the previous ones, remained within me silent. *What of my own books?* The cultural portraits, the novels, above all the novel—*The Bridegroom Cometh* had just been published in London—if I take this task, I'll be submerged as I was by the *Seven Arts*. Only that was a year, this would be at least five years. It might well be while I and the magazine lived.

So the magazine was never born.

Now as I think back to that decision, I find doubts about the accuracy of our motives. Did we suspect that we were hiding the depths of a hesitation from our own view? It was true: we wanted to write our books and that would be hard, at best, if we bore too the responsibility of a serious magazine, a great magazine that we felt ourselves equal to creating. But did we perhaps fear our own collective unconscious which was pleading with us to turn away, to stay away from an undertaking that our unconscious knew was doomed. We were in a time of storm (the bomb was already in us). And we pleaded with ourselves to give precedence to our books. Were we saying: *sauve qui peut*—the cry for survival which dared not lose itself in the dark night ahead; which needed to make a world simple, direct as possible.

The world crisis had been gathering since Van Wyck Brooks in 1917 quit the *Seven Arts* and said the time has come to write books. And we let the *Seven Arts* die. Nothing had changed since then; only everything had become more itself. To our weakness we had sacrificed our magazine in 1917. We were now aborting this one because of the world's threats, soon to be made concrete in a bomb exploding.

6

Two Faces or
Hart Crane and Norbert Wiener

The 1920s in America were disserved by their most conspicuous writers. Hemingway and Faulkner, Mencken and Sinclair Lewis, O'Neill and poets, seemingly as remote from each other as Frost and Edna St. Vincent Millay, shared the decade's sense of thanksgiving that the war to end all wars was won. They went to the feast of life with gusto and revealed, one and all, under the brilliant colors poison and death. Think of the era's masterworks: *Spoon River Anthology, Winesburg, Ohio,* the lacquers of Amy Lowell, *North of Boston, Babbitt, The Great Gatsby, Desire Under the Elms,* and *Moon Calf,* all revealing the dire fate of the individual in an atmosphere made by the machine.

To the same category belongs *The Unwelcome Man.* That book, like the others I've named, has pessimism for its keynote. The lot of the sensitive man is to lose and vanish. In the depiction of the hero's walk across Brooklyn Bridge, the treatment of the machine-made world surrounding Quincy Burt awaits the sense of revelation in my later stories. But in the second novel, *The Dark Mother,* the tears are already penultimate. The whole matrix of the work is fecundity and hope. Except for the generous and prophetic reviews of such men as Clarence Day in the *Metropolitan Magazine* and Van Wyck Brooks in the *Dial, The Unwelcome Man* drew little attention. *The Dark Mother* drew even less, although I remember an enthusiastic discussion in the *Boston Transcript* by Mary Antin. *Our America* which came out in 1919 already had a positive dimension called, pejoratively, "mystic"—which made my fellows turn away from my work and made me turn away from theirs.

To me, in the perspective of three more decades, the emblematic men of this period—those who reveal most accurately and deeply the life of the time with its irresistible implications for the future—were a mathematician and a poet: the scientist, a most impure one in that he projected his symbols into social problems such as peace and communication and was deeply troubled by what he saw. This unorthodox scientist was Norbert Weiner, and this poet was Hart Crane. Both are now dead. Neither probably knew the other's name, but they belong together in the portrait of this decade.

Wiener I knew slightly, as one can only know a man who speaks an idiom strange and impenetrable—in this case mathematics. I knew him deeply with the empathy of the knowledge that what frightened me frightened him. Hart Crane became my close and beloved friend.[32] Wiener I first met, if my memory is just, at Edmund Wilson's home on Cape Cod. On later occasions I saw him in Provincetown, Boston, and Cambridge. I recall his explaining to me the impossibility of a true science of eugenics because man the observer lives no longer than man the observed. Objective control is beyond reach since it shifts with every generation. He invited me to see his "girl friends" at M.I.T. by which he meant, of course, that he would explain the principle of his computers each of which had a girl's name. For a felicitous flickering instant a veil barely lifted, and I saw with Wiener's eyes the literal possibility of man's losing control of man. Then the darkness fell again on my ignorance of mathematics and mechanics.

One could see that Wiener's body was not built for long lasting. He had an extended stomach and an overtense nervous and social structure. I would have gauged that his blood pressure was either too high or too low. His beard, square-cut, reminded me of the prophets whom his logic rejected and whom his heart could, nonetheless, not despise. His head, perhaps, was not in danger; but his relationship with his community was solitary like the original John the Baptist. He foresaw, of course, some of the fruits of the computers and automation. He feared that the machine might come to dominate the spirit of the flesh, and he did not hide his fear. He shared it with many. His contribution was to reveal the exactness of the danger: that the human use of man might be entirely lost or indeed never broached in the new civilization.

The last time I saw Norbert Wiener he became an emblem for me. I was going up the steps of an old Boston publishing house, and he was coming down. For a moment he did not see me, and his face which he thought was unobserved expressed devastation. Wiener had been an infant prodigy. As he matured and his age was no longer a stunt center of interest in him, he became a man in a hurry. He saw where the "cybernetics" he had developed might lead. . . must lead unless a deeper consciousness directed and moved us. He had no method of living or technique like the revealed religions. He saw vast energies released without restraint, and his empiricism held him back from the new dimension which might have armed him. If a man says, "God is within this self" and means it, a shift begins in his histology. So Wiener at last was in a hurry. At twelve when he entered Harvard with honors he had not been hurried. When he collaborated with the mathematical engineers of Mexico, Japan, and Europe he had not been hurried; but when he came home and saw what was happening in a cybernetic age, whatever it was, it frightened him and made him hurry. Did this have a bearing on his early death?

The picture is clearer when it is drawn by a poet. For as Rainer Rilke wrote, "the poet hates the approximate." He seeks precisions and finds them in verse, often also in his life. For the scientific fact lacks a dimension, forever, in the open ambiguities of space and time, and they must be found in art. This was the case with Hart Crane who died young (by his own act), and his life of a brief thirty years is beginning to haunt the American intellectual now that he is gone. Crane looked the part of the American poet. Fairly tall, he dressed neatly but informally and managed to be clean without the ostentation of being machine scrubbed. During one brief part of his life, when he left Cleveland, he worked in advertising agencies in New York; and from a distance he seemed to belong there. His eyes when one came close dispelled the illusion, for they were both tender and clouded; and Madison Avenue avoids both extremes like death. (It was Randolph Bourne who first taxed what we call Madison Avenue with not caring enough for anything even to sin for it.) His square head captained a body so sprightly and spring-like that it did not obviously suggest the black thunderstorms to which he was addicted. He was closely tied and not at all attached to the middle class. (His father made a fortune from his candy stores in Cleveland and lost it in the great depression.) But these roots were shallow and yet just strong enough to disturb his devoted passion, the fire burning passion of his true Promethean nature.

Crane was a homosexual with a weakness for fresh sailor boys. And when drenched with drink he needed strong reverberations to become a song. He was capable of throwing a chair out of the window. Sober, which was most of the time, he was as cool as a field of daisies. Aroused in protest of some stupidity in government or literary criticism, he became excoriating and bawdy. He had no politics, and he missed it. Spengler's *Decline of the West* greatly disturbed him because he needed to know it to be wrong. And I recall a letter Hart wrote urging me to answer it. This I did; and, if my memory is correct, my essay was published in *The Menorah Journal*.* There was no room in the universe of the grim old Prussian for the hot, hopeful parabolas of Crane or other apocalyptic poets in verse and prose. He needed reassurance, and I seemed able to give it.

The literary avant-garde of the 1920 and 1930s, unlike that in music and painting, seemed to be just beginning when Sylvia Beach published Joyce's *Ulysses* in Paris. The avant-garde was split into many factions. There were followers of Tristan Tzara's *Dada* who later joined the Communists. There was Ezra Pound. (When the *Seven Arts* was born Pound suggested himself as the foreign editor. I of course refused.) There were other expatriates whose duty it was to buy dinner for Harold Stearns. There was a poet, T. S. Eliot, whose cosmos was erudite literary vapors; and the greater poet, Dr. William Carlos Williams, whose universe was a small town in New Jersey. There were rhetorical purists (Kenneth Burke), playboys, and brilliant intellectual clowns (Matthew Josephson). There were apocalyptic critics, among them Gorham Munson whose book, *Waldo Frank, A Study*, came out in 1924. Munson identified me as a continuer of the tradition of Walt Whitman in full assault against such rationalists as V. F. Calverton who reduced literature to a subsidiary department of Marxist economics. And Sidney Hook who in Calverton's magazine answered my *Rediscovery of America* (appearing serially in the *New Republic*) with a positivist declaration: "there is no Whole, there are only wholes."

At this period I was a constant reader of Spinoza, whom I joined with Walt Whitman.† In my language of the times, *Leaves of Grass* was a "proof of God," as were all my works of the 1920s and 1930s, modulating from the lyrical novels: *Rahab, City Block,* and *Holiday* to *Virgin Spain* and *America Hispana*. So Crane took them to be within his own apocalyptic vision.

Much has been written about Crane since his death. He has been the object of memoirs and biographies and the subject of erudite interpretations.‡ My part in all this included an analysis

*And in the volume of essays *The American Jungle* published by Farrar and Rheinhardt.

†See my essay "With Marx, Spinoza" in the *New Republic* and in the volume *In the American Jungle*.

‡As I write a documentary film of his life is being made for television.

of Crane's use of metaphor which appeared in the *New Republic* when Crane's first volume of poems, *White Buildings* (dedicated to me), was published and the introduction to his complete poetry which I edited after his death.

This is not the place for emendations but there remain facts, intimate and poignant, about his life which until now are not known and should be known. Hart resolved to go to Mexico. His purpose was to write—more accurately to find, in the troubadour and trouvère sense of the word, a poem on the last Axtec emperor Montezuma—and to continue the parabola of the *Bridge* whose relation to the *Rediscovery of America* and, more specifically, to my *America Hispana* is self-evident.

Otto Kahn, the exemplary banker who called banking "an over-paid profession," gave Crane a couple of thousand dollars; and he went. I knew facts about Mexico which Hart only surmised. I knew specifically that the Aztec cult of death was not originally shared by the other cultures of the country: the Toltecs, the Zapotecs, the Maya; but I knew also that this cult had suffused the entire land when the Aztecs conquered it. It seemed to me that I knew this personally; for I met no Mexican on my various visits who did not reveal, as we became friends, traces of this bloody cult, the death wish. And it would be a danger for Hart Crane before he was prepared to meet it.

Crane was long since a confirmed drinker. He drew from alcohol a sleep that was a promise and the sense of a death. There was so much in daily life that was death to the life he sought! In the drab wastes of Cleveland or of Brooklyn and Manhattan (when he came East), he had achieved an equilibrium of sorts between the "macadam deserts" of the American existence and the ecstasy from his own dark conduit, from it to cosmos, that was recorded by his poems. I feared Mexico might upset this equilibrium with its own strong stamp of both life and death, unless Hart's own idioms were given time for self-assertion. In a big-brotherly fashion I therefore extracted a promise from Hart Crane: for the first month in Mexico, while he was exposed to the first raw blow of his encounter, he would drink no alcohol. After that I presumed he would take care of his own adjustments.

Hart gave me the promise—and broke it. I did not hear from him directly, but I got a troubled letter from Leon Felipe Camino.* He had gone up to him in a restaurant and found him very drunk and hostile as if Leon Felipe were the reminder of some guilt. He

---

*The great Spanish poet who translated *Virgin Spain* and other of my books.

was, according to Leon, going around with a crowd of young Communists and fellow travelers.

Hart's sense of exile bothered him. He wanted to belong to America; and he wanted, no less keenly and sharply, to disassociate himself from the America of his candy-making father. These hierophants—the Communists—of a new-mystical-inevitable-order seemed to have the only forward looking answer. So Hart, like many of the intellectuals of the twenties and thirties turned toward communism. Many of the best poets of America Hispana and Europe did likewise: either joining completely like Pablo Neruda, Picasso, Nicolás Guillén of Cuba, and Louis Aragon of France or declaring their friendship without joining like the Nobel Prize winner from Chile, Gabriela Mistral. He never joined because he was too close in his ideas to me to accept some of the Marxist dogma, particularly its aggressive antimysticism which equated its own mystique and the romantic notion of Rousseau that man was naturally good until society corrupted him. But he loved the young Communists. For a few pesos—surprisingly few —he bought a one room 'dobe house in a village neighboring the capitol. He threw the door open to his new allies in his war against the middle class. At the central Mercado he bought—also with the money Kahn had given him—pieces of sculpture made of clay or straw and pots and plates for the rudimentary cooking of tortillas and enchiladas (it was cheaper, he learned, to drink tequila than to eat). Meantime in his head the union shaped itself of what the poet meant by Montezuma and by the comradeship of persons close to Whitman which underlay them all.

The poet's father died, and Hart was called back to Cleveland for the settlement of the estate. The candy man had over extended himself. What was left from the bankruptcy in those early bleak 1930s went to his widow whom he had recently married, but there was enough for the poet to get back to Mexico, and in Mexico there was a house that was his, and above all there were the friends and comrades with whom he had left the key to the house telling them it was theirs to enjoy in his absence. In the spirit of tender acceptance and thanksgiving for what he had, he turned south toward Veracruz, climbed the high *meseta* toward his new home. At last there it was, the one room house that was his, standing alone among the cactus. It was interesting to note how important this personal possession was to this lone swan. He observed that the door was ajar. He had given his friends the right to use the house, not to let it fall into respectless lands; and he was certain that he would find at least one friend inside. The

244 | "Death" of Waldo Frank

hinges creaked as he pushed the door wider. They had been there, the friends! Shards of pots lay on the floor; a window was shattered; a pad of his sumptuous paper on which he prepared his poems was riffled, crumpled, and scattered on the floor.

Hart closed the door—from the outside, leaving the key in the door—and went back to the city. He must have been desperately wounded by the assault of ugliness and hate, or could it be merely carelessness? He had been moving in the direction of purpose. This revelation of the cult of death, he must have known, did not apply merely to Mexico. It was the world's condition to the young poet who aspired to love.

He turned back to the America of his origins; he decided to go home. He made an effort, I learned later, to overcome his homosexuality which he had always gladly accepted as the mark of his self. Now as the steamer *Orizaba* left behind the America of the poem he envisaged, he felt the drawing close of the America emblemized by the chilling waters, by his father; even so it is doubtful that he was ready for his final deed. After all he was young, resilient; he had already a publisher and readers. He could perhaps write articles for a living. Yet he knew that his prospects were slight. The water which alone could save him from them was getting colder. Then came the grain of sandstone that blinds. His attempt to normalize his sex life must have been pitiful. He stretched out his hand to close his cabin, and the door slammed on a finger. The whole universe flooded with pain, seemed to be pain: there was no escape from its ubiquity. He was part of it, and there was no Whole but pain. In the last quarter of the night, after the ship left Havana and when it was nearest the northern waters, a sailor on watch saw a figure clad in pajamas rapidly cross to the stern deck, mount the aft rail, face south only an instant, and then leap into the sea churning valveless.

The two faces converge upon me, they belong together: the poet and the mathematician Norbert Wiener, thinking he is unseen, letting his face speak. He has just made arrangements for the publication of his book: Can man be trusted to make human use of man? And if not, what will happen when its present ego and collective ego continue with insuperable genocidal weapons to inherit, employ, and rule? Hart Crane in the moment between the earth and death sees beyond life and death, faces the end by death that is beyond him. Each face sees the other and is aghast. "Begin again, give up and try again." But the distinct world of other dimensions overwhelms, and all he can conceive before all goes is the dark.

Notes

1. For an earlier version (1925) of the material covered in this and in the following two chapters, see the autobiographical essay, "I Discover the New World," *In The American Jungle* (New York, 1937), pp. 3–15. William Bittner, in *The Novels of Waldo Frank* (Philadelphia, 1958), provides an excellent account of the autobiographical elements in Frank's fiction, as well as a fine summary of the period covered in this chapter, pp. 20–32.

2. According to Jerome W. Kloucek, *Waldo Frank: The Ground of His Mind and Art* (Michigan: University Microfilms, Inc., Ann Arbor, Michigan: 1958), p. 13. Frank was named Waldo David in honor of Ralph Waldo Emerson and Henry David Thoreau—an interesting fact in view of his life-long identification with these writers, and doubly interesting in regard to the name of his phallic-centered "continent." Bittner reports (p. 24) that Frank's brother recalled Waldo's proclaiming, about 1901, "a new 'Waldensian religion of which he was going to be the prophet." The name is an intriguing conflation of Waldea and Walden.

3. For an account of Frank's years at Yale, especially their contribution to his intellectual growth, see Kloucek, pp. 23–52. According to Kloucek, "what profited Frank most at Yale was his introduction to formal philosophy, beginning with a survey course in his sophomore year. William Ernest Hocking was then on the faculty and seems to have impressed Frank more than any of the English instructors; at any rate, after he left Yale, Frank continued an intermittent correspondence with Hocking on philosophical problems and readings for several years." It is not clear why there is no mention of Hocking in this chapter—or anywhere in the *Memoirs*. Hocking had been a student of Josiah Royce; in 1912, Frank's last year at Yale, he published *The Meaning of God in Human Experience*, which responds to the challenge of pragmatism and realism to idealism. Frank would surely have been open to the appeal and influence of such a man. Kloucek

also discusses in detail Frank's unpublished M.A. thesis, 'On the Spirit of Modern French Letters."

4. See below, pp. 229, for a full account of this episode.

5. Frank collected his *New Yorker* "profiles" (he apparently invented this standard feature of the magazine) in a volume published anonymously as *Time Exposures, by Search-Light* (New York, 1926). The section on Phelps appears on pp. 23–30. The book also contains a portrait of Thomas Beer, pp. 71–78.

6. The murder of Herman Rosenthal on the steps of the Hotel Metropole occurred during the summer of 1912. Police Lieutenant Charles Becker was convicted of masterminding the killing, and was executed in 1915; he insisted on his innocence to the end. See Andy Logan, *Against the Evidence* (New York, 1970).

7. A recollection of the Baghdad Club by Frank, presumably delivered in conversation, appears in Mark Schorer, *Sinclair Lewis, an American Life* (New York, 1961), pp. 196–197.

8. Frank's published portraits and discussions of Stieglitz include the following: *Our America* (New York, 1919), pp. 180–187; *Time Exposures* (New York, 1926), pp. 175–182; "Alfred Stieglitz: The World's Greatest Photographer," *McCall's*, LIV (May, 1927), pp. 107–108; *Rediscovery of America* (New York, 1929), pp. 177–178; "The World in Stieglitz," in *America and Alfred Stieglitz*, edited by Waldo Frank and others (New York, 1936), pp. 212–224; "Alfred Stieglitz," in *Stieglitz Memorial Portfolio, 1864–1946*, edited by Dorothy Norman (New York, 1947), pp. 18–19. In addition, an extensive correspondence between the two men is located at Yale University and the University of Pennsylvania.

9. Margaret Naumburg, Waldo Frank's first wife. In 1913 she studied with Montessori in Rome and founded The Children's School (later The Walden School) in New York in 1917. For a portrait of Margaret Naumburg and her work in education, see Paul Rosenfeld, *Port of New York* (New York, 1924), pp. 117–133, 302–303.

10. For an earlier discussion of the *Seven Arts* by Waldo Frank, see his contribution to 'Symposium on the Little Magazines," *Golden Goose III*, 1 (Columbus, Ohio, 1951), pp. 20–22. For recollections by another founder of the journal, see James Oppenheim, "The Story of the *Seven Arts*," *American Mercury*, XX (1930), pp. 156–164. In "Herald of the Twenties," *Forum* XXX, vii (University of Houston, 1961), pp. 4–14; Gorham Munson recalls the impact of *Seven Arts* and the role of Waldo Frank in particular. Van Wyck Brooks recounts his relations with the journal in his *Auto-*

biography (New York, 1965), especially pp. 273–276 and passim. The brief career of the magazine is treated in Frederick J. Hoffman, Charles Allen, and Caroline F. Ulrich, *The Little Magazine* (Princeton, 1946), pp. 86–92. See also Henry May, *The End of Innocence* (New York, 1959). The most exhaustive study of *Seven Arts*, its aims, its achievements, and its place in twentieth-century cultural history, is Claire Sacks, *The Seven Arts Critics: A Study of Cultural Nationalism in America*, 1910–1930 (Ann Arbor: University Microfilms, 1955).

11. *Waldo Frank, A Study* (New York, 1923). Munson also edited, the same year, a special issue of the little magazine *S4N* titled "Homage to Waldo Frank," issues 30, 31 (September, October, 1923; November, December, January, 1924). In the foreword to this issue Munson wrote: "My attempt was nothing less than to provide the exacting reader with a durable monument of esteem for the man I consider America's most significant novelist." Among the contributors were Hart Crane and Jean Toomer. See also Munson's "Herald of the Twenties," op. cit., and "The Fledgling Years, 1916–1924," *Sewanee Review*, xl (1932), pp. 24–54.

12. The Non-Partisan League was founded in North Dakota in 1915, as an agrarian political organization and a revival of populism; it was active until the early 1920s, revived in the 1930s, and eventually affiliated itself with the national Democratic party.

13. After studying briefly at the University of Wisconsin and City College of New York, Toomer (1894–1967) found his "stride in writing," as he put it, and contributed to a number of little magazines. Born in Washington, D.C., the grandson of P. B. S. Pinchback, the Negro leader during Reconstruction in Louisiana, Toomer said about himself in a letter to the editors of *Liberator* in 1922: "Racially, I seem to have (who knows for sure) seven blood mixtures; French, Dutch, Welsh, Negro, German, Jewish and Indian. Because of these, my position in America has been a curious one. I have lived equally amid two race groups. Now white, now colored. From my own point of view I am naturally and inevitably an American. I have strived for a spiritual fusion analogous to the fact of racial intermingling." (Quoted in Arna Bontemps, "Introduction," Perennial Classic edition [1969] of *Cane*.) Through his writings Toomer became friends in the early 1920s with Frank, Hart Crane, Gorham Munson, and others. His relations with Frank were especially close and mutually fruitful. The visit to the South Frank describes was, Toomer writes in the autobiographical letter, "the starting point of almost everything of worth that I have done." The trip apparently confirmed his identification as a south

ern Negro writer, at least for the time: 'I heard folk-songs come from the lips of Negro peasants. I saw the rich dusk beauty that I had heard many false accents about, and of which, till then, I was somewhat skeptical. And a deep part of my nature, a part that I had repressed, sprang suddenly to life and responded to them." *Cane* appeared in 1923 with a foreword by Waldo Frank. It preceded by many years, and undoubtedly influenced, many of the works associated with the Harlem Renaissance by figures like Langston Hughes, Zora Neale Hurston, and Wallace Thurmond. See Bontemps, op. cit., for an appraisal of *Cane*. For interesting contemporary responses to Toomer, see W. E. B. Du Bois and Alain Locke, 'The Younger Literary Movement," *Crisis*, xxvii (1924), pp. 161–163; Eugene Holmes, "Jean Toomer, Apostle of Beauty," *Opportunity*, iii (1925), pp. 252–254, 260; Gorham Munson, 'The Significance of Jean Toomer," *Opportunity*, iii (1925), pp. 262–263 (an expanded version appears in Munson's *Destinations* [New York, 1928] pp. 178–186); Paul Rosenfeld, *Men Seen* (New York, 1925), pp. 227–233. According to Rosenfeld, Sherwood Anderson and Waldo Frank "helped rouse the impulse of Toomer." See Bontemps for a biographical account of Toomer, especially during the period of his "'disappearance" from the literary scene.

14. George Ivanovich Gurdjieff (d.1949) was a Russian emigré living in France who developed a practical method of mysticism based on yoga-like exercises. He had many followers in literary circles in France, England, and America in the early 1920s, including Katherine Mansfield. A chief disciple was A. R. Orage, a London editor. Another was P. D. Ouspensky, author of *Tertium Organum* (1934). Gurdjieff visited America with a group of disciples in 1924 and gave demonstrations of dances and exercises in New York and Chicago. Toomer spent a period of time at Gurdjieff's Institute for the Harmonious Development of Man at Fountainbleau. For Frank's criticism of Gurdjieff see *The Rediscovery of Man*, pp. 424–427.

15. The "Generation of '98" was a group of writers who responded to the defeat of Spain in Cuba in 1898 as an opportunity to initiate a searching analysis of Spanish life. They introduced a new critical spirit, drawing on influences from France, England and Germany, and opened the way for a flourishing modernist literature in Spain. See Gerald Brenan, *The Literature of the Spanish People* (Cambridge University Press, 1951), 417ff., and Guillermo Diaz-Playa, *A History of Spanish Literature* (New York, 1971), pp. 312–324.

16. *Salvos*, pp. 103, 115. In *Our America* Frank acclaims Chaplin as "our most significant and most authentic dramatic figure," but does add: "There are sophistications in Chaplin's work that are not healthy," (pp. 214–215). Frank wrote a much fuller portrait of Chaplin in 1929 (*In the American Jungle*, pp. 61–73) after the visit to Hollywood described in this chapter. Chaplin comments on his friendship with Waldo Frank and through him with Hart Crane, in *My Autobiography* (New York, 1964), pp. 267–268.

17. Waldo Frank's lecture tour of Mexico and South America in 1929 resulted in the remarkable volume of tribute, *Waldo Frank Hispana* (New York: Instituto de las Españas, 1930). The volume includes newspaper accounts of his lectures, appreciative essays, and poems in his honor. Especially revealing discussions of Frank's great success on this tour and his continuing importance in America Hispana are the contributions of M. J. Bernadete, pp. 1–18, and Federico de Onís, pp. 243–249.

18. Baal Shem Tov ("Master of the Holy Name") was the title held by Israel ben Eliezer (c.1700–1760), founder of Hasidism, the Jewish pietist movement which stressed joy, love of nature, and personal communication with God through ecstasy.

19. Adolph Oko (1883–1944) was a noted Spinoza scholar and editor. From 1906 to 1931 he served as the librarian of Hebrew Union College, Cincinnati. See "Frank: Commemoration," *Contemporary Jewish Record*, VII (October 1944), pp. 451–453.

20. See *Harlan Miners Speak* (New York, 1932) for a full account of the Dreiser Committee and of Waldo Frank's subsequent testimony before a Senate committee hearing in Washington.

21. For other accounts of the same incident see Edmund Wilson, "Class War Exhibits," *New Masses*, VII (April 1932), p. 7; Malcolm Cowley, 'Kentucky Coal Town,' the *New Republic*, LXX (2 March 1932), pp. 67–70; and Matthew Josephson's memoir of the 1930s, *Infidel in the Temple* (New York, 1967), pp. 110–113. The story of Frank's beating appeared in the *New York Times*.

22. Essential background for the events and personalities covered in this chapter is Daniel Aaron, *Writers on the Left* (New York, 1961), especially Part Two, "The Appeal of Communism," which includes a chapter on the League of American Writers and Frank's role within it.

23. In 1932 Frank joined with Edmund Wilson and about fifty other writers and artists in an open letter declaring support of the

Communist party presidential ticket of William Z. Foster and James W. Ford. The open letter was published as a pamphlet, *Culture and Crisis*. See Aaron, pp. 213–215.

24. An excellent account and appraisal of Waldo Frank's debt to and criticism of Freud—especially in his fiction—is in Frederick J. Hoffman, *Freudianism and the Literary Mind* (Baton Rouge, La., 1945), pp. 250–263.

25. See especially *Major Trends in Jewish Mysticism* (New York and London, 1946), and *On the Kabbalah and Its Symbolism* (New York and London, 1965). Scholem is Professor Emeritus of Jewish Mysticism, Hebrew University, Jerusalem.

26. In the Table of Contents accompanying his final typescript of the *Memoirs*, Frank noted: "Part Three is partly unfinished and partly not written." He indicates a seventh chapter (which would confirms the symmetry of the book; three "parts" with seven sections each), but leaves it untitled. Chapter Six, "Two Faces," seems by all evidence to represent the last work Frank performed on the book. That he sensed a waning of his ability to continue is suggested by the fact that while the chapter deals with a subject ostensibly out of the chronological line of Part Three, its deeper subject is the "death" of the poet. It should be pointed out that Frank attached particular meanings to the word "death" in the title of Part Three. In an early manuscript draft (September, 1963) of the discussion of "superstition" (now included in the opening chapter of Part Three), Frank recalls that in a now-lost notebook kept during his high school years he had anticipated his own death at age 56. It occurred to him much later that 56 is a multiple of the magical number seven—a number he has always thought of as "his"—and that his fifty-sixth year fell in 1945, the year of the bomb, when "hundreds of thousands had died." "Perhaps everyone has died in the sense of the end of an era," he writes. And perhaps his adolescent fantasy had been a voice of the collective unconscious. "The collective voice needs to say: Mankind reaches a death—and a birth, and can say only 'I shall die." His own "death," then, at 56, might be a symbolic token of the desperate need for a collective rebirth after the atomic bomb. He wrote: "It is not impossible that some chamber of Frank's mind was involuntarily thrown open like a shutter, to say in the instant of a seemingly unnoticed flash of light; 'When you are 56, the world you have lived in, thought in, and felt in, will die.' The mind, then, takes up the reports and knows the observation to be not individual at all. *I* will die in the sense that my world will die and I will live to see the death. We have lived, all, to see it

—and do not know it. A major transformation has been thrust upon man, not by chance, but by the nature of his will which has taken the shape of science." This passage casts considerable light on Frank's intentions in his title, in the emphasis placed in Part Three on Victorianism—the "old world"—and violence, and in the emblematic confrontation of the "two faces" of science and poetry in the concluding chapter.

27. The following episode occurred in 1948.

28. George Santayana, "The Genteel Tradition in American Philosophy" (1911) in *Winds of Doctrine* (London, 1913).

29. See Harold Clurman, *The Fervent Years* (New York, 1945) for a history of the Group Theatre, and especially pp. 20–22 and pp. 44–50 for Frank's association with the enterprise.

30. The following pages, to the end of Chapter Two, were not included in Frank's final typescript, but added with editing from his manuscript.

31. See "Resignations Accepted," *New Republic*, VII (10 June 1940), pp. 795–796.

32. Frank's friendship with and influence upon Hart Crane is well documented, especially in John Unterecker's biography of Crane, *Voyager* (New York, 1969). Frank wrote the introduction to *The Collected Poems of Hart Crane* (New York, 1933), pp. vii–xxix. For an interesting study of their intellectual relations see Robert L. Perry, *The Shared Vision of Waldo Frank and Hart Crane*, University of Nebraska Studies n.s. no. 33 (Lincoln, Nebraska, 1966).

Bibliography

BOOKS PUBLISHED BY WALDO FRANK
(American Editions)

The Unwelcome Man: A Novel. Boston: Little, Brown and Co., 1917.

The Art of the Vieux Colombier. Paris and New York: Editions de la Nouvelle Revue Française, 1918.

Our America. New York: Boni and Liveright, 1919.

The Dark Mother: A Novel. New York: Boni and Liveright, 1920.

City Block. Darien, Connecticut: by the author, 1922.

Rahab. New York: Boni and Liveright, 1922.

Holiday, New York: Boni and Liveright, 1923.

Chalk Face. New York: Boni and Liveright, 1924.

Salvos: An Informal Book about Books and Plays. New York: Boni and Liveright, 1924.

Time Exposures, by Search-Light: Being Portraits of Twenty Men and Women Famous in Our Day, Together with Caricatures of the Same by Divers Artists, to Which is Appended an Account of a Joint Report Made to Jehovah on the Condition of Man in the City of New York (1926) by Julius Caesar, Aristotle and a Third Individual of Less Importance. New York: Boni and Liveright, 1926. Published anonymously.

Virgin Spain: Scenes from the Spiritual Drama of a Great People. New York: Boni and Liveright, 1926.

New Year's Eve: A Play. New York: Charles Scribner's Sons, 1929.

The Rediscovery of America: An Introduction to a Philosophy of American Life. New York: Charles Scribner's Sons, 1929.

America Hispana: A Portrait and a Prospect. New York: Charles Scribner's Sons, 1931.

Dawn in Russia: The Record of a Journey. New York: Charles Scribner's Sons, 1932.

The Death and Birth of David Markand: An American Story. New York: Charles Scribner's Sons, 1934.

In the American Jungle (1925–1936). New York: Farrar and Rinehart, 1937.

The Bridegroom Cometh. New York: Doubleday, Doran and Company, 1939.

Chart for Rough Water: Our Role in a New World. New York: Doubleday, Doran and Company, 1940.

Summer Never Ends: A Modern Love Story. New York: Duell, Sloan and Pearce, 1941.

Virgin Spain: The Drama of a Great People (Second Edition, revised). New York: Duell, Sloan and Pearce, 1942.

South American Journey. New York: Duell, Sloan and Pearce, 1943.

The Jew in Our Day. New York: Duell, Sloan and Pearce, 1944.

Island in the Atlantic: A Novel. New York: Duell, Sloan and Pearce, 1946.

The Invaders: A Novel. New York: Duell, Sloan and Pearce, 1948.

Birth of a World: Bolívar in Terms of His Peoples. Boston: Houghton Mifflin Company, 1951.

Not Heaven: A Novel in the Form of Prelude, Variations, and Theme. New York: Hermitage House, 1953.

Bridgehead: The Drama of Israel. New York: George Braziller, 1957.

Rediscovery of Man: A Memoir and a Methodology of Modern Life. New York: George Braziller, 1958.

Cuba: Prophetic Island. New York: Marzani and Munsell, 1961.

Index

Frank in, 108–12, 147, 196
Frank's empathy with, 125,
127–28, 132–35, 173, 214
Spanish Civil War, 130, 132
Spengler, Oswald, 241
Spingarn, J. E., xvi
Spinoza, Baruch, 32, 142, 176,
184, 201, 216, 242, 251
Spoon River Anthology, The, 62,
239
Stachel, Jacob, 189
Stalin, Joseph, xxii, 178, 190–92
Stanislavsky, Constantin, 220
Stearns, Harold, 242
Stein, Leo, 88
Stendhal, 142
Steuer, Max, 61
Stieglitz, Alfred, viii, xxv, 63–64,
146, 212, 248
Stirner, Max, xix, 10, 183, 187
Stix, "Hans," 39
Stoicism, 141
Stolberg, Ben, 192
Stout, Rex, 193
Strachey, John, 193, 227
Strasberg, Lee, 220
Strasborg, Bobby Lewis, 222, 225
Strauss, Richard, 7
Stravinsky, Igor, 73, 76, 119
Success Story, The, 153, 221
Sumner, John, 140
Sunday, Billy, 152
superstition, 211–12
Supervielle, Jules, 122
Sur, 171
surrealists, 108, 116, 122, 179
Swift, Jonathan, 32, 142
Swinburne, Algernon, 23, 32, 40,
114
Switzerland, 26, 28–29, 118, 173
symbol, 33, 70, 92, 134, 147, 171,
203, 216
Symphonie Pastorale, La, 117
Synge, John, 72, 223–24

Taft, William Howard, 59
Taine, Hippolyte Adolphe, xviii
Talmud, 32, 174
Tammany Hall, 22–23, 58, 189
Tangiers, 125, 128
Tantrism, 204
Tapper, Bertha Feiring, 65
Taub, Allen, 181–82
Tennyson, Alfred, Lord, 10, 23,
41
Tessier, Valentine, 79, 114, 121,
223

Texas, 149, 232
Thackeray, William Makepeace,
9, 32
Thaw, Harry, 21
Thayer, Scofield, 93
Theater Guild, 67, 153, 223–24
Théâtre du Vieux Colombier, 74,
79–80, 95, 98, 113, 120, 165,
223
Thomas, Augustus, 47, 66
Thomas, Dylan, 227
Thomas, Norman, 187
Thompson, Francis, 40
Thoreau, Henry David, 42, 98,
108, 118–19, 123, 143, 160,
199, 247
Thurmond, Wallace, 250
Tierra del Fuego, 164
Times, The (London), 173, 217
Tinker, Chauncey Brewster,
40–41, 43, 49
Titian, 108
Tocqueville, Alexis de, xxvii
Toledano, Lombardo, 194
Tolstoi, Alexis, 193
Tolstoi, Leo, xviii, xxv, xxvii,
9–10, 24, 26, 31, 42, 45, 48,
62, 68, 80, 118, 128, 141–42,
183
Tone, Franchot, 222
Toomer, Jean, viii, xxvi, 102–108,
249–50
Townley, Arthur, 100–101
Trachtenberg, Alexander, 189
Traherne, Thomas, 46
Traubel, Horace, 183
Trotsky, Leon, 184, 186–87,
190–92, 194
Truro, Mass., 177, 188, 196, 231
Turgenev, Ivan, 26
Tuskegee Institute, 103
Twain, Mark, 83
"291," 63
Tzara, Tristan, 115–16, 179, 242

Ulysses, 122–23, 242
Unamuno, Miguel de, xv, 112,
129–31
United Artists, 150
United Mine Workers, 180
University of Berlin, 175
University of Buenos Aires, 164
University of Mexico, 153
University of Salamanca, 112
University of San Marcos, 171
Unterecker, John, 253
Untermeyer, Louis, 84–86, 91

Index | 267